The TALL Book

The 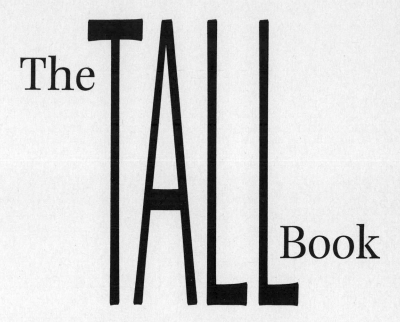TALL Book

A Celebration of Life from on High

ARIANNE COHEN, 6'3"

Illustrations by Myra Fourley

BLOOMSBURY

NEW YORK • BERLIN • LONDON

Published by Bloomsbury USA, New York

All papers used by Bloomsbury USA are natural, recyclable products made from wood grown in well-managed forests. The manufacturing processes conform to the environmental regulations of the country of origin.

LIBRARY OF CONGRESS CATALOGING-IN-PUBLICATION DATA

Cohen, Arianne.
The tall book: a celebration of life on high/Arianne Cohen.—1st U.S. ed.
p. cm.
Includes bibliographical references.
ISBN-13: 978-1-59691-308-0
ISBN-10: 1-59691-308-8
1. Stature, Tall—Psychological aspects.   2. Stature, Tall—Social aspects.   I. Title.

QP84.C63 2009
612.6'61—dc22
2008048215

First U.S. Edition 2009

1 3 5 7 9 10 8 6 4 2

Designed by Rachel Reiss

Typeset by Westchester Book Group
Printed in the United States of America by Quebecor World Fairfield

For tall people everywhere, and honorary tall person Bre Levy.

_____

*In memory of Sandy Allen, the world's tallest woman,
and the best tall ambassador the earth has ever seen.*

Contents

Part IV: Tall Quandaries, Explained

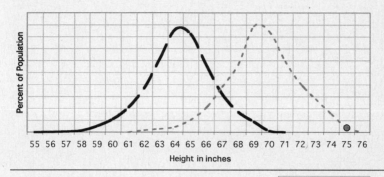

Because everyone asks: What is the definition of tall*?*
You are tall if you're taller than the people
around you. Height is relative.

Tall World Starts: Here

You could say that this book began at the Bethlehem Public Library in Delmar, New York, in 1989, when I discovered that no library in the universe carried a book about tall people.

This was a devastating blow to a 5'3" eight-year-old. Up until that day, the stacks had cleared up a host of childhood confusions about birds and bees and bases, particularly *The Dictionary of Slang*, which I consulted regularly. I had great faith in the library.

But that afternoon, I had a more important concern. A morning visit to the pediatrician had prompted him to add another dot on my growth chart and announce, "You're gonna be taller than the president!" That would be Ronald Reagan, 6'1". I just nodded. Of course I would be taller than the president. That's totally normal.

For the rest of the day, the line bounced around in my head, accompanied by a freakish image of me towering over Ronald Reagan and his petite wife Nancy, roughly the size of my then-right thigh, while I endured a typical school afternoon of standing at the back of the line and responding to the name Amazon Ari.

As soon as the bell rang, I trotted myself over to the card catalog to investigate this tallness thing. The subject cards skipped from *talkov—igor* to *tall buildings*. The Dewey Decimal index *didn't even assign a classification number* to tall people. Surely the world kidded.

I alerted the reference librarian that a pivotal subject card had fallen out of the card catalog. She waddled over and examined the situation through her bifocals. "Dear, I don't think that's a topic that authors write nonfiction books about. But we do have a few books about short height. Would you like to see those?" No, thanks.

"What about *Sarah, Plain and Tall*, dear? Have you read that novel?" Yes. And Sarah's not particularly tall.

Igor Talkov, by the way, is a Soviet rock 'n roll artist with a political bent. And the then-world's tallest building was the Chicago's Sears Tower.

When there's no book about your topic, it's like your whole issue doesn't exist. My concerns were deflated, automatically relegated to a topic of no particular importance, which made me feel dumb. I was left to scrounge for information from my surroundings. My mother's thoughts on the matter were concise: that I was "a tall glass of water" and that "it's what's on the inside that matters." Meanwhile, my classmates spent all their time telling me how freaking tall I was, as dutifully noted by five million inquiries of "How's the weather up there?" Mixed messaging.

So for the next two decades I decided to drink the Kool-Aid and tell myself that it's what's on the inside that matters. I assured my mind that being tall was just another trait, like the texture of my hair (frizzy) and the color of my skin (ashen), an inconsequential exterior beyond my control. I thought about it often, but then told myself that I had more important things to think about. My height was the elephant in the room. Telling yourself not to think about the elephant is not a good long-term strategy.

I graduated into the adult world, and my inner monologue often went something like this:

> Wow, I feel really awkward towering over my short friend/ boyfriend/boss . . . Arianne, just act normal. Why did everyone in the restaurant turn around and look at me when I walked in? Is my fly open? . . . Arianne, they stare at everyone.

And on and on, silently in my head, for twenty years. This is why tall people are a quirky bunch.

And then in 2005, my book agent spoke those magical words: "Is there anything you'd like to write a book about?" Well, actually, now that you mention it.

Early in my research, I attended the annual European Tall Club convention, Europatreffen. Only in a room full of tall people does it become apparent that height is a pivotal piece of identity, that height was the most defining force in our lives. I told how my height had determined my choice of sports (swimming) and boyfriends (tall), my social circle (tall), my college (tall), and my personality (big enough to fill the tall).

There's a lot, I learned, going on in Tall World. Talls annually earn $789 more per inch than our average-height counterparts, racking up $1.5 million in extra assets over forty years. We are smarter, safer, and more powerful than our neighbors, and we live longer than they do too. We are also evolutionarily favored, are rarely victims of crime, and excel in professional, academic, and athletic arenas. We are the CEOs, presidents, and captains of industry, leaders who control the majority of the world's wealth and fill up the enrollment registers at top universities. In summary, we're wonderful, successful, and fun. Remember, the root of *Amazon* is the same as that of *amazing*.

Being tall, I learned, has meaning far beyond just seeing over people's heads. We share the balancing act of being the chosen people, yet we live in a society that is not built for us. How many times have you thought: *I am a nice, friendly tall person who obeys laws and pays taxes. Why can't I fit into a bus seat?* It's a ripe paradox.

I was floored to find that all these details together create a firm cultural context for tallness. *Whoah,* I thought. *There's a tall culture.* Seven days of living within that culture changed my life. It reaffirmed all the weird thoughts I'd had in my head for twenty years. I became an unabashed tall person. My inner monologue became empowered: *Short friend/boyfriend/boss, stop making me feel physically uncomfortable!* The elephant took its last breaths.

This project began because ever since the library let me down, I had some pressing questions. I wanted to know *why* tall people are 12 percent smarter (chapter 1), and how come tall men are the most sexually successful group on the planet (chapter 13), and *who the hell* is behind those airline seats (chapter 16). And I wanted to talk about the fifty-year secret history of the pharmaceutical stunting of tall children, which is ongoing (chapter 11) and the little-known story of the tallest women in the world (chapter 4).

I found lots of people who wanted to talk tall: athletic coaches, clothing executives, furniture designers, nonverbal communication experts, psychoanalysts, economists, evolutionary scientists, tall lobbyists, America's top tall dominatrix, and the guy who orders Manhattan bus seats. And I found a remarkably friendly social circuit of talls from Brooklyn to Beijing, who tossed me up to the world's tip-toppers: America's tallest woman, the world's tallest comedian, the WNBA's tallest player. At the top, everyone sort of knows each other, and their perspective on tall life is fine-tuned. My tall book was alive and well in their heads, fully formed. I just needed to go collect it.

This book is a backbone of the tall life, a synthesis of the vast knowledge that is tucked away in high-up corners around the world.

A 6'6" Dutch woman told me about her first visit to a tall club. "It really changed something in me. It gave me the knowledge that I'm not alone, and that I have tall sisters all over the world. And I think it gave me something in my back. Spine." *Tall spine.* That's what I hope to develop in this book.

Arianne Cohen
New York, May 2008

PART I

Tall Context

CHAPTER 1

A Primer on the Tall Life
Smarter, Richer, Longer, and Better

Let's jump right into the good news: Tall people make a lot of money. Buckets more than shorter people, for the same work. I announced this to my hairdresser, Donna. She peered over my head at the mirror. "*Hmmm*. Yeah, I could see myself paying you more than I pay me." She kept snipping. "How much more would I pay you?"

"About two and a half percent per inch."

Donna paused to do the math.

"So you're eight inches taller—that's like what, twenty percent more than me?"

Yep.

"Are you making this up?"

Nope. It's well documented.

For every additional four inches of height, talls enjoy about a 10 percent earnings increase, says Princeton economist Christina Paxson, one of a handful of researchers to separately study four half-century American and British salary surveys and put a price tag on height: $789 per inch per year. The premium holds true for fat talls, thin talls, female talls, and male talls.

Short people always respond to this news as if I've personally attached a siphon to their bank account. Twenty minutes later, Donna hollered over the hair dryer, "Is it always *exactly* $789 per inch?" Well, no. Of the tens of millions of workers included in the surveys, the premium ranged from $728 to $897 per inch. Paxson ran the numbers based on today's U.S. median income of $35,000 and came out with $770 per inch; a study of MBAs found a similar figure. Which means it's very safe to say that we earn a $740-to-$800-per-inch premium.

Donna turned off the hair dryer. "Can I start charging you more?"

"Nope."

She pointed the hair dryer at my face.

To save your wealthy brain some calculating, here is a chart of how much you, as a tall person, make compared to the average 5'5" U.S. worker. These figures are based on median U.S. incomes: the *average* 6'1" person will rake in $6,312 more annually than the *average* 5'6" person. Which means that half of talls are banking even more. The chart stops at 6'6" because there is some evidence

YOUR HEIGHT (IN INCHES)	EXTRA CASH EACH YEAR COMPARED TO A 5'5" WORKER	EXTRA CASH AMASSED OVER 40 YEARS	EXTRA CASH AMASSED OVER 40 YEARS + INVESTED AT 6%
5'6"	$789	$31,560	$130,094
5'7"	$1,578	$63,128	$262,190
5'8"	$2,367	$94,680	$394,285
5'9"	$3,156	$126,240	$526,381
5'10"	$3,945	$157,800	$656,475
5'11"	$4,734	$189,360	$788,571
6'0"	$5,523	$220,920	$920,666
6'1"	$6,312	$252,480	$1,052,762
6'2"	$7,101	$284,040	$1,182,855
6'3"	$7,890	$315,600	$1,314,951
6'4"	$8,679	$347,160	$1,447,047
6'6"	$10,257	$410,280	$1,709,237

that, NBA players notwithstanding, income does not increase indefinitely and flattens out at 6'6".

While it's fun to inform your best friend that your bank account will top hers by a cool $1.3 million, when looking at this data from a national perspective, tall incomes look less like a joke, and more like empire building. That $789 per inch, spread over three hundred million Americans, means that $170 billion is transferred annually from the shortest quarter of Americans to the tallest quarter. "It's on the order of the gender gap or race gap," says University of Pennsylvania economist Andrew Postlewaite. Imagine: A 5'8" person makes 14 percent less than a 6'1" person. The wage gap between black and white men is 15 percent.

None of this surprises me in the slightest. I learned the golden tall rule early: *Never talk dollars with short people.* In college, I always made a dollar more an hour than my friends on the same library jobs. Since then, my professional life has been rather blessed, plunking me on the high end of the salary continuum when all other things (age, education, gender) were equal. Granted, the writer's salary continuum is not impressive at any height. But I typically earn 15 percent more than my peers.

The obvious question is whether tall people are earning more because they have better jobs, or because they're better compensated for the same work? The answer is both. The graph on page 10 shows the average hourly wages of thirty-two to thirty-nine-year-old white men by height.

A few trends jump out: Tall workers are unlikely to earn the lowest salaries and are much more likely to take in higher salaries. And overall, talls are earning 16 percent more than shorts, averaging $17.28 per hour, versus $14.84. This means that for some reason talls are shifting to the right of the graph, and taking higher-paying jobs. Tall workers particularly dominate the highest salaries, those over $55 per hour. Less than 5 percent of the population makes $55 to $82 per hour, but those who do are doubly likely to be 6'3" or over. Which is incredible given that only 3 percent of white men are 6'3" or taller.

These figures are, of course, for men, which is usually the case with salary figures—nothing messes up income statistics like maternity leave. But tall women benefit from height just as much as

Wage distribution of adult white males in the U.S. by height

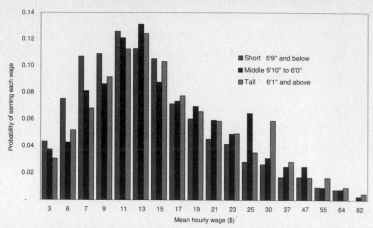

SOURCE: Gregory N. Mankiw and Matthew Weinzierl, "The Optimal Taxation of Height," Working Paper, April 13, 2007, p. 28, based on the National Longitudinal Survey of Youth.

men, if not more. A 2001 study from the Minnesota Twins Registry showed that tall women earn an astounding 3.5 to 5.5 percent more per inch than their shorter counterparts, while other small studies find the $789 to be roughly accurate. This news is diluted by the fact that the gender gap stubbornly sticks around regardless of height, meaning that tall women still earn 17 percent less than tall men. The gender gap is not a height issue, as has been hypothesized.

The tall income advantage jumps even further for jobs involving physical labor, because tall healthy bodies are more "productive, especially in activities requiring prolonged intense physical labor," writes anthropologist Sara Stinson. It's easiest to track this phenomenon in cultures that put price tags on people—always a popular human rights tactic. "We know that in slave economies tall, muscled people are worth much more than short people," Nobel Prize–winning economist Robert Fogel told me. Talls, particularly women, also have comparatively large stores of energy. Imagine, a 6'0" woman carries roughly twice the fat stores of a 5'4" woman yet uses only a third more energy. This means that she can not only work well but store a lot of fuel in case of upcoming food shortages; she can provide more energy for a developing fetus, which researchers say is why babies of tall mothers have a higher likeli-hood of thriving. This information is all valuable. Not surprisingly, tall Sudanese tribal women are worth twice the dowry of shorter brides, an extra twenty to fifty cows.

So *why* do talls make more money? I always assumed the obvious: when you're tall, people don't mess with you. This was the reigning theory in the academic community as well. "People have known for a very long time that tall men make more money," says Postlewaite. "It's been attributed to something along the lines of 'taller men command more attention and authority, and are therefore able to earn more money.'" Plausible, but not very scientific.

A few other potential explanations floated around. Perhaps talls are better educated, or are taking advantage of family job con-nections, or are mysteriously promoted into higher jobs immedi-ately. None panned out. Talls are only marginally more educated than shorter people—Ph.D.'s are just 1.5 inches taller than high school dropouts. Family job connections can't be the cause, be-cause tall children from short families go on to earn the same amount of money. And though talls are indeed sometimes promoted—talls are about 10 percent more likely per inch to be white-collar workers—that still doesn't explain why tall people make more money than their colleagues with the exact same job. So what exactly *is* behind the tall advantage?

In 2003 Postlewaite and two co-researchers decided to comb through male American and British salary data and look for trends. They noticed something funny. The heights of boys at age sixteen accurately predicted their adult incomes. "Being tall as an adult isn't really what matters," he says. "Being tall as an adolescent matters." Tall sixteen-year-old boys, years later, make more money. This is slightly odd, because as you may recall from your junior year, some tall sixteen-year-old classmates went on to become very tall adults, while others stopped growing right there and are barely able to see over bookcases. Postlewaite published a paper in 2003 saying that adult height doesn't matter—only age sixteen height.

He concluded that tall teens' lifestyles must somehow lead to big bucks, and he put his money on extracurricular activities as the culprit. "It's known that short male teens participate less in school government, hobby clubs, and athletics," he says. "Kids who participate in few activities have fewer opportunities to develop interpersonal skills and self-confidence. Athletics alone accounts for one-third of the income differential."

Academics agreed on his numerical findings—that tall teens become wealthy adults—but his self-confidence explanation wasn't popular among female economists, who noted that women weren't included in the study, and that many tall teens struggle with social activities at age sixteen regardless of height. "There's good reason that age sixteen height correlates to adult earnings," says Paxson. "The boys who are tall at age sixteen are the ones who had a really good start to life. If you look at poorer kids and kids with health problems, you see that they're not only shorter, but their adolescent growth spurt is delayed." In 2006 Paxson and her Princeton colleague Anne Case published a study, largely in response to Postlewaite. They traced male and female adults who had been cognitively tested as small children, so that they had decades of data following height, smarts, and income. Their data showed that the kids with the higher IQs ended up making more money—and a disproportionate number of them were tall. The paper opens with one of my favorite sentences: "We offer a simple explanation: Taller people earn more because they are smarter."

Smarter

Case and Paxson are, as you might guess, my favorite researchers ever. They are not the first to suggest that talls are smart. Two large Swedish and Danish studies in the 1990s found that intellect increases with height. The numbers are astounding: for example, of 76,111 Danish men, those over 6'3" scored 19 percent above the group's average IQ, and a full 44 percent above the shortest men, 5'4" or under. This is not to say that all talls are brilliant—I assure you that there are some memorably low-IQ tall people wandering about—but it's less common. A Honolulu study found that short older men (ages seventy-one to ninety-three) were three times more likely to score poorly on cognitive testing than tall older men;

25 percent of the shorts bottomed out on their test scores, versus 9 percent of the talls.

Case and Paxson found slightly more muted IQ benefits than the Scandinavian studies. "There's not a huge association between height and IQ, but it's definitely there," says Paxson. For every standard deviation increase in height, she found a one-tenth standard deviation increase in IQ, which looks roughly like this:

U.S. HEIGHT PERCENTILE	HEIGHT (WOMEN / MEN)	AVERAGE IQ PERCENTILE
50th	5'4" / 5'9"	50th
84th	5'7" / 6'1"	54th
97th	5'9" / 6'3"	58th
99th	5'11" / 6'4"	62nd

Note that the last category is a 12 percent IQ boost simply for being tall.

The week that Case and Paxson published their study, they became international media sensations. Reuters ran the headline "Taller People Are Smarter—Study." Paxson and Case were bombarded with e-mail, mostly from angry short people who did not want to hear that they were less smart, less wealthy, and still short. Some were rather dramatic, including e-harpoons like, "You have loaded a gun and pointed it at the vertically challenged man's head."

Which was unfortunate, because Case and Paxson weren't trying to say that talls are inherently smarter. They're not. They were trying to say that talls are more likely to be smart because *the same childhood environments that make kids smart also make them tall*. In a nutshell, talls are more likely to come from better home environments than shorts or average-size people. "There's a lot of indication that the factors that affect cognitive ability, like prenatal care, nutrition, and exposure to disease, also effect growth in childhood, and adult height," Paxson told me. "This was a hard thing to get across to reporters. But let me put it this way: If you have two children with the same cognitive test scores, one tall and one average, they're gonna earn the same amount on average."

Twins are helpful in pinpointing precisely what combination of environment and genetics creates tall-smart kids. Conveniently, Scandinavians obsessively catalog their twins. By comparing twins reared separately and together, they found that *two-thirds* of the smart-tall connection is caused by healthy environments, where children are well fed and academics are emphasized. This means that tall kids are smart largely because they're often raised well.

The remaining third of tall-smartness is attributed to tall genetics, which is a bit less understood. Here's what we know: Some talls are smart from the beginning. Long five-to-twelve-month-old babies do significantly better on cognitive tests, even after controlling for babies that came from troubled pregnancies or low-educated parents. The reigning theory is that one of the growth factors, insulin-like growth factor (IGF-1, discussed extensively in chapter 9) also affects the brain's learning and memory. Children in the 99th percentile are known to be particularly flooded with IGF-1. No one is quite sure of IGF-1's effect on the brain, but a connection between IGF-1 and smarts would mean that smartness in some very tall people is essentially encoded in tall genes.

Tall Longevity

That same IGF-1 is also suspected to be the cause of tall longevity. "Tall people live quite a significant amount longer," says health economist Sir Roderick Floud, president emeritus of London Metropolitan University. "It's not just a question of people who are very short having shorter lives. There's a clear linear relationship, so that as you get taller, your years of life increase up to 6'2" or so for men. Once above 6'2", mortality begins to increase again. It's basically a U-shaped curve."

Floud's talking about a well-known study tracking 1.8 million Norwegian adults. In 1984 researcher Hans Waaler found that a 5'0" man has nearly double the risk of mortality at any moment than a 6'2" man. Other studies across centuries have backed up Waaler's U-shaped curve, including a study of Union Army soldier deaths, and a 2003 study that followed 2 million Norwegians for

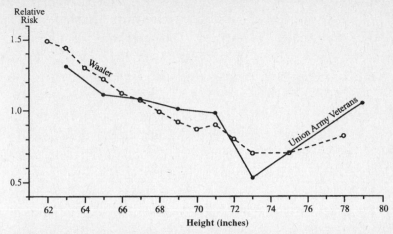

SOURCE: Robert Fogel, *The Escape from Hunger and Premature Death, 1700–2100*
(New York: Cambridge University Press, 2004), p. 23.

twenty years. You can see the above graph of both male Norwegian and Union soldier mortality chances. A 1.0 is the average risk
of death for the general population.

Keep in mind that health standards in the Union Army were not
profound. Army records talk about cantaloupe-size hernias; neither incontinence nor left-eye blindness was a ground for dismissal
(right eyes were needed for musket shooting). No one, tall or short,
was a bastion of health. But tall soldiers lived longer. In modern
populations, for every two male inches, mortality decreases by 9
percent, according to a 2000 Finnish study of 31,999 people. Even
among middle-aged and older men, who obviously have a higher
rate of death, their risk of mortality is 4 percent lower for every
two inches. The figures are similar for women.

Now, all of these studies simply look at the age at which people
die. They don't explain *why* talls live longer. In fact, averaging the
deaths and heights of millions of people can obscure underlying
causes of death—for example, if a bunch of short people happened
to live in landmine country, it wouldn't be apparent. "I think it's
quite pointless to do Waaler's kind of research," says one economist.
"There's a lot of error." Yet there's little research on the causes of
tall longevity, such as studies of tall twins with the same genes,
which would shed light on *why* talls are living longer. There is,

in general, very little tall medical research. I find this quite frustrating—what's more clinically relevant than preventing death?

Here's what we do know about why tall people live longer: Statistically speaking, tall men are unlikely to die from accidents and violence. Those are the domain of shorts, though it's unclear why. Talls also have substantially lower rates of lung and cardiovascular disease. The good childhood living conditions that produce tall people also produce bodies that are more able to resist time's ravages. And tall people tend to be richer, which is pivotal—wealth is a strong predictor of mortality. In summary: If you're tall, you're statistically likely to live for quite a while, but we're not quite sure why.

Unless you're a super tall man, in the top quarter percentile. Super tall men seem to die earlier, which is likely a function of the fact that very tall men have more chronic health conditions. In fact, graphing chronic medical conditions versus height (see below) looks suspiciously like the graph of mortality. Men at 6'3" have the fewest chronic illnesses.

Very tall women, in the top percentile, are another story, and research has been contradictory. The 2003 study of 2 million Norwegians found that women's longevity spiked among the tallest women, essentially holding to the same pattern, inch per inch, as men's: those just over six feet tall lived the longest. A separate study found that the tallest women had higher chronic illnesses, much like the men's graph, particularly musculo-skeletal illnesses.

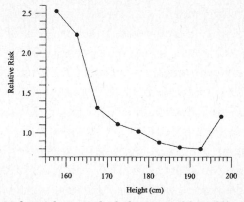

Male Height vs. Risk of Chronic Health Problems

SOURCE: Robert Fogel, *The Escape from Hunger and Premature Death, 1700–2100* (New York: Cambridge University Press, 2004), p. 28.

The clashing findings indicate that an underlying factor is probably at play—some tall women are genetically or environmentally prone to certain, as-of-yet undefined illnesses.

As the height economist John Komlos summarizes, "It's good to be tall, but not too tall."

I came across an intriguing theory explaining this longevity difference between the very tall and the super tall. Often called the Rate of Cell Division Hypothesis, it says that from the time humans are conceived, cells are preprogrammed with a set maximum number cell divisions. This would mean that aging is less a matter of time than of how many cell divisions the body goes through. IGF-1 causes growth, but it also pushes cells into dividing quickly. Who has a lot of IGF-1? Children in the 99th percentile of height (see page 115). They may be smart, and they may grow a lot, but their cell divisions also happen quickly. Flies and mice with low levels of IGF-1 have been shown to live substantially longer. This is largely speculative, but if true, it has one main upside for the super tall: When injured, the tallest heal faster, a boon for pro athletes. And it has a downside: earlier death.

Better

Based on all this information, it's not a stretch to say that on the whole, tall people are *better*. I am biased. But even nonbiased researchers have concluded that we are smarter, richer, more educated, longer living, and physically superior. Take the 1999 study of 32,887 Swedish men, which found that men above the 98th height percentile performed superiorly on intellectual, physical, and physiological stress tests and had fewer illnesses and lower morbidity rates, and were more suitable for leadership roles. If that's not a seal of all-around betterness, I don't know what is.

I'm sure that there are some gaps in our betterness. We're resource guzzlers, consuming more food and goods, which make us expensive and environmentally damaging. We take up space and sometimes break things when we sit on them. There's no word on whether tall people are nice or not. But on average, talls are doing pretty damn well.

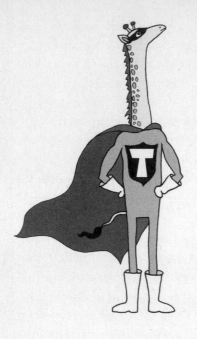

Given our betterness, it's not surprising that talls populate the upper echelons of the elite. "Men who are powerful in our society—CEOs, presidents, politicians—are almost without exception taller than the average American man," says Kory Floyd, an evolutionary psychologist at Arizona State University. "It doesn't mean that a short person couldn't acquire resources and become a CEO, but it means he wouldn't have the advantages that a tall person might have."

Talls are the most powerful people in the world, bar none, and always have been. "Political leaders throughout time have been tall, dating at least to hunter-gatherers," says Loughborough University anthropologist Barry Bogin. "Tallness has been seen as a social, economic and physical dominance over others." This is true of both men and women. Power is mostly a height game: a 6'0" man and a 6'0" woman are perceived as equally powerful. We know this based on photo studies. If the woman is taller, she is unanimously considered more dominant. Our brains are wired this way, which we know because when children as young as three are shown similar photos, they also pick whoever is taller as more dominant. The societal ideal that men are more powerful is a myth—it's just because only 15 percent of women are taller than men.

This plays out in the professional world, where the farther up the flagpole you go, the taller people get. It doesn't matter what industry. Take academia. Assistant professors are 1.24 inches above average heights, associate professors 1.5 inches taller, and department chairs 2.14 inches taller. Two inches skips over 20 percent of the population. As the researchers wrote, "Height is important not in itself, but because it is a predictor of social dominance."

The truth about tall betterness has leaked out over the years and has entered the zeitgeist to the point that better talls are *expected*. A Harvard professor told me an anecdote about Drew Gilpin Faust, 5'11", who was named the first female president of Harvard in 2007. "When it was announced, a male colleague leaned over and said, 'You know, tall people are much more successful.' As if *that* made her successful. He was relating her success solely to being tall."

His mistake is understandable. At first glance, talls are automatically assumed to be in charge. "Tall people are given a little more deference or credibility," says University of Missouri psychologist Miles Patterson. "Tall people stand out and get your attention. You combine that with the tendency to see the taller person as a leader type, and such a person carries greater influence over others." The tall-leader connection is so ubiquitous that it boggles the mind to imagine the exceptions. Adolf Hitler, at 5'8", and Lenin, at 5'5", both employers of shoe lifts and raised podiums, who more than one historian has suggested possibly felt the need to compensate on the job for their shortness.

The tall advantage is now taught at universities, where it's further magnified. "I learned in Psych 101 that it's the hallow effect," says Chris Rovzar, 6'3", a *New York* magazine editor and Yale graduate. "If someone's tall and good looking, you attribute other good qualities to them."

I didn't realize how pervasive the assumption of tall dominance is until respected experts began extending the tall advantage beyond its actual boundaries. A well-known academic psychotherapist told me, "There've been all these studies on how tall people are more liked and more successful." Actually, tall people aren't any more well liked than anyone else. A pediatric endocrinologist commented, "There's always a biological advantage to being tall." Actually, there's not—a well-cared-for, smart shorter person will do just as well.

But the glow of smart, rich, long-living talls has been irreparably reflected onto all talls and become embedded into our cultural consciousness as a truth: *Talls are great, as proven by science.* Which gives us a bit more credit than we deserve.

And here in that glow is where the true benefit of height lies. "Power has a way of being self-reinforcing," says Floyd. "Tall people are perceived as more dominant and often get treated that way, and if people treat you as dominant, then you de facto become more dominant in that group." It's a self-fulfilling prophecy. And that is the tall advantage.

CHAPTER 2

Tall People Around the World

Misery produces short people.
—Louis-René Villermé, 1829

The year I was twenty-three, I spent much of my time attending press conferences in Phnom Penh, Cambodia, where I worked as a newspaper reporter. I walked into meetings to find fifty men and twenty cops milling around, the tallest of whom reached my armpit. All stared. I never quite figured out how to manage this situation.

I was the tallest person anyone had ever seen. Taller than the locals, taller than the expatriates, and taller than what locals remembered of the American GIs. I assumed that after months of frequenting the same markets with the same saleswomen, they would eventually get over it. Never happened. Every time I entered a market or passed any Cambodian, I ran a 75 percent chance of invoking a comment about height, *"Bpee metres!"* (Two meters!) followed by a swift sucking in of the breath. I was considered so tall, and therefore exotic, that I didn't get a gender—I was just an enormous *barang* (foreigner), a sort of *über*-large white mutant.

Tall hazards are never quite what you expect. One Monday I awoke in Phnom Penh with a bit of stomach pain and soon found myself in an airplane headed to Bangkok General for an emergency appendectomy. The surgery went smoothly, and I landed in an extralong bed on the Foreigner Floor. A nurse handed me my belly button ring, which had apparently caused fifteen minutes of operating room commotion, as no one knew how to remove it.

The resident English-speaking doctor, Dr. Singh, explained that my surgery had been successful. Then he informed me that they had found an "unspecified mass" on my pancreas. He wanted to let me rest, then perform another CAT scan the following day, focusing on the pancreas. He also ordered blood work to look for tumor markings. He held up an image of my pancreas and pointed to where it should end. Mine extended six inches past his finger. He said it could just be inflammation—but that he'd asked the nurses not to mention it.

I knew perfectly well that pancreatic tumors are bad news. Of the approximately thirty-seven thousand Americans diagnosed with pancreatic cancer annually, the five-year survival rate is 3 percent. But I consoled myself with the free-flowing morphine and the knowledge that I would have an answer tomorrow.

While I pondered the fact that I was potentially dying of pancreatic cancer, Dr. Singh took a five-day trip to China. I was put on the Foreigner Diet, which consisted of cream of corn soup breakfast, cream of chicken soup lunch, and cream of spinach soup dinner. One night, cream of cream arrived. Then the CAT scan machine broke. Nonetheless, in preparation for morning CAT scans that never materialized, too-young nurses starved me every night.

When you think you have a terminal illness at age twenty-three, this is what you do. First, you want to wave a magic wand to make your bodily problems go away. You poke at your pancreas and wonder why you can't just reach through the skin and fix it. Then you remind yourself that you will never have sex again, and that the rest of your life will be painful, boring, and short. It was over.

On day seven, a relaxed-looking Dr. Singh appeared. I was very hungry, having fasted yet again. He was smiling. "Good news, your tumor indicators were within normal limits," he said. I asked if I could go home. He said no, I was on "high-priority standby" for a CAT scan. I was so bored that I watched *Showgirls* in Chinese.

On day eight I had my CAT scan. A green-turbaned Dr. Singh appeared a few hours later and said that all was well. "You do not, my dear, have a pancreatic tumor."

He explained that down in the basement, the radiologists who review the X-rays and scans have little charts glued to the wall, telling them how many centimeters each organ should be. "My dear, as you know, you are very tall. So, I think that maybe they looked and thought your pancreas was very large for a Thai person. You probably had a bit of pancreatitis too, but you are okay now." I glared.

"You do not have a tumor, my dear." He smiled. "You are just tall."

My U.S. health insurance distinctly did not cover my pancreatic cancer scare in Bangkok, under the explanation, "Incorrectly diagnosed with terminal illness due to height," and then denied my request for mental health visits. Instead I returned to Cambodia.

Cambodians are extremely short—women frequently come in below 5'0". But there is a wide range: Some tribal villagers are a full four inches shorter than those in a town a mile away, a scenario that repeats across Thailand, Vietnam, and Laos. Perhaps this variation is why Southeast Asians are particularly height obsessed. They like to quantify it: In Thailand your shoe size is of pivotal importance. In Cambodia, getting-to-know-you chatter includes your weight and height. Newspaper classifieds specify, "Wanted: Female 5'5" hostess."

Turns out that Cambodians are not genetically short, and neither is anyone else. "Most of the ethnic differences in stature appear to be environmentally driven," Stanford pediatrician and growth expert Ron Rosenfeld told me. "That doesn't mean that there aren't genetic factors. There are, but environmental factors are much more important." Thais are inherently no shorter than Norwegians, Swedes no taller than Columbians, Mexicans and Guatemalans no shorter than the Dutch. Cambodians, he explained, are short mainly due to substandard health care, malnutrition, poverty, poor shelter, and endless rounds of feast or famine.

If everyone in the world grew up with reasonable health care and nutrition, every ethnic group and population would average roughly the same height: pretty tall. Well-fed children worldwide vary in height by only a half-inch. The World Health Organization growth standards for children "show no differences for Africans, Asians, North Americans, or any other children," says the anthropologist Barry Bogin. "All the kids measured for these standards are well-nourished and breast-fed, and they all grow exactly the same."

This means that—gasp—us tall folk are not actually all that tall. It's just that the majority of the world's six billion people aren't anywhere near their maximum height potential. In a world of perfect childhoods, a 5'10" woman or 6'3" man would be mildly above average, around the 65th percentile.

A few rare, exceptional groups are genetically destined to be short, such as the Efé African Pygmy people. They produce unusual hormone levels and, as a result, will never be tall, no matter how lush the environment. And a few small populations do skew a bit taller. "If you took East Africans from Kenya or Rwanda where there's a history of taller-than-typical tallness, and brought them up in the best conditions, with the best schools, the best medicine, and the best emotional environment, perhaps East Africans might be a bit taller on average than the Dutch are today," says Bogin. But these exceptions are few and far between. On the whole, humans are encoded to be wonderfully lanky and tall.

This is hard to swallow after years of assuming that Eskimos are naturally squat, and Swedes naturally lanky. Think of it this way: Imagine a pile of six billion tree seeds. You scoop a few thousand in your hands and plant them all over the world. The soil and weather will differ broadly, and the trees will grow to widely varying heights. It's the same with people.

What does this mean for individuals? Say you study two trees that are planted next to each other. One is eighteen feet taller than the other, despite growing up in the same soil. The difference is genetics. The taller tree likely started off with a greater genetic maximum height potential. When you're looking at height differences in individuals, you're looking at *genetics*.

But say you get in a helicopter and fly over a tract of a thousand trees, and you notice that they're all extremely tall. Their excellent growth is a reflection of the *environment*. Perhaps the soil was nutrient-rich, and the weather favorable. It's the same with people. When you look at the people of Cambodia, who average nearly eight inches shorter than the Dutch, you're seeing the results of their environments. A rule of thumb for large populations: Tall people are shorthand for thriving; short people are shorthand for suffering.

The medical world caught onto this only recently. Until the early 1990s it was widely assumed that certain populations, like the Dutch, were just genetically tall. Bogin proved otherwise by studying short people, because height is easier to quantify in its lack. He's an exceedingly friendly guy who gets excited about phrases like "growth velocity."

Bogin's discovery began when he read a 1992 newspaper article about seven drowned Mayan men in Florida. He had been working in Guatemala since 1974 measuring Mayans, the so-called "pygmies of South America," who average 5'2" for men and 4'8" for women. Guatemala was in the midst of a civil war. "The one thing I couldn't do was prove that the Maya were very short because they were suffering," says Bogin. "Most people said it was just genetic."

The article mentioned that the drowned Mayans had lived among a five-thousand-person Mayan community in Florida. Bogin grabbed his tape measure and went there. He found that the Mayan children born in Florida were nearly *five inches* taller than the same-age children in Guatemala, and that the second-generation Florida Mayans grew to equal American heights, with 15 percent topping 6'0". To give you a sense of how enormous that five inches is, Eastern European immigrants to America increased only two to three inches over *three* generations. "It was clearly not genetic," says Bogin. "They're not limited in their growth potential."

Bogin noted that the Florida Mayans had particularly long legs. Healthy babies' legs grow faster than their other body parts, shooting out tadpole-style from the age of six months. If the environment is bad (poor nutrition or health care, poverty or emotional abuse), the part that grows the fastest is most affected. "On average tall people have longer legs, women particularly," says University of California at San Francisco pediatric endocrinologist Melvin Grumbach. "If you stop growing earlier, your legs fuse and your spine keeps growing a little longer." Thus many short people from poor countries have long torsos, while tall people have longer shins. Long legs are a sign of good childhood health.

Height is such an accurate indicator of well-being that the United Nations uses it to monitor socioeconomic progress in developing countries. The UN can track not only the health of a group of children from year to year but also the relative well-being of one generation or village as compared to another, as well as access to food, sanitation, and health care. All with a tape measure.

The obvious question is, why do so many ethnic groups in America still average short, even after a couple of generations here? And why are most very tall Americans either white or black? Shouldn't all kids who grow up in good homes get tall? I asked Bogin. It's a historical issue: most whites and blacks have been in America for over four generations, and they no longer show the environmental suffering that can be passed on from generation to generation. "The suffering experienced in the previous generation gets passed on not genetically, but in how the metabolism of your body functions," says Bogin. "It's an intergenerational effect of poor nutrition and poor health, and it takes three or four generations to get rid of that."

It works like this: Imagine a pregnant woman in Beijing or Johannesburg or Delhi in 1945. Her nutrition is poor, and her damaged metabolism primes the fetus's brain, pancreas, and ova for starvation. The daughter grows up, immigrates to California, moves into a McMansion, and gets pregnant. It doesn't matter how great her environment and health are, because her ova are already predetermined. "Her body was damaged by the suffering experienced by her mother," says Bogin. Her child, a first-generation American, will likely be taller than she but shorter than the neighbors. It will take another generation or two to shake out the stunting. As a rule of thumb, only third-to-fifth-generation Americans are very tall. I am a textbook fourth-generation American. My great-great-grandmother was a 5'2" immigrant, my great-grandmothers 5'4" and 5'6", my grandmother 5'8", my mother 6'0". I'm 6'3".

I think. I could be 6'2". Or nearly 6'4". My doctor's office measurements have varied from 6'1" to 6'3.5". This is relevant because it's extremely complicated for researchers to figure out how tall, say, the 14 million people of Cambodia are. Seventy percent of doctor's office measurements are significantly botched. Measuring is so fraught with error that the National Institutes of Health held a whole conference on the topic in 1985, where they declared a protocol: Trash the tape measure and instead use a stadiometer, which is accurate to a sixteenth of an inch and is calibrated to the floor daily. Doctors are trained to measure three times to the apex of the skull and then find the average—in centimeters, which prevents the eye from rounding to the nearest inch. (The most accurate height measurement for large groups is actually from floor to knee, which correlates with full height and stays consistent throughout life. But only academics know this.)

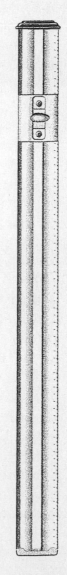

An added complication is that height is a moving target. During the day people lose 1 to 2 percent of height from spine compression—more for overweight people and book bag carriers—which means that people need to be measured first thing in the morning. The average person also loses a half-inch every twenty years, though that's heavily impacted by socioeconomics—one study showed that black American males lose 1.7" every twenty years. And there are gender differences. "Women shrink more than men, a couple inches between thirty and eighty," says economist Richard Steckel.

Which is all to say that whatever height you think you are is ballparked, and that the country height averages coming up in this chapter are, by definition, estimates.

At the top of the height hierarchy are our favorite windmill lovers, the Dutch. The men average 6'0.5", the women 5'7", and they have not yet reached their peak. "We will not go through the ceiling," Dutch height expert Hans van Wieringen told the *New Yorker*, "but it is possible that we will grow another four inches." Their stratospheric rise began 150 years ago. In 1865, Dutch army recruits averaged 5'4.9"; in 1965, young men averaged 5'9". A mere fifteen years later the mean male height increased to 5'11.7".

The Dutch are genetically just like any other Northern Europeans. "Everything is just longer," says Bogin. "Their heads, necks, abdomens, everything. There's nothing special genetically." And no, the Dutch are not tall because they need the extra height to survive the cold—that's an old wives' tale. The Dutch are indeed tall, skinny people who periodically use their legs to walk very quickly across Holland. But they didn't start getting tall until 150 years ago, so their height can't possibly be an evolutionary adaptation. Think about it: Mammals in cold climates tend to be short-limbed and thick-trunked, to minimize surface area. Polar bears thrive in the cold; giraffes thrive in the heat.

Dutch height is a tribute to their health care and social services systems, which are run on a per capita income that is 75 percent of America's (roughly $34,000 per person, versus $44,000). They are, as a culture, quite pleased about their height. If talls are a people, then the Netherlands is our adopted homeland. Visiting is like falling into tall heaven and glimpsing what the world could be like: long legs everywhere, numerous heads above the six-foot mark (and the 6'5" mark). "I would like to give everyone who's tall three weeks of vacation in the Netherlands," a 6'6" woman at Europatreffen told me. "They'd be so relieved."

Now that we know that height indicates childhood and mother well-being, the following charts are no longer just a cheerleading exercise for the Dutch. The peoples on the left are thriving; those on the right are suffering. And somehow the Italians and British (and the French and Spanish, who are roughly the same height) are getting less childhood care than the Scandinavians and Americans. A 2000 Dutch study of European heights concluded, "The persistence of international differences in average height indicates a high degree of differences in childhood living conditions."

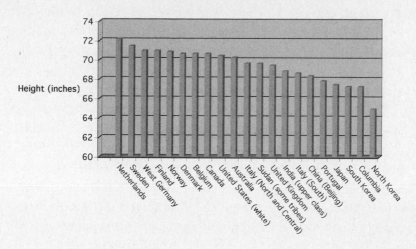

Male Heights Around the World

You might notice that the United States, the richest country in the world, ranks seventh and ninth. It wasn't always so. From colonial times Americans were the tallest in the world, and steadily grew healthier and taller from the late 1800s through World War II, when Americans were still two inches taller than the average German soldier. The Dutch surpassed us around 1930, and the

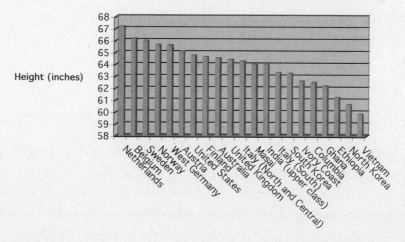

Female Heights Around the World

SOURCE: Figures courtesy of John Komlos, economist, University of Munich.

postwar Danish and Germans soon followed. Americans stopped growing in the 1950s and haven't grown taller in almost sixty years. This seems contradictory—the U.S. economy repeatedly doubled in that timespan—but all the money in the world doesn't matter if its not spent on health care and childhood care.

Today, the average U.S. man is 5'9.2" and woman 5'3.8". Women have declined by 0.3 inch over forty years, which is significant. "It's amazing—no, *astounding*, that heights would have declined at all at a time when both income and medical knowhow were improving markedly," says economist John Komlos. Only black men have grown significantly, purely a reflection of the slow four-generation recovery from slavery's malnutrition. You can see the visual below:

So why have American heights stagnated? "If you want to explain the height differences between these countries, it's simply because the medical provisions are not adequate for a large part of the U.S. population," says J. W. Drukker, a Dutch height economist. "In the Netherlands we have a good welfare system and good social policy, with a safety net for people from the lower strata of society. If you have a baby, you immediately get a mailer that you have to report with your child, and they check the child for illness, control its feeding status, give you advice, and ask you to come back. The same applies for Sweden and Norway, which are also very tall." In the United States, a number of our babies miss pre- and postnatal

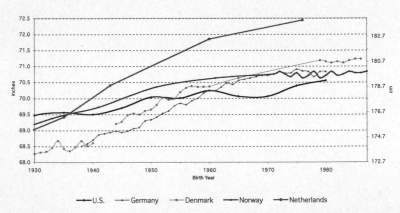

SOURCE: John Komlos and Benjamin E. Lauderdale, "The Mysterious Stagnation and Relative Decline of American Heights in the Second Half of the 20th Century," *Annals of Human Biology* 43, no. 2 (2007): 206. The U.S. lines are uneven because U.S. data were collected every ten years.

care altogether. Someone should run for president on the slogan "Universal health care will make you taller." It's true. Talls are found wherever childhood health care is top notch, mothers get months off after birth, and social services abound.

Height experts find the American height slump rather maddening, like watching an ongoing train wreck. "In the U.S., obviously something's very wrong with the health care system, and there's no reason," says Komlos, who wrote a paper about Americans called "From the Tallest to the Fattest." "Some of the other evidence is really preposterous," he continues, like our life expectancy ranking, twenty-eighth. We're two to four years behind European countries and Japan. We're also malnourished: Two-thirds of U.S. children are deficient in vitamins and minerals, despite being 20 percent obese. (A diet of Cheetos has that effect.) And nearly a third of Americans live in poverty, versus 5 to 10 percent in Scandinavia. "American infant mortality rate is about twice that of Sweden," says Komlos. A recent UNICEF report ranked the United States in twentieth place for child well-being, and the Dutch first. A coincidence? No. Plenty of Americans come out of the womb programmed to be super tall—they just never reach their maximum height potential.

Economists blame our market-oriented welfare policies, and the tendency of capitalism to distance large swaths of the population from nutrition and health care. "Scandinavians keep improving the environment where they grow up, so that raises [the heights of] the bottom," says Bogin. "In America our bottom is very low, because some people don't have food the last week of every month."

I had looked forward to visiting Bogin at the University of Michigan, only to find that he had just moved to England. And John Komlos also hopped the pond to Munich after over four decades in America. Height researchers, it turns out, are rampant socialists. "Have you ever run into an American who says, 'My health insurance is really great'?" asked Komlos. "I'm one hundred percent insured here, by the way. For dental and everything." And the Germans are the third tallest people in the world.

Shortly after my pancreatic cancer debacle, I lived happily upright in Phnom Penh for four weeks—until I developed a hallucinatory

fever. My neighbors filed in and out without knocking and speculated that I might be too tall to have a proper immune system. I
turned out to have dengue fever; I was unwittingly breeding mos-
quito larvae that carried the virus in a water bin in my bathroom.
My neighbors speculated that I might be too tall to have a proper
brain.

Through my profuse sweating haze, I periodically felt a sizable
hand holding mine. I'd crack my eyes open and see my Cambodian
teacher, Morivan Ly. At 5'6", she was considered a giantess and
dwarfed my middle-aged landlords, who were not much taller than
my bed. They liked to hold their feet up in comparison to mine,
which hung far off the bed.

Height has great cultural nuance in Cambodia. Which is slightly
odd for a place where no one actually knows how tall they are. The
government measures only childbearing-age women, a public health
strategy to gauge labor risks from small pelvises, which go hand in
hand with low height. A quarter of women are 4'10" or below; researchers think men average in the 5'3" range. Suffice it to say that
it's a very consistent place. Everything is short: the trees, the people,
the cattle, the alcohol supply.

Yet height serves as a visual litmus test of where individual
Cambodians were during the Khmer Rouge war. Those who were
young teens during the war, from 1975 to 1980, and spent their
adolescent growth spurts starving, are notably short, averaging
under 5'0". "Women who were in their early teenage years in 1975
appear to be the shortest and most likely to be stunted, which is not
surprising given that nutrition during adolescence is an important
determinant of stature," write researchers. These individuals have
a distinctive body: they are short-legged, long-torsoed adults, with
very short shins, the physical calling cards of stunted growth.
Those who were babies during the war are notably larger, because
most babies didn't survive, and those who did were nourished by
baby formula in refugee camps.

Which is to say Cambodia is a weird place to be super tall. Everyone knew at a glance that Morivan was born after the war (1981).
At the markets, people asked her what she ate and yelled, *"Tom!"* I
thought it was a nickname. It means "big." She faced dating diffi-
culties, because Cambodian men assume that a tall woman will

make them appear inadequate. Morivan ultimately dodged this fate by marrying a six-foot American reporter and moving to New Jersey.

I did not realize how ingrained the cultural bias against tall women was until Morivan told me Cambodian folktales while I was ill. These fables are serious business, believed quite literally. At birth each baby, based on a six year rotation of birth years, is deemed a giant, a human, or an angel, each male or female regardless of the baby's gender. Future marriage depends on this labeling. Two female giants can marry because they both have magic; a human and a human are okay; a human and an angel will start a relationship and then separate; two male giants will fight all the time. And a giant and a human are disastrous. "Usually the giant will eat the human," Morivan gravely explained. "Very bad."

I eyed her, trying to figure out whether I was hallucinating. She launched into the folktale of people-eating she-giants:

> Once upon a time in a land far far away (presumably Cambodia), a prince left his castle and went to study. He became a hermit, studying all he needed to know to be a good future prince. Once he had completed his learning, he began the long walk back to the castle through the (presumably Cambodian) jungle. After a day of walking, he found a clearing to sleep. While he slept, a female giant spotted him and hid behind the thick foliage to look him up and down. She thought, "I haven't had a boyfriend for a year! And here's a cute prince!" But there was a problem. "If I come out like this, he will maybe have a heart attack. So I should come out looking pretty, changing myself to look like a beautiful woman."
>
> When the prince awoke, he found a beautiful woman perched beside him. She was so gorgeous that he decided to bring her to his castle, to become his princess. They finished the journey together and were greeted at the castle with great celebration.
>
> She moved into the castle, but another problem appeared: The "princess" was hungry. And so she began having night binges and eating the townsfolk. One by one they

began disappearing. The villagers would later find the bones. The townspeople were anxious about this, so they began hiding at night, to see who was eating the neighbors. Dozens of townspeople watched as the princess sneaked out of the castle, transformed herself into a female giant, and ate a sleeping child. Then she transformed back to her beautiful self and sneaked back into her husband's bed.

The next night, they armed themselves and surrounded the female giant, and just as she was about to eat another neighbor, they killed her. Then they celebrated a lot.

"And that's why it's not good between a giant and a human!" Morivan chirped. "The giant will eat the human." She gestured toward my body. "And when people say at the market, 'You tall like giant!', this is what they're talking about." I had no idea. And this is why a height measurement, in inches and feet, is only a small fraction of the tall experience.

CHAPTER 3

The Birth of Tall People
A History

The dawn of tall people did not begin on an impressive note. Our predecessors five million years ago, the hominids, were roughly three feet tall, the height of a big toddler. They spent their days roaming the African savannah, hiding from predators, scrounging for food, and often, dying. Our predecessors had a hard time not becoming extinct.

You see, the hominids had a problem: big cats kept eating them. When being chased by a lion-type creature, a prehuman with a maximum wingspan of 2.5 feet and twelve-inch legs has limited self-protection options. He's bait. He's likely to climb a tree, and good tree-climbers have short legs. Which, evolutionarily speaking, reinforces the shortness. Hominids were diminutive for the next 4 million years. Lucy, who lived 3.2 million years ago, was 3'6" tall and weighed sixty pounds.

Yet many modern benefits of talldom are directly connected to this extended period of shortness. Had hominids shot up in size immediately, they might have taken to wandering around alone, as many large animals sometimes do. That would have been disastrous. Loners do not tend to develop extreme intelligence (think dinosaurs, giraffes, elephants). Instead our slow-growing progenitors used teamwork to survive ("you be the bait, I'll climb the tree!"). In the process of fooling the big cats, they developed social skills and intellect, which paved the way for modern smart tall folk.

"There's not a lot of good data about when people got tall," says Harvard anthropologist Dan Lieberman. "We say that the big shift was around two million years ago with homo erectus, based upon one skeleton, the Nariokotome Boy. He's nine years old, and would've been about six feet tall when fully grown."

Now, hominids probably would have eventually grown relatively tall anyway—species grow until they either max out their skeleton capacity or are blocked by a larger creature in the food chain. But prehumans quickly doubled in size for two reasons: to lower their body temperature, and to run. Nariokotome Boy's body was exquisitely designed for the savannah, where a day in the sun could mean literal frying. "People who live in those hot climates are long and thin, and it's because height maximizes the surface-area-to-volume ratio—they can stay quite cool by perspiring," says Lieberman. But Nario was also now too big to hide in trees and needed to be able to move. Fast. "If you have longer legs, you're more economical when you locomote. You're using less energy per kilometer."

With the 100 percent increase in size came a 100 percent increase in caloric needs, met by hunting. And in order to hunt, even longer legs were needed. "We argue that the ability of humans to run marathons is not a fluke. We're the best endurance runners in the world, and it's for hunting," says Lieberman. It's called persistence hunting, jogging after prey for hours on end, if not days. The tall hunter-gatherers who could adeptly do this were more likely to survive socially—no one kills their meal ticket—and more likely to reproduce, producing tall savannah babies.

Jump ahead another million years. The true exaltation of tall people (the size! the mystique!) began a few hundred thousand years ago, when hominids developed the ability to walk and carry things at the same time—and promptly grew another twelve inches, averaging nearly today's heights. Nomadic hunting-gathering is a much healthier lifestyle than you might think. "They ate a wide variety of food, they exercised every day, and they didn't have infectious diseases, desk jobs, or stress," says anthropologist Barry Bogin. "They basically had the bodies of athletes."

From the beginning, talls were powerful within their tribes. Taller bodies have larger skeletons and more muscle mass, so tall hunter-gatherers could command more resources and physically control their fellow tribe members, stealing food when needed. "Dominance is the ability to affect another person's behavior," says Kory Floyd, an evolutionary psychologist at Arizona State University. "Physical strength is the natural correlate of dominance, and there's an inherent respect for the large organisms in a species."

The question is why women grew too. Most female mammals are 30 percent smaller than males, which is also the case in ancient hominoid skeletons. "Women's evolutionary niche has been more in terms of nurturing offspring," says Floyd. "In the evolutionary scheme it's not as big a deal whether a woman is tall or short." Today boys and girls are within millimeters of each other until puberty, and adult men and women are just 8 percent apart. Experts hypothesize that women had to grow wider hips to accommodate the large heads of smart human fetuses. And most of the time wider hips were attached to taller women. People are like trees—as they grow taller, they also grow wider trunks to support the weight. Thus the existence of today's tall women, such as your author.

The evolution of tall people was not all smooth sailing. Famine was a killer. Tall bodies need more calories, and when there's a long-term calorie shortage, talls bite the dust. Similarly, talls don't excel at hiding from predators, or at camouflage. "But those are exceptions," says Floyd. "The general favor goes to tall people. There is a preponderance of evidence. I would argue that an evolutionary favoritism goes along with height."

We smugly assume that we are the tallest humans to ever grace the earth. Quite the contrary. The Cro-Magnon people living thirty thousand years ago were about our size and 10 percent more muscular. Hunting-gathering, when food sources were abundant, was an exquisitely healthy lifestyle.

Heights plummeted because of a little tall disaster called civilization. "Heights go way down when we go into state society," says Bogin. "When Egypt conquered the Nile area, the height of peasants fell dramatically. They moved from having access to a wide variety of foods to growing what the Egyptian state demanded. Their bones show lots of deficiencies in minerals and iron." The same stunting happened repeatedly throughout history. As late as the 1800s, male Cheyenne Indians, who hunted bison and collected berries, averaged a whopping 5'10", towering above even today's Americans, not to mention General Custer's cavalry, which averaged 5'7", and the period's wealthy European monarchies.

Cities, both ancient and modern, were a particular breeding ground for short people. A trip to modern Guatemala is an object lesson. Many Latin Americans are about as tall today as they were eight thousand years ago, says Bogin. "Their height went *way* down when the empires appeared. They're only beginning to recover." More recent studies of the industrialization of London, Chicago, and New York indicate the reason, and it's not disease. When city goods suddenly become cheaper, people buy whatever's cheap. And instead of eating well-rounded farm meals of fruits and vegetables, grains, dairy, and meat, they skip the pricey shipping and eat bread and potatoes.

Early civilizations lauded the one trait they rarely had: tallness. It was quickly upgraded to a matter of morality. Caesar and Tacitus considered height virtuous, attached to a morally superior mind. The Bible and New Testament make similar pronouncements and are quite height-conscious—many of God's favorites (Jesus, Abraham, et al.) are tall men who tower over their people. King Saul got his job because "from his shoulders and upward he was higher than any of the people."

Firm height data start appearing in early Europe in A.D. 800, when King Charlemagne's people were a mere half-inch below today's heights. King Charlemagne himself was 6'4", despite having a father named Pepin the Short.

And then came the downfall. From 1100 to 1800 Europeans shrunk, with average men sometimes approaching the 5'0" line, as did late-1700s French soldiers. As economist Robert Fogel says of the soldiers storming at Bastille, "They looked like thirteen-year-old girls." The soldiers averaged 5'0" and weighed one hundred pounds.

The particularly swift height plummet between 1500 and 1650 was caused by a small ice age, disease spread by trade (bubonic

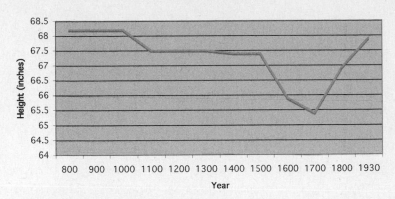

Male Height in Europe, 800–1930

This height graph is called a U-graph. My rendering is a "V" because data are available only for certain data points.

SOURCE: Richard Steckel, "New Light on the 'Dark Ages,'" *Social Science History* 28, no. 2 (2004): 211–29.

plague), and infighting among Europe's many principalities, which harmed food production. Parenting habits didn't help. Nineteenth-century British babies and children were often sedated with over-the-counter narcotics like opium, morphine, and laudanum, which are now known to have stunting effects.

Through it all, Europeans adored talls. We know this because the word *tall*, which made its 1374 debut in Chaucer, maintained positive connotations for six centuries. The Oxford English Dictionary surmises that the word is derived from the suffix of the Old English word *getæl* (or ge-tale), which meant "swift" or "prompt." Tall people, of course, are swift, particularly when they are marching across Europe in armies, a common activity at the time.

The early uses are amusingly lusty:

(1374) *Sche [Venus] made him [Mars] at hir lust so humble & talle.* Translation: Venus made Mars lust at her humbleness and tallness.

(1450) *A fayre qwene . . . bothe ffresche and gay upton to loke, and a talle man with her.* Translation: A fair queen, both fresh and gay to look upon, and a tall man with her.

(1592) *That such a base slave as he should be saluted by such a tall man as I am, from such a beautiful dame as you.*

It's unclear whether *tall/talle* really did have sexual undertones. Perhaps fifteenth- and sixteenth-century writers were just lusty, or perhaps the editors of the Oxford English Dictionary are lusty. But it remains a distinct possibility that *tall* meant "hot."

Between 1600 and 1800 *tall* had many meanings. It quickly morphed to connote bravery and boldness, and at one point meant "skilled," as in the phrase "tall of his hands," which was all the rage around 1600. For a while, it seems, writers wrote only about tall inanimate objects, like tall trees and tall ships (well, *Talle shippes, furnished with vitayles municions and all thynges necessary*). Tall became grounded in its current meaning around 1800, with a few winning usages along the way:

(1796) *Tall as giants, hairy like bears.*

(1861) *A man is called tall when he is above 5.754 feet in height.*

The dictionary makes quite a hullabaloo about *tall, dark, and handsome*. The phrase was launched into popular parlance when Mae West dropped it in 1933's *She Done Him Wrong*, referring to Cary Grant.

Nowhere did talls get more appreciation than in the military. Long before basketball courts existed, armies recruited tall troops, and military schools were a magnet for talls. "They generally overrepresent taller folks," says Scott Carson, a University of Texas historical economist. "Lincoln used to say that a cavalry commander had to be 5'10", but 5'4" would do in a pinch. In peace they recruited taller folks, but recruited anyone in war."

The leading tall recruiter was King Frederick William I of Prussia, who reigned from 1713 to 1740. Though he himself was 5'5", fat and sedentary, he developed what one biographer called "an almost pathological love for tall soldiers." At a time when the average European male was 5'5", he created the Grenadier Guards, a battalion with a six-foot minimum and a 6'5" mean. He was said to adore having the troops march through his private chambers.

Frederick had a problem: recruitment. Only a tiny fraction of Prussia's population fit his Grenadier needs. So he sent agents to comb Europe for tall young men—precursors to NBA scouts. But this process proved pricey, so Frederick turned to a more cost-effective strategy: mating his soldiers with tall women to create tall soldier babies. This undertaking turned out to be both slow and unreliable, though it ultimately produced hundreds of extremely tall country children.

Frederick's tall tastes were the talk of Europe, and neighboring rulers like Peter the Great began providing him with tall men as gifts and bargaining tools. If they wanted a favor, they gifted him with a giant. Yet Frederick felt his Grenadiers still had taller potential. So he took to kidnapping talls from across Europe. This was a special time for tall people. Imagine stepping out of your front door and having two Prussian agents jump you, drag you into their carriage, and take you to Prussia for enlistment in an army headed by a 5'5" fat man. The king's neighbors were not amused, least of all the British monarchy, which did not take well to a roly-poly king stealing tall Brits off the streets of London. The Grenadiers grew to a force of two thousand men, many close to seven feet tall, at the expense of diplomatic relations.

Yet it is arguable whether tall soldiers had any actual military value beyond a few moments of intimidation. The approach of the Grenadiers was said to be terrifying, and their longer limbs meant they could march faster and bayonet without being bayoneted more easily. But the Grenadiers were also much larger musket targets, not to mention an enormous expense to feed. When King Frederick's son, Frederick II, came to power in 1740, he focused on extending the size of Prussia, not the Grenadiers. The Grenadiers were disbanded.

Later militaries have also shied away from the Grenadiers model, opting to be organizations of uniformity. Leggy recruits who do not fit regulation military apparel and equipment are routinely placed in office assignments or discharged. U.S. Army boots fit up to size 15, and pants up to size 46. Many tanks and cockpits simply do not fit very tall bodies. When Leonid Stadnyk, currently the world's tallest man, arrived for his compulsory Ukrainian military physical in 1996, at nearly eight feet, the military doctors didn't have a long enough tape measure. Stadyk was excused from duty under the explanation "too tall."

Perhaps Frederick's greatest legacy is that his obsessive scouting served as something of a pan-European advertisement for the value of talls. His scouts put advertisements in newspapers and paid NBA-level prices for talls—transactions that were widely talked about and written up in newspapers. Slam dunk.

New military recruits typically spend their first hour of serving their country by getting measured. If you think about it, it's odd. The iconic image of enlistment isn't, say, a soldier being handed a gun, but a fresh-faced recruit stripping down to boxers and standing against a wall ruler. The tradition is a holdover from the pre-Polaroid days, when height was the equivalent of an identification badge, a prime way of identifying battlefield casualties and AWOL soldiers (as well as missing prisoners, citizens, slaves, and students). Militaries have always recorded troop heights with particular, um, military zeal, especially the Dutch. The chart on page 43 is a compilation of thousands of handwritten military height logs, condensed into one chart.

No one realized that the records behind this chart were a gold mine of financial information until the late 1970s, when one J. W. Drukker, 6'1", a Dutch economist, brought a stack of Dutch military records into his office. The records were notable only in that they showed the Dutch to have been among Europe's shortest people until the later 1800s, when colonial riches flowed in. One day he had his idle assistants plot soldier heights against Dutch per capita income from 1800 to 1950. Drukker still can't believe this actually worked. "My colleagues said, 'Height and income, ha. When are you gonna do storks and birth rate?'"

They stopped laughing when they saw his data. The soldier heights tracked precisely with income. Each time the Dutch grew taller, their incomes also grew larger, and vice versa. In other words, he could pump in a list of average heights and get a snapshot of per capita income. The correlation was so perfect that Drukker

Average Height of Male Soldiers Born in the mid-1800s

Australia	5'7.7"
Canada	5'7.3"
United States	5'7.3"
Norway	5'6.5"
Ireland	5'6.1"
Scotland	5'6.1"
Sweden	5'6.1"
Lower Austria	5'5.7"
United Kingdom	5'5.4"
France	5'4.9"
Russia	5'4.9"
Germany	5'4.6"
Netherlands	5'4.6"
Spain	5'3.8"
Italy	5'3.4"

SOURCE: Richard Steckel and Joseph Prince, "Tallest in the World," *American Economic Review* 91 (2002): 287–94.

worried he'd repeated a variable in the equation. He hadn't. His work was later validated by a separate multimillion-dollar archival study of the Dutch economy, which found the same per capita income figures that Drukker had extrapolated from a free list of heights.

Economists around the world tested the correlation, called a Yassis curve, in their own currencies. The results are markedly precise, largely because average heights have such a small range. Mean heights in Europe over the last three hundred years vary by less than eight inches. This means that a half-inch fluctuation reflects a major economic shift.

The "Average Height of Male Soldiers" chart, then, is not just a height list but an at-a-glance summary of the economic health of fifteen countries with fifteen different currencies. It's an enormous aid to economists, who struggle to measure the prosperity of regions with different currencies and metrics, not to mention tribes with no currency at all. It also allows some eerily accurate income estimating. For example, we know that the wealthiest nineteenth-century Londoners and Parisians reached today's average American heights, so we can easily extrapolate that more than a century ago their quality of life (food, health care, etc.) was approximately at today's middle-class American standards.

The Yassis curve was the academic high point of Drukker's career. "You don't have breakthroughs all your life," he told me. "The Yassis curve was a breakthrough."

Predicting per capita income with height is just the beginning of the fantastic amount of information embedded in height, enough to warrant an entire field. The father of anthropometric history—the study of human height over time—is the economist Robert Fogel. Economists are forever sticking their fingers into fields in which they don't really belong, which is how Fogel landed in a media hailstorm in 1974. His book, *Time on the Cross*, argued, among other things, that slavery was an economically sound system, 25 percent more profitable than the northern economy, and that slaves were often well fed and cared for. The *New York Review of Books* relegated the book to "the outermost ring of the scholar's hell," and another critic called it "simply shot through with egregious errors." Four academics pledged to put together their own book "refuting every word." When I talked to Fogel, now in his eighties, he looked back at this period with a sense of amusement. At the time it was not funny.

At particular contention was his claim that most slave women did not have children until age twenty-one. This ticked off many historians, who had long argued that slaves were mated as soon as they were physically capable. In an attempt to save his career, Fogel fled to London and dug into slave-ship-manifest height records. Much like military records, slave heights were tracked with extreme detail for use in identification; the business itself centered on height, valuing slaves for their size.

In an effort to prove the age twenty-one bit, Fogel learned from biologists that girls usually become fertile exactly three years after their growth spurt. Fogel graphed slave girls' height charts and extrapolated that slave girls were fertile at age fifteen. Birth certificates indicated that most didn't have children for another six years—blowing away the long-held assumption of forced young motherhood. For these and other efforts, Fogel went on to win the Nobel Prize.

Fogel's work suggested that much more information was probably locked in height records, but no one was sure what. Graduate students are ideal for sifting through millions of potentially meaningless statistics, so Fogel gave lectures at the University of Chicago, telling students where to find height data. Two of those students were fledgling economists John Komlos and Richard Steckel, who were both seeking research topics. Anthropometric history was the perfect niche: small enough that they could be world experts, yet meaningful enough that their findings could have broad implications. They both fell under Fogel's tutelage.

Komlos is not tall. He describes his height as "closer to five-seven," which he blames on his malnutrition as a Hungarian Jewish baby during the Holocaust. His mother was pregnant with him while the Nazis occupied Budapest, and she gave birth in a hospital in 1944 with fake papers before returning to the family's hideaway, where he spent months crying for food. His father did stints of forced labor and jail time before the family fled to America in 1956, by which point Komlos's destiny as a short man was sealed.

He is now one of the world's preeminent height economists and a military record junkie. When I visited him at the University of Munich, his double-high office walls were lined with hundreds of thousands of brittle pages scribbled with the heights, ages, occupations, and addresses of, say, the British German Legion in the Crimean War.

Both Komlos and Steckel tried to limit their data-entry time by looking for exceptions: finding very tall populations and seeing what was different about them. Their discoveries seemed, at first, random. Steckel discovered that slaves were five inches taller than Africans of the time, implying that they were healthier. Komlos found that East German girls were a half-inch shorter than West

Germans, suggesting that the socialist East German government provided a particularly troubling environment for girls. Komlos found that in the 1800s the students at the elite Royal Military Academy Sandhurst (which Prince William later attended) were a full nine inches taller than the working-class Marine School, showing that the upper classes really did look down on the lower classes.

As the information piled up, a fuller picture of what tallness means emerged. Komlos, being an economist, was able to quantify an equation for populations *defining tall*:

Tall People =
High Per Capita Income + Income Equality +
Low Disease + Reasonable Food and Goods Prices

When all of these variables are maximized, populations reach their full genetic height potential. "There's a biological maximum to height—no one expects humans to reach four meters when the GDP doubles," says Drukker. But an average male of 6'4" is conceivable.

Steckel's findings, meanwhile, created some general rules about what can be gleaned from height:

- **Personality:** Tall children are frequently the rambunctious ones. Malnourished children are quieter and less demanding. "On slave plantations, this may have been very deliberate," says Steckel. "They likely had one elderly woman looking after lots of children."
- **IQ:** Tall children average slightly superior intelligence. Stunting, particularly in early childhood, is a sign of cognitive defects.
- **Resource allocation:** Tall children are receiving adequate food and health care. Girls who are comparatively shorter than boys (or vice versa) can indicate distribution inequities.
- **Chronic illness:** Tall people are healthy. Height is perhaps the only historical measure that accounts for chronic ailments. "Just because you're alive doesn't mean you're healthy," says Steckel. "Death is a kind of extreme event."

- **Life expectancy:** Height at age twelve has a very strong
  correlation (0.85) with life expectancy.

Based on these rules, the social inferences that can be made
from tallness (or its lack) are astounding. Steckel is currently working on a controversial theory of postslave intelligence, based on
slave height records. "Slave children were extremely small, below
the first percentile of modern height standards, among the smallest children ever measured," he says. "I think that people who grew
up as slaves were malnourished as children, and were cognitively
less capable and docile as adults." Though slave teens caught up in
height, presumably well fed once they began to work, a good deal
of evidence from developing countries shows that similarly sized
children grow up with diminished intellectual abilities. Steckel's
point is strengthened by the fact that the black children born just
after slavery were not only much taller but grew into vehement social and civil rights activists in the late 1800s. "The next generation had very different personalities, as did their children. The Jim
Crow laws were created as a backlash against these very capable
young black men." Steckel has weathered equal doses of criticism
and acclaim for this theory, but he plans to charge on, dipping into
whatever arenas height data lead him. "I think there's really no
limit in the information you can draw from height data," he muses.
"Is there a topic that height doesn't impact?"

Most of the tall advantages that we've racked up since our salad
days on the African savannah—everything from our intimidation ability to our speed-walking skills—are actually evolutionary
hangers-on, former survival tools that have outlasted their original
utility. Evolutionary psychologist Marjaana Lindeman compares
tallness to other behaviors that are now of little effect, like the way
our hair bristles when we're frightened (useful to a gorilla) and
our instinctive fear of spiders (useful against an ancient poisonous
arachnid). "Biological evolution is very slow," she writes. "As a con-
sequence, we have numerous reactions and behaviors that are now
of no use but have been adaptive for millions of years. The height
effect is an ancient remainder from our evolutionary history."

Ancient, but still beneficial. The same tricks that worked 2 million years ago work today. "If all else fails, you can influence others' behavior through brute force," explains Floyd. "It doesn't mean that you *will*, but it means that you *can*." He conjures the image of a celebrity surrounded by bodyguards. "When you approach those bodyguards, they're not going to persuade you to not hurt their client through logical reasoning. They are taller and stronger. They're going to protect that person with their height." Talls are, and always have been, our own bodyguards.

The net result of historians' work is that rather than simply asserting that "tall people are great," we can actually quantify the greatness in dollars and IQ points and life expectancy and labor value. We can prove that there has always been an evolutionary bias toward the tall and, as Floyd puts it, "that all other things being equal, you've got a better chance being tall than short." And we can, finally, define what tall really is: lucky genes, generations of good provisions and care, a strong economy, and one heck of a wild ride to the top.

PART II

The Tall Life

CHAPTER 4

The Secret Life
of the World's Tallest
A Look in the Stretch Mirror

As you know, I am rather tall. I am not, however, among the top quarter percent in the world, or super tall. This became apparent one afternoon when I was a sophomore in college and came across a classmate who does rank among the world's tallest—at 6'11". I made a genial comment about how nice it was to meet a fellow tall. "You're not tall," she said. "You're not even 6'5"."

Only later did I realize that she wasn't kidding. Her tall world has little in common with mine. My world is similar to everyone else's, except that pigeons take off directly at my head. Her world is always dirty, because no one cleans the dust and mirror spots above 6'6". And it's a tiny world, with just a handful of peers sharing her perspective worldwide. She is so tall that other tall people (me!) break the unspoken code of tall people and tell her how tall she is. Most important, her public identity is pre-chosen: tall. We merely tall folk have a choice, and always get a modifier, such as tall *writer*. She's just tall. This is, I think, the true line between very tall and super tall—the point at which height is so striking that people see it as an identity rather than a physical trait.

It's a lot to deal with. "Developing the ability to overcome people's attitudes toward me has been the defining force in my life," a 6'7" British woman, Belinda Nokia, told me. "You are always meeting people for the first time. My height comes first; every other characteristic comes a very dim and distant second. It's just now, at age thirty-four, that I am really starting to come to grips."

It's also a very *public* life. I learned this when dating Alan, a 7'2" man I met while researching this book. Within five days of his arrival in New York, he was a neighborhood celebrity, and hundreds of neighbors knew who I was and where I lived. He was permanently in the public gaze, and by extension so was I. It was pleasant but unexpected—certainly not a conscious choice.

I had previously found the city to be a place of refuge, where I could walk around anonymously. The opposite is true for super talls. "If you put an extremely tall person in the center of urban anonymity, he'll draw tons of attention," says Rosemarie Garland-Thomson, a body studies professor at Emory University. "But put that same person in a small town, and he would become somewhat unremarkable. I believe a number of giants have lived in small towns, relatively unbothered." Sure enough, our Thanksgiving trip to a quiet suburb was a calm affair. The whole block did a double-take the first time we walked the dogs, and then promptly returned to their festivities. Not surprisingly, the world's top-five tallest men and women live in rural small towns.

Height has always been in the public domain. Unlike weight or ethnicity or looks or disability, social mores allow bystanders to stare and/or verbalize whatever they're thinking about height. Any tall person can verify this fact, but what surprised me was bystanders' general attitude that Alan was a public entity. On our first date, the waitress seated us, and the entire restaurant stared— just as they do when he goes shopping or walks into a movie theater or pretty much does any human activity. When we walked together in Midtown, seemingly polite, lovely people would whip out their cell phones and photograph him or us without asking. Which drove me nuts. Plenty of nice folks came up and said friendly things, which he loved. Because of this, he analyzes the personalities of his potential new neighborhoods carefully, because in the wrong neighborhood his days will be racked with rude interruptions. People want to talk to super talls, whether the super tall in question is buying diapers at midnight or taking a girl (named Ari) out to dinner. It's a wide-open life.

Super talls have always been rather visible, so it's easy to trace how they landed in their current public domain. Had Alan been born two centuries earlier, he would've been given a one-way ticket to the circus. It wasn't a bad career for those who took the bait. The path was paved by the most famous tall person of all time, Canadian Anna Swan, a circus performer for P. T. Barnum. She thrived on the sideshow circuit with her husband Martin Bates, 7'2". It's tricky to pinpoint how tall Swan was, because she was billed as an Eight-Foot Lady. Pictures show her a few inches taller than Bates, perhaps 7'5", and at times over four hundred pounds. They met on a ship in 1870 and shared a remarkably lucrative road show and museum career. As P. T. Barnum wrote of her, "She was an intelligent and by no means ill-looking girl, and during the long period she was in my employ, she was visited by thousands of persons." The two married and had two children, both of whom died immediately, at eighteen and twenty-two pounds, the latter the largest newborn on record. She died at age forty-two in 1888 of heart failure. Their home in Seville, Ohio, with its fourteen-foot ceilings, can still be seen.

Other job options for super talls were dismal. Before mass media, super talls were considered such an anomaly that no employer would hire them, and they struggled to find work that didn't exploit their height. This was a major problem for the typical 300-pound super tall, in need of expensive food, wardrobe, and medical arrangements. Thus a well-paying gig as the Seven-Foot Woman or Eight-Foot Man was the default career path; these sorts of jobs later expanded to include monster or big-person roles in theater and B-movies. The current tallest woman in the world, Yao Defen, 7'8", thirty-five, is a Chinese former circus giant.

The cities, particularly Manhattan and nearby Coney Island, were a moneymaking vortex for extreme bodies. "You could call the sideshow a New York City art form," says Dick Ziguns, owner of the Coney Island Sideshow. "There were eight sideshows in Coney Island, plus all the shows that traveled around the country were cast out of here." And the Ringling and Barnum circuses in Madison Square Garden, featuring giants alongside little people, Siamese twins, and bearded ladies.

New York provided not only the requisite audience number but also the sense of difference required for extreme bodies to profit. "Part of what makes someone extreme is the surrounding context," says Garland-Thomson. "It depends on comparison. If you've got seventy-five people walking down the street, someone really tall is going to appear even more so. The visual landscape of the city is much more intense." In other words, the city essentially creates super-talldom as an identity.

Until the 1950s, extreme height struck the public as mysterious and intriguing. Doctors didn't quite understand Anna Swan's growth (likely the result of gigantism), and she was considered a miracle worth paying admission to see. But starting in the 1960s, audiences' baseline understandings of medicine put a damper on supertall circus careers. Modern audiences saw giants as sufferers of a medical ailment, and people like Shaquille O'Neal as the product of tall genes, not divine intervention. At the same time, zoo-style objectification—quintuplets, hair-covered men, giants— went out of vogue.

One of the last of the world-famous circus giants was a guy named Eddie Carmel. A Jewish kid from the Bronx who liked to read, he grew to 8'5". As a twenty-something in the late 1950s, he set his eye on entertainment and started commuting into Manhattan daily to break into show business as the world's tallest comedian—he did streetcorner performances and comedy clubs. But the sideshow paychecks beckoned, and he inevitably ended up there, billed as the tallest man on earth by the Ringling Brothers' Sideshow at Madison Square Garden, where he performed until 1969. His feelings were mixed about this. He identified as an average guy, contained in a big body, and he was ambivalent about his objectification.

He is immortalized in the Diane Arbus photo, "Jewish Giant at Home with his Parents in the Bronx, NY, 1970." In the photo, his 8'5" frame is hunched under the ceiling, his two short parents looking up at him among the small sofas of a dark, middle-class living room. The photo emphasizes both Carmel's normalcy as a

young Bronx man and his abnormalcy as a giant who doesn't re-
semble his parents or fit in an apartment. Carmel died in 1972
at age thirty-six, before gigantism was treatable, the same year the
photograph ended up in the Museum of Modern Art.

Toward the end of Carmel's life, the perception of super talls
shifted dramatically, thanks largely to televised NBA games. By
1975 pretty much everyone had seen super tall people on TV, in
the context of being celebrated in front of sold-out basketball arenas. This new frame of reference could not have been more positive. By 1995 Shaquille O'Neal was known as The Man of Steel,
not the Traveling Human Giant. The idea of super tall people as
freaks was replaced by the idea of super tall people as amazing
athletes.

The impact of this is not to be underestimated. Though we all
grumble when the bazillionth stranger asks, "Do you play basketball?," the question suggests a cultural comfort with tall people. Yes,
height is too strongly associated with basketball, but it's much better
than "Are you in the circus?" It's a leap in the right direction. The net
effect is that when a typical employer in Somewhere, U.S.A. meets
a 6'10" applicant, he's seen lots of similarly heighted people before.
On television. Of the five seven-footers I met while researching this
book, all work desk jobs.

Workplace advances have come before social improvements. The
public doesn't yet take super height in stride and treat it with the
same respect afforded to any other visible difference. "When you
meet a fat person, you might say something like, 'Oh, are you from
the same town as me?'" Alan commented. "But with tall people, it's
the element of being unusual that's commented on, and exaggerated." We need to focus on similarities.

Margo Dydek, 7'2", is perhaps the most visible super tall in the
world, and her height is constantly commented on and exaggerated. She prefers that people not comment on her height at all. At
thirty-three, she is the longtime tallest player in the WNBA, a thin
Polish woman with pale skin and Slavic eyes and long beautiful
limb lines. Super talls, in and of themselves, are beautiful; it's only
when a 5'8" guard enters the frame that she looks awkward. People stare at her until their eyes fall out. "I was at one of her games,
and she was in the stands afterward," a 6'5" woman told me. "And

me being tall, I know exactly what it's like to be stared at. And I *couldn't stop staring*. I was right there, saying *Wow, is she ever tall*. I just couldn't stop."

Dydek is what we might call a third-wave super tall. She doesn't want to be seen as tall, or assumed to be an athlete. She wants people to see her as a person. Her method: She deflects all questions related to tallness. When I met her, I asked how basketball affected her tall experience, and she answered by talking about the time-management skills she's gained playing hoops. When I asked her advice for tall teens, she suggested that all teens should find their passion. When I asked her if there's anything she doesn't fit into, she replied, "I don't have any problems in regular life. I can fit in the car. I can fit in airplanes." (When I told this to Alan, who is the same height, he shrieked, "She's lying! Totally lying!")

She provided just one thought on tallness: "Some people, the first time they see me, are obsessed with my height. When I was younger, it was a problem. But I'm so used to it, it's just my life now. I don't think about it. I just prefer my friends or whoever to see what I'm doing, and what I am rather than just my height. I don't want to say anything more."

Dydek's approach wasn't an option for America's tallest woman, Sandy Allen, 7'7.25". She was born in 1952, a period of ambivalence and confusion over super talls' place in the world. She lived in her birthtown of Shelbyville, Indiana, until her death in 2008.

When I was a child in Delmar, New York, Allen occupied my imagination as a superhero (Sandy Allen! America's tallest woman! Five inches taller than Shaq!). I always imagined her in a cape. Thus I was surprised to find her in 2007 in a small convalescence-home room, made smaller by her eight-foot bed. She was nearly bedridden from the ongoing health consequences of gigantism. To get to her, I walked past some of the oldest people I'd ever seen. (I was later informed that one was, indeed, *the* oldest living American, Edna Parker, 115.) I continued on through the Alzheimer's unit, where a hundred dead-eyed residents were locked in by coded doors.

Yet the moment I entered her room, Allen cracked a joke: If I ever wanted the ceiling painted, I should put a hat on her head and tell her which way to walk. She had a deep voice and a maternal aura that compelled me to hug her, which was difficult given her overwhelming size. Her legs were too weak to hold her 400 pounds, so her wheelchair weighed another 360 pounds. To give you a sense of her mass, her shoulder width was double mine; she had 75 trillion red blood cells, 50 trillion more than average; her thighbone was twice the size of the average woman's. (Gigantism compels growth in all directions, not just upward.) She had recently summoned the fire department to lift her off the floor after sliding off her bed. Her cheekbones protruded, and her skull furrowed behind either temple, from facial bone overgrowth. There was a large silvery scar over her thyroid. She spent her days interrupted by nurses providing piles of pills to normalize her hormone levels. She was the oldest living giant, the first to make it past fifty, which she considered a major accomplishment.

Becoming the world's tallest woman is a rather anticlimactic affair. It's mainly a matter of informing the people who measure these things that you're super tall. In her first letter to Guinness World Records in 1974, she wrote, "I would like to get to know someone who is approximately my height. Needless to say my social life is practically nil, and perhaps the publicity from your book may brighten my life." Guinness verified her height, and a certificate arrived in the mail shortly thereafter, deeming her the world's tallest.

Incredibly, Allen, then nineteen, was still unclear why she was so tall. Her family is average sized. ("I didn't know what to think.") She had weathered an inconclusive hospital stay when she was ten years old and 6'3". She returned to elementary school, became tetherball queen, and shied away from basketball because she was afraid of hurting someone. This was a devastating blow to the high school coach, because Allen was a 7'1" freshman. Despite Allen's confusion, her religion allowed her to remain serene about her growth. "There have been two times in my life when I've looked up and said, 'Why me, Lord?' One was at my sixth-grade roller-skating party. They didn't have any skates for me, and I was watching everyone else skate. I was heartbroken. I remember crying on my walk home because I didn't get to have any fun." The other time came in high school driver's education, when she couldn't fit behind the wheel. "Oh God, was I upset. Years later I drove an old '67 Chevy Impala. I literally wrapped my legs around the steering wheel to drive it. That's sheer willpower."

When she was twenty-two, CAT scans became available. Doctors detected a sizable tumor on Allen's pituitary gland, pumping out excessive amounts of growth hormone. They convinced her to undergo brain surgery by insisting that the tumor would eventually press against her optic nerve, causing blindness, not to mention strain the body with lifelong growth and hormonal chaos. They performed surgery through the top of her head. A later follow-up surgery was more successful, through the top of her mouth, removing the tumor entirely.

The difference between being a super tall girl in Shelbyville and *the* tallest girl in the world is profound. The Guinness record was a boon to Allen, putting her on a new path. She soon met lots of tall people, beginning with her first date, a seven-foot man from Illinois. She realized brief fame in a Federico Fellini movie, playing a woman who has been sold by her husband to arm-wrestle in bars in Rome. ("I beat 'em all, of course.") She embarked on a spree of international media appearances with Guinness and acquired a van with "World's Tallest Woman" painted on the side, pulling over at truck stops to prove her height to disbelieving truckers. She temporarily lost the title to an eight-foot teenager, who died at age seventeen, returning the crown. She began making school appearances, preaching the wonders of difference, with the help of her size-22 shoes for kids to try on, provided courtesy of Shaquille O'Neal, who wears the same size. "I think that I'm this way so that I can encourage people not to give up if they've got problems in life," she told me.

"Sandy thinks of herself as a carrier of the Lord's message," says Harry Augenblick, a friend of thirty-five years who periodically helped her financially. "Guinness gave her a platform, and she preaches good messages, but not at all in an obnoxious way."

The same decency was not returned to her. Thirty years later Kim Blacklock, 6'7", who knows what it's like to be gawked at, still talks about walking a Manhattan block with Allen. "People weren't kind. Just the screaming. It was like—that kind of shock where they can't even stop their mouth to think that a human being is going to be the recipient of their reaction. In New York people sort of don't look where they're going, and all of a sudden, boom, there she is, and there's a scream of surprise. I imagine that would be hurtful."

Still, Allen trusted everyone, including the tabloid the *Globe*, resulting in a fabricated story claiming a sexual affair between her and the world's shortest man, and their future engagement. Numerous similar stories followed. The Web was particularly unkind to her. The first time I looked her up, a Web site popped up with someone comparing the size of her genitalia to a small Japanese truck. To be super tall is to have thick skin.

Allen attracted a stunning amount of sexual curiosity. She was well trained in rebuttals from eight years of delivering auditorium speeches at the Guinness Museum in Ontario. "A lot of times, more intelligent questions come from kids. Adults ask everything from how's your sex life to how you sit on a toilet." Howard Stern was a particular offender. He had her as a radio guest and asked her on air if her sex organs were large. (In fact, lack of puberty is a common symptom of gigantism.) Allen deadpanned, "Howard, you know what hotel I'm staying in, come over and see me." He commented about her presumed toilet-stuffing abilities. Allen retorted, "Any elephant would be proud. Next time I feel one coming on, I'll call you." He asked if she's married; she said that with a size-16 finger, she couldn't find a sucker rich enough to put a stone on her hand. Then Stern backed her into admitting on the air that she was a virgin. She was not pleased.

But she let the comments roll off her. What bothered her was inappropriate behavior, particularly in the form of men attempting to lay the world's tallest woman. "You know what really makes me mad? Guys call up and want to go out for dinner and then go back to the hotel and have a good time. Unh-unh, that's not me. I got a lot of good dinners out of that."

Allen always instinctively understood that she had an important role to play, Ambassador to Tall People Everywhere, and that this was an upbeat job. She played the part admirably well, publicly maintaining a sunny outlook at all times. That was invaluable to someone like me, a 5'3" eight-year-old, who looked up to her.

I wondered how her life compared to those of her cohorts on

the world's tallest list. I found that the happiest super talls have both accepted their height as a full-fledged public identity and *use* it to their advantage, such as Bao Xishun, a Chinese herdsman from Inner Mongolia. At age fifty-five, he's 7'8.95" and the world's second-tallest man. Though his parents are 5'2" and 5'10", Xishun does not appear to have a growth disorder. He enjoys publicity stunts and happily talks to anyone. He's a media darling, unafraid to pull headline-making stunts, such as when he reached into two aquarium dolphins' stomachs and pulled out plastic shards to save their lives. Xishun gained further attention when he placed marriage ads worldwide, eventually marrying 5'6" Xia Shujian, twenty-nine, in 2007, with whom he had a baby in 2008. He held the "world's tallest" crown from 2005 to 2007, by eking in two millimeters above Tunisian Radhouane Charbib, another super tall who also thrives on publicity and cash.

On the less satisfied end of the spectrum is the current tallest person in the world, Leonid Stadnyk, 8'5", thirty-six, a veterinarian with gigantism. Though he underwent pituitary surgery when he was twelve, some of his tumor remains. The press found him in 2004 in a small Ukrainian village, where he lives as a recluse with his mother, traveling by horse and cart. He refuses to visit a city and cash in, and for years refused to be measured by Guinness, therefore allowing Xishun to maintain the "world's tallest" title. Stadnyk is still growing, on a path to become the tallest man in history (8'11") unless he has expensive surgery. His eyesight is in danger from his enlarged pituitary gland. It is unclear why he has not undergone further treatment.

Stadnyk is also a contender for world's most depressed man. Headlines about him include "Hard Life and Isolation for World's Tallest Man," and he says things like, "This is my punishment from God. What sin I have committed, I do not know. I dream of being just like everyone else. My height is my curse." He suffers in misery, wishing for the one thing he can never have: a 5'11" body. He fundamentally fights his tall identity.

On this continuum, Allen was in the middle. "God makes people for a reason. I believe I am tall to help people," she told me. She didn't fight it. But like Stadnyk, she hadn't figured out how to *use* it either, and certainly not cash in. She lived on Social Security and

Medicaid, which left her fifty-two dollars in monthly discretionary income, and no Internet connection. Her main entrepreneurial success came when she let people take photos at Pacers games for donations, until the team asked her to stop. At one point an agent "co-wrote" a book about her, for which she never saw a dime. "Once in a while someone will send me twenty dollars in the mail, which is awful nice," she said.

As dusk fell, the smile that Allen put on for the media began to fade. Her life had recently been quite hard. To be the world's tallest woman is, in many ways, to be alone. No amount of visiting friends from Shelbyville could change that. Allen suffered from a lack of the hormone cortisol, which set off a chain reaction of troubles resulting in low blood pressure and a lot of bladder infections and hospital stays. It was confusing to her. "It terrifies me," she said. "I don't understand it, and the doctors don't either. It's a crazy circle. Maybe I should donate my body to science." Her minivan, which was outfitted with a motorized lift, had recently been stolen.

Looking at her features from the side, I could see that without the excessive hormones, she would have been a classic midwestern beauty: button nose, smooth pale skin, clear blue eyes, strong bone structure. Instead, she spent her time attending nursing home activities: bingo, storyteller, library lady, and nails & tales.

I asked her what she would've done with her life had her gigantism been treatable. "I've never really thought about that," she said slowly. "I probably would've gotten married, settled down, and had umpteen million kids. Like I said, I've always accepted my way of life. Now the only thing I hate about my life is that I can't get around very well. I suppose I'd maybe want to be about 6'0"." She paused. "I so admired you when you came up to the door. If I could, I'd stand up all nice and straight like you do."

Dinner arrived, and she ate three cheeseburgers, which seemed to be her main source of evening excitement. "I'm awful at night. Sometimes I eat four bags of popcorn. It's terrible." She broke off. "I have my down days, especially living here. I'm not always up-up-up. There are times I get depressed sitting here by myself, nothing to do, nothing on the old boob tube. It's not always easy. But you know, I've gotten so used to it."

Which made it all the sadder that no one had told her that she

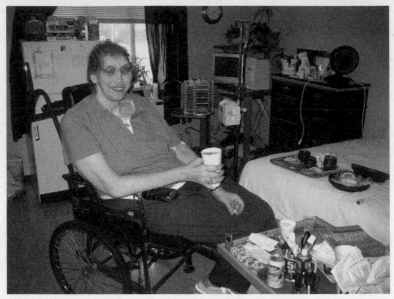

Sandy Allen, within a super tall arm's reach of her hobbies, in July 2007.

was no longer the world's tallest woman—just America's tallest. Yao Defen, 7'8", who is equally ill, topped the world's chart. And of course, Allen could no longer stand and had shrunk over the years under her tremendous weight.

To the end, she never strayed from her ambassador role. As we said our goodbyes, she nodded at me. "Be proud of it. If you're gonna stand out, people are gonna look up to you, so give them something to look up to."

Allen's happiest memories came from a period in her twenties and thirties, when she was busily working for Guinness, with numerous outlets for her tall energies. That seamless integration of career and height is not an easy balance for today's supertalls to hit. There's no *Super Talls: A Manual* lying around, outlining how to cope when people see your height as an identity. This challenge was illustrated vividly when I met Blacklock for coffee. She's the world's tallest comedian, a 6'7", three-hundred-pound woman. I saw her coming two blocks away. The whole street stared, in a neighborhood that shares sidewalks with Woody Allen and Soon-Yi, and Naked Jogging Man. Eyes bulged anyway. Just as Blacklock, age fifty, spotted me, a woman stopped her to ask her if she was famous. I understand the instinct. When you look at Blacklock, you think, she *must* be famous. But she isn't. Just public.

Blacklock plopped down in the booth across from me and summarized her career. Born to a 6'6" defensive tackle father and a 6'0" mother (they met at a 1952 Tall Timer's Club meeting in Syracuse), she played professional basketball in Europe and then floated around for two decades, teaching, house painting, landscaping, adopting some kids, deejaying, catering. This lifestyle seems to be typical of many super talls, who float around for extended periods, perhaps a manifestation of floating above society, feasible because super talls can always capitalize on their height to make money in a pinch. Blacklock's pinch came in Hollywood, where she landed bit parts in television as "female trucker" and "mountain woman" in *Revenge on the Highway* and *Brotherhood of the Gun*, respectively.

She only recently found her comfort spot, when she was asked to perform a comedy routine at a barbecue pit outside Santa Fe penitentiary. She instantly recognized the opportunity to transform what could otherwise have been bruising experiences into comedic gold, and she promptly billed herself as the World's Tallest Comedian (motto: "Prove me wrong"). She's one of dozens of super talls in entertainment: the rocker SixSeven, sideshow star Eric the Gentle Giant, That Tall Juggling Guy. What manager wouldn't want to bill the World's Tallest _____?

I went to see her perform at Caroline's Comedy Club in New York. When she walked onstage, the crowd let out a gasp. The world sees tall, so she gives them more tall, starting with her refusal to raise the microphone above her breastbone. She began with a bit about how she came about, the result of her Samoan princess great-grandmother falling for a merchant marine. "She *should not* have been doing it with a marine off a ship. That would've been death by clubbing with your own arm." She mocked some short male celebrities and then talked about her experiences as a 6'7" woman on Match.com. The crowd ate it up.

It comes down to this: the world treated Blacklock as if she were on a stage, so she jumped onto that stage, on her own terms. She subverts what the world gives her, repurposes it, and projects it all outward. She plays the hand she was dealt, as do the happiest super talls, whether they're office managers or truck drivers.

The climax of her act is a facial expression, the I'm-tall-not-stupid face. When the manager flashed the fifteen-seconds light, she put it on one last time. "Tom Cruise, *Mission Impossible*. He's 4'7". What was the mission? Get something off the top shelf?" The crowd howled. "Thank you very much! You've been a great audience. I'm Kim Blacklock, the world's tallest comedian. I'm having a great night, and I hope you have one too."

CHAPTER 5

A Brief Interruption for a Tall People Convention

Before the celebrated publication of this book, if you wanted to explore tallness, you joined your local tall club. It's a kooky premise, sort of a cross between the Rotary Club and the 4H Club, but for women over 5'10" and men over 6'2", who dance, party, and quite frequently produce more tall people. Some clubs are quiet and civic-minded, lobbying airlines and retailers for size-appropriate products; others are purely social. Most are a half-century old, a place where people's parents met.

I had intended to begin my tall journey perhaps with the Golden Gate Tip Toppers, or the Sarasota Tall Sunsations, but in my online research I came upon a proliferation of Web sites for German tall clubs: twenty-three city clubs, with tens of thousands of members attending monthly discos, pub trips, and bowling expeditions, plus "youngster" outings for the twenty- and thirty-somethings. Photos were posted promptly following events, documenting the fun had by the tall people. Tall people playing volleyball. Tall people petting zoo animals. Tall people roasting a pig.

I wanted to meet these people who were so intensely organized about their tallness. Conveniently, most of the Web sites were bannered with advertisements for the 2007 European Tall Club convention, with a logo of smiling trees. Europatreffen (European meeting) was slated for spring, in Freiberg, Germany, the annual gathering of Europe's fifty-five tall clubs from Ireland to Austria, the world's largest such gathering.

So I flew to Freiberg. When I first spotted the crowd of towering Germans a block away, I was scared. They were waiting at a bus stop, the men's heads approaching the seven-foot bus sign, the women a head shorter, their harsh umlauts floating toward me. Fifty towering Germans is a terrifying sight. I wanted to return to my hotel. But I forced myself to walk toward my chosen people. They were huddled in conversation, their backs turned. When I approached, they were so tall that *no one noticed me*. This had never happened before. They prattled on, and I stood there, recognizing one word, *Bahnhof.* Bus station.

On cue, a bus appeared. The bus door hissed open, inviting me into the vertical vortex. Everyone on the bus looked like me. Large heads, large shoulders, everything 20 percent larger. I stared at the women the way you might stare upon unexpectedly meeting your identical twin.

Americans are the black sheep of Europatreffen. Prone to mono-lingualness and cultural tone-deafness, our presence is carefully vetted. I was eyed tentatively at first, but within an hour I was in continuous conversation with tall people from ten countries, seated at the popular table at the restaurant. On that bus, and later that evening at dinner and dancing, for the first time ever I camouflaged. On the dance floor, I melded right into the middle of the crowd, such that no one watching would have recalled me. I had to wave both arms to catch a waitress's attention. This had never happened before. Giggles, I learned, are particularly contagious when coming from a foot above—they sort of cascade down around you. It was an evening of unexpected firsts.

When I walked back to the hotel that night, standing straighter than I ever had before, I noticed that my feet were throbbing. Unusual. I realized that I never stand and socialize. I'm always looking for a chair.

To be bluntly honest, I was in Germany for the same reason most tall people attend: I still had, for lack of a better term, my tall virginity. It's a psychological badge that must be shed. Of course I was already tall—I'd been tall for twenty years, but I had never made any effort to shed that angst about my size, and was still periodically uncomfortable. And I'd certainly never explored being tall before. It had always just been a fact. I am tall. I buy tall clothing. I date tall men. I can reach high things. The end. But when towering over the grocery store checkout line or out with my friends, I still felt like I didn't quite fit into the group. I had never particularly melded into my height and I certainly hadn't celebrated it. Like other virginities, you have to do something to lose your tall virginity. You have to get lucky.

The standard line about Europatreffen is, "I can't explain it. You just have to go." A whole new world opens up to you. Which is how I found myself, at 8:30 A.M. the next morning, charging along steep ridges in the Rhine Valley with three dozen tall people speaking German. It looked like the final scenes of *The Sound of Music*, where the Von Trapps are walking over the Alps, except we were a herd of umbrella-toting six-to-seven-foot tourists. We stopped for a rest, and I was squished behind a 6'5" woman and the brown poncho of a guy who resembled Tall Jesus. I couldn't see the tour guide. I didn't know what to do. This had never happened before. Annoying. Yet fascinating! In my journal, I wrote, "Couldn't see!"

We spent the rest of the day as we did all other Europatreffen days, with drinking in various forms. People who weigh 180 to 350 pounds can drink like fish. First came a bakery tasting of Black Forest cake, which in its native land is comprised of 30 percent alcohol. (The "black" is short for "blackout.") Then came the schnapps distillery, followed by a wine-flooded dinner with double servings and triple drinks. At each introduction heights were established, and then height was never mentioned again. This, I decided, is the secret of tall club: When everyone is tall, height is negated, and you lose your identity as The Tall Girl. You're judged on your underlying qualities, the ones others never see. This feels both naked and freeing at the same time.

By evening, the talls had been drinking for six hours, and the men and women jostled for each other, seemingly the organizers' way of saying, *Come on tall people, make more tall people.* Tall conventions are a secret international dating circuit. To call the men "romantically predatory" would be an understatement. Attendees are rather blunt about this. As Arjan Rooyens, 6'7", a Dutch life coach who spent the entire week talking to women, put it, "I'm hunting tall women. This is like my candy store."

I had by this point dropped all intention of having a work-only trip. For the first time every man in the room was an option, and I felt free to ask any of them to (ostensibly) translate. All were happy to teach me to ballroom dance, something else I'd never tried due to lack of tall partner. Also new was the oodles of unwanted romantic attention, offered most pointedly by a guy named Torson, who grinned at me so hard his eyes squeezed shut. I escaped to a circle of the three tallest men, all over seven feet, who take great pride in being the Three Kings of Tall Club. One of them, Alan, a 7'2" Brit in his thirties, was glum because the largest man anyone had ever seen, a thick 7'5" man, had arrived that day, thereby bumping Alan into fourth place. It was an experience he'd never had. "Don't you ever feel a little sting when you see someone taller?" he asked. Nope, I said. He looked at me. Really, no.

The conception of tall clubs was unplanned. In the spring of 1938 Kae Sumner Einfeldt, 6'3", was spending her days curled over a desk at the Walt Disney company, painting the dwarfs in *Snow White and the Seven Dwarfs*. The vocation made her particularly attuned to matters of height and proportion. The dwarfs owned special furniture, with miniature chairs for their miniature femurs, and miniature desks for their miniature torsos and arms. So why was Einfeldt crunched into an office chair, elbows sprawled across her desk?

Einfeldt, then twenty-two, had no plans to become the mother of Tall Clubs International. Her plan, in its entirety, was to write and illustrate a *Los Angeles Times* article relating tidbits about tall life. As an afterthought, she closed the article with an invitation for tall folks to contact her. Letters poured in. Being the social gal that she was, she invited them to a gathering at her home. Nine appeared, and the evening became the founding meeting of the California Tip Toppers.

The Tip Toppers were an industrious group, with a sense of mission to improve life for all of tallkind. They chose a campaign to induce manufacturers to produce furnishings for talls as their raison d'etre. They took to the phones and lobbied for tall products. Their first success was with mattress companies, who particularly liked the logic that not only would talls appreciate bigger mattresses, but so would overweight sleepers and families sharing beds. The California King mattress was introduced in 1941 and became a major hit.

Einfeldt's kooky concept of tall clubs spread first to Kansas in 1939, and then, thanks to a 1940 photospread in *Life* magazine of tall people dancing, sixty U.S. and Canada clubs by 1945. Einfeldt was en route to Europe to spread the concept further when the United States entered World War II, and the government told her to hightail it back to California.

The war forever rerouted the purpose of tall clubs. The initial furniture lobby was pushed aside, because U.S. manufacturers now had higher priorities, like supplying an army abroad. By the close of the war, the clubs were social organizations. Einfeldt met her husband, George, at a Tip Toppers event; they married in 1948 and went on to be a tall club members for fifty-eight years, with children and grandchildren also in the clubs.

One hundred fifty U.S. clubs have launched since. These days there are sixty active clubs, with names like the Skyscrapers, the Timberlines, and the Tall 'n Terrifics. Each club centers on its annual Tall Weekend, a four-day party and tourist-activity blowout; the club's Tall Queen serves as master of ceremonies, wandering around in a tiara.

The Miss Tall International pageant is the crowning event of the U.S. tall club annual national convention. The premise: One tall queen is chosen by pageant judges to represent the beauty and virtues of tall women everywhere. It's a pageant for non-pageant people. The crowd hoots as gowned contestants teeter through turns and pauses. Then each performs a humor skit and answers impromptu questions from the judges. Backstage you can find contestants, ages twenties through sixties, squeezing into extralong dresses, slathering themselves in makeup, and experimenting with duct tape.

As one Miss Tall International, Lisa Lightener, told me, "I entered because I thought I might meet people. When you're wearing a sash and crown at the mall, people talk to you."

After Einfeldt's trip was foiled, Europe waited another decade to start its own clubs, first in Germany in 1953. The clubs launched with an early sense of tall activism (pushing for bigger bus seats, taller school chairs, more tall stores), which they've maintained. Each club mirrors the local nuances of tall life. A Finnish club member lectured me on the cultural insecurity among Finnish tall men. A Dutchman pointed out, "The German clubs are about good beer, and the Holland club is about good clothes and good chairs." All together they create a mass worldwide network of diverse tall folk.

It's hard to put your finger on why, exactly, gathering these folks together at Europatreffen works. There's an inherent Wonka-like level of absurdity to Tall Clubs. The random activities, like the high ropes course (tall people in trees!) and Nordic walking (tall people with ski poles!) are so unorthodox that they are a source of bonding. Attendees still talk about a legendary Europatreffen at Edinburgh, where one activity involved dogs herding ducks through an obstacle course, followed by dogs chasing tall people through an obstacle course. ("If you had seen it, it would've been the only thing you talked about for the next year.")

By rights, a bunch of similarly sized people speaking eleven languages shouldn't become the best of friends. But they do. I asked psychoanalyst Susie Orbach why. "If you feel like you're physically out on a limb, then you get some comfort from being with similar people, and you relax. There's a basic understanding because everyone's like that. It's no different than any other specialized grouping." Relaxing into normality.

The cumulative effect is sort of like tall rehab. You are forgiven all your tall sins. I had previously thought myself rather well adjusted. But I discovered that for the past twenty years, I had been using an entire universe of behaviors and movements to compensate for my height. I sat as much as possible; I casually slipped off shoes at every opportunity or stood with my legs in a V. Upon first introduction, I started talking as early as possible, to give people something to think about beyond "tall woman." I eschewed heels.

But at Europatreffen, I stood up stick straight. I announced my thoughts in my full voice and presence. I ate until I was full. I kept my heels on. I towered over locals, making no effort to minimize my height. All at once I stopped adjusting myself for others.

I thought I might get to the root of the magic that is tall club in its boardroom. After four days of 8:30 A.M.-to-1 A.M. tourist activities and all-day drinking, representatives from a dozen countries filed into a conference room at the crack of dawn for the annual board meeting. I sucked on my coffee and hoped that they would talk about their plan for tall worldwide domination.

Instead, first came a round table of country updates, which was like a shorthand newscast of what's going on in the tall world, translated into French, then German. The Austrian club shared its success in forming partnerships with dance clubs, thus explaining the only adept dancing I'd seen. A Swiss representative outlined the lack of tall clothing options due to retailers' reluctance to cross the border into Switzerland. The Swedish club earnestly explained its identity as a Web site organization with few active members; the British said that 90 percent of their seven hundred members are Web only. The gripes were the same ones heard in hobby group boardrooms across the world: tall club is struggling to attract young members, now that Google and Match.com provide the same shopping and dating opportunities that used to entice members. "When young people do come, they enjoy it, but it's a matter of getting them there," mused a British rep.

I considered raising my hand and suggesting that they advertise themselves as a weekend/weeklong tall trip organization. That is essentially what Europatreffen is: a free tourist agency where all you need to do is show up, with the added benefit of spending time with actual locals who are hugely tall. It's a wonderful deal. Slogan: *Do you look like us? Come take over a European town for a week.*

My brainstorm was cut off by the bickering phase of the meeting. Far-flung delegates (Finland) suggested that holding Europatreffen in central Europe every year makes travel expensive;

near-flung delegates (Germany) suggested that hosting Europatreffen in Germany three of the next four years was perhaps excessive. Some delegates (everyone but Germany and Finland) adamantly agreed that Germans are born to run Europatreffen. A German representative, who had personally organized four Europatreffens, reminded everyone how much it costs to feed tall people. Then the former president (Switzerland) announced that there were too few representatives at the meeting to make decisions.

And then everyone stood up abruptly and stretched their legs. I thought it was a coffee break, until the room emptied. On to the next event. The magic of tall club continued.

On the final afternoon of Europatreffen I was hungry and Alan was following me around, as he had since day one, an experience not unlike having a helium balloon attached to my belt loop, always hovering above. So he followed me to a café. We were a Europatreffen couple by this point, a vague distinction that could mean all sorts of things. His legs sprawled out awkwardly from under a faux-antique wooden table. He ordered, ate, then ordered again, and summarized: "Food is not so much an issue as being hungry is an issue." Europatreffen put me in my place. I had previously thought that my life was dictated by being tall. It's not.

Alan had avoided Europatreffen for years, thinking that height was a superficial trait. Now he wished he'd made an appearance earlier. "My first Europatreffen was a turning point for me. The sheer quantity of people up at my height. Once you find out that you're not the only one, then you don't want to change it. I'd never been around that many tall people, and I smiled for days afterward." I pushed him on what, specifically, was so magical about Europatreffen. "I think if you're struggling with your self-worth in dealing with your height, the first Europatreffen can be rather medicinal."

Attendees come to feed various interests: some want to meet tall partners, others want to dance with talls, others like the mix of travel and tall people. And then they make friends, and once friends are made, they keep coming back. I asked how he described tall club to outsiders. He paused, then emerged with my favorite sentence about tall club: "Tall club is like a special interest group, except there's no special interest."

Then we got up, and the patrons and passersby gaped. He didn't notice.

The crowning event of Europatreffen is a formal ball. The *Bahnhof* was crowded with two hundred tall people in very formal formalwear. Silk ballgowns. I wore a not-so-little black dress, purchased at The Tall Girl Shop the week before, and was underdressed. Alan had finally figured out that if he stopped following me around and just stayed put, I would probably come back. Everyone on the trip was old friends.

The buffet held enough grub to feed a thousand average people, or three hundred and fifty tall people, and it became clear that I was apparently the first ever participant to lose my name tag. (*You don't have your name tag?*) They let me eat anyway. Everyone unabashedly pigged out in their fancy outfits and joked about the organizers, who took on military intensity. Everyone agreed it was the best-run trip they'd ever been on.

I seemed to be attracting a lot of attention. Dave the 6'11" Irish trucker told me, "I'm sure you'll have lots of requests to dance tonight." A minute later Rooyens joked, "You're leaving behind a trail of jealousy." Honestly, I'd never been surrounded by enough tall men that such a situation could present itself. Usually my dating life is a numbers game. I walk into a room and find one male of appropriate height; here there were fifty. I had never had reason to develop a protocol for choosing men. It took me a whole week of Europatreffen to figure out how to handle the situation.

A whole bunch of people asked me to dance. And I got the sense that this was what my life might be like if I looked exactly like I did but stood 5'3". This was, in a way, gratifying, a brief chance to experience the other side, quickly dispelled by the evening's various announcements and presentations about upcoming tall club events. Next year's Dutch conference hosts gave an earnest PowerPoint presentation about All Tall Together 2008. Everyone clapped, then danced more.

And then it was 2 A.M. and the bus was honking outside. It was over, with Alan promising to follow me back to America, which he did.

When you leave Tall World, it's like leaving a tall bubble. There's lingering evidence that you were there. You stand up extremely straight for the rest of your life, and you know how to ballroom dance. You have tall friends around the world. You regularly look around and think, *Damn, everyone's so friggin' short.* Something strange has happened that you can't quite articulate.

And being tall was a nonissue. Not only did I no longer consider myself particularly tall, but I had taken ownership of my height. It turns out that it's hard to love being different until you discover the one place in the world where you are not different. Somewhere in between the archery (tall people with arrows!) and the endless dinners (tall people eating!), something pivotal happened: I ceased to see myself as an exception.

CHAPTER 6

Growing Up Tall
You and Your Growth Chart

Height, as I know it, began in 1981. I was a bit long (twenty-two inches), a bit skinny (seven pounds), and a bit premature (a month). My formal debut as a tall person came two hours later, with baby footprints. My inked toes and heel extended beyond the lines of the state-regulated footprint box, and my blackened fingers stretched clear off the page. On my hospital identification certificate, I appear to be a four-fingered child.

Like most babies, I spent a lot of time curled up in a ball. Which is to say that everyone was surprised when, around age two, I stood up and towered over the other toddlers. The early words spoken around the house were *arachnoid*, doctorspeak describing my spiderlike fingers, and *simian*, Mom terminology to describe my toes. As in "They look like they could be curled around a branch."

Toddlers don't know that they are tall. My first conscious awareness came in prekindergarten, when my teacher took Polaroids of the class. All the kids were photographed without incident. Then my turn came, and she had to stop, put down her camera, and move the letters on the bulletin board behind my head. Later that summer I was riding training-wheeled bikes with my best friend Jeni, and I tried her bike. My knees hit the handlebars. I knew I was tall. But it was just a fact, like that I liked frosting. It had no meaning.

The pieces began to fill in when I learned to read. My main exposure to tall folks came from the library, often a big brown book of Grimm's tales. Every night I read about tall ogres, monsters, and giants. Sample motto: *Fee-fi-fo-fum. I smell the blood of an Englishman.* Not exactly role models. The plotline is always the same: A cute little person slays a tall person who is in possession of some sort of treasure. The heroines are always tiny: Little Women, Little Red Riding Hood, Thumbelina, the Little Mermaid. This is not a coincidence. "The small size is a proxy for the fact that it's a child who has lost power," says Harvard folktale professor Maria Tatar. "Giants are always the villains in fairytales. It's the association with adults. Every adult is a giant to children." This inference wasn't clear to me. I just thought that all heroines were little and cute and thoroughly unlike me.

The tall characters were also idiots. Roald Dahl's BFG was a few settings short of a picnic; Paul Bunyan was lucky he was ambulatory. Even today Harry Potter's half wizard/giant Hagrid can barely handle watching some keys. And not one of these guys was attractive. "In folklore, the little guy is often the trickster, and the giant is the buffoon," says Tatar. "He may have the brawn, but he doesn't have the brains. And certainly not the looks." These are larger metaphors, I think, for the human belief that genetic gifts don't come in pairs. They couldn't be tall *and* smart.

I wish I'd spent my bedtimes being lulled to sleep by a set of wacky fairy tales featuring awkwardly tall heroines with superpowers. But tall characters never get supernatural powers, because their bigness is considered power enough.

School has a way of exacerbating height. When I entered kindergarten, I was the permanent caboose in line, the constant back-row presence, the ongoing example used when learning about big versus small ("Imagine Arianne standing next to Napoleon"), always in the back row. I noticed that I wasn't just taller than the girl who sat next to me. I was taller than *everyone*.

It was precisely at this moment that my obliviousness to the battle of size taking place below me began. Until writing this book, I had no idea that other little kids were keenly aware of their height rank. If you ask adults, particularly men, they can list their size rank over the years—who was bigger, who wasn't, how that dictated the playground hierarchy, and how it changed from year to year. It was all very, very important. That sense of being powerful or neutered stays on faintly forever. Everyone sees themselves, at least a bit, as who they were at recess.

Towering above the crowd, albeit somewhat awkwardly, I was blind to the squabbling below. In *Gulliver's Travels*, Gulliver is baffled by the power-maneuverings around the King of Lilliput, who is only "taller by almost the breadth of my nail than any of his Court, which alone is enough to strike awe into beholders." Those nail-breadth differences were completely irrelevant from above, because to me my classmates were all so very short. I was #1. Easy enough to remember.

The Elementary School Years

My small-and-adorable years were a fleeting experience, as they are for all talls. They end the instant the preschool growth spurt propels you upward, and the cute chub evaporates. The roly-polyness is gone, and with it slips away much of your adult-manipulation power. I slid from cute toddler to annoying elementary schooler over the holidays when I was four, and suddenly my strategy of pouting cutely to get picked up was over. My mother, luckily, was on my side, because she remembered the same thing happening to her. As she puts it, "I remember when you took ballet. There was this adorable little kid. She was tiny and precious, and everyone fawned over her. And I *hated* her."

Once no longer cute, I was swiftly assumed to be older. Five meant eight, and eight meant eleven. Such assumptions worry pediatric endocrinologist Naomi Neufeld: "My patients are four years old, with the height of eight-year-olds. People come away from that child saying, 'Boy, is that a stupid eight-year-old.'" There's a choice: either act older, or be presumed dumb.

Many tall kids experience a distinct loss of childhood. Playing hide-and-seek is no longer a valid use of a Saturday. Helpfulness is mandatory. I was the third grader asked to rearrange desks with the teacher, the pre-teen roped into volunteer work. I began babysitting at age nine, which never would have happened had I actually looked my maturity level. (Note: Nine-year-olds have horrific decision-making skills. Really.) Many of my childhood screwups came when I was given the responsibility of a teen.

The upside is that adults consider tall kids to be one of their own. I loved this. Swim coaches told me about their bank accounts, camp counselors told me about their debauchery, my mom told me about her co-workers. I knew all the gossip and how to relate to adults. In psychologyspeak, height "has the effect of accelerating social development, which can be a good thing if the child has the cognitive wherewithal," says David Sandberg, a University of Michigan child psychologist specializing in child size. For me, cuteness was replaced by a new kind of power, the ability to operate in an adult world.

This is a very good thing, and one of the great blessings of being tall. You gain a sense of worldliness that stays on permanently. I have a theory that many talls are assumed to be leaders as adults not just because they're tall, but because they've been treated as adults from the beginning, both by parents and by other kids, and they instinctively act as the grown-up in the room. When the world gives you a role, you play the part.

The Middle School Years

My middle school held Friday-night socials, where seventh and eighth graders hung out in a pool-tabled root beer bar below school. One night I arrived too early and found no one to talk to, which is the seventh-grade social equivalent of roasting in the desert alone. I lingered in a corner for a while in my signature stance, the Hip

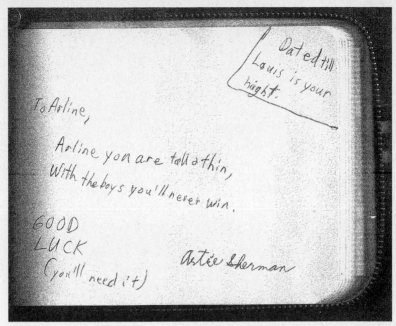

*Tall childhood has been the same for eons. To wit: my mother's
sixth grade yearbook.*

Drop: with my legs in a V, I shifted one hip downward, so the socket dropped down; along with significant slouching, it made me five inches shorter. Nothing is more unattractive than the Hip Drop.

When my hips started to ache, I awkwardly strolled my 5'9" self around the room, passing two older kids (real names: Katie Pelletier and Justin Barrios) at a pool table. I have blotted from my mind what exactly was said, but the take-home message was "You're a tall hideous she-man and no boy will ever date you." I cried hysterically that night, a typical closing to a social.

There was no benefit to my tallness in middle school. The many advantages of height are predominantly adult pleasures. Any positives—maturity, athletic prowess—couldn't possibly counteract the trauma of the social and were rendered invisible by the hormone fog. And as with most tall kids, my gawky stage was protracted. Tall-kid development goes like this: cuteness is curtailed, on one end, puberty delayed on the other, with tall kids reaching puberty an average of six months later. In the middle, we have one-plus years to put the gawk in gawky. There was a welcoming committee waiting when I hit puberty. I recall being constantly teased about being tall, more so than other kids, for roughly a decade. Teen teasing is based on visual difference, so the more visually different a kid looks, the more they're teased. I was a walking bull's-eye. Standing there in my Hip Drop, I resembled an upside-down exclamation point. I would've made fun of me.

When I told my tale to the psychologist Sandberg, he suspected that my memory was mistaken: I likely was teased the same amount as anyone else, just *differently*. He recounted what likely happened in my school hallways. When Big Billy Blaisedell, the resident bully, approached Average Kid, he'd call him a jerk one day, stupid the next day, and ugly the third day. "The average kid doesn't take it personally," says Sandberg. "He says, 'I'm not stupid,' 'I'm not a jerk,' and it rolls right off."

But when Billy saw me, his brain leaped to the same conclusion every day: tall! And then, *Hey Ari, you look like a giraffe.* The next day: *Hey Amazon Ari.* The next day: *Are you a man, Ari?* It hit a weak spot every time. Because in my head I *did* look like a giraffe. I went and looked in the mirror and saw all the things he said. I *was* boy sized, I *was* an Amazon. And I was very, very worried about it. Every comment was wounding and remembered, particularly the more searing, nuanced comments that tween girls were adept at serving up. It was psychologically upsetting. Even teased baboons have chronic pathological stress.

Meanwhile my body was sprouting like a pine tree. Sandberg says that smarter kids tend to cope with the whole taller-than-everyone-else scenario better. I spent much of my fledgling brain power on prayer: "For the love of God, *please* let me stop growing. *Please* let the growth chart be *very very wrong.*"

I thought I had things under control again in ninth grade, when I spent a lot of time with my swim team. One day at swim practice I was standing in the pool balcony doing flies with hand weights, where you lift your arms straight out to shoulder level and drop them repeatedly. I apparently looked like a big tall bird flapping for liftoff. For the next three years I was followed by crowlike cawing wherever I went. Just in case I didn't get it, I was periodically reminded at full volume that *birds of a feather flock together.* In retrospect, I find this hilarious. But at the time I assumed that since the boys' team thought I looked like Big Bird, I was destined to be single and alone forever, just as Katie Pelletier and Justin Barrios had said I would. It was reinforced on all sides.

The Prom and Beyond

The iconic moment of tall teenhood is the prom photo, that permanent documentation of tall awkwardness: the lack of tall-flattering formalwear, one date awkwardly towering over the other. My prom date was Amir, a Bosnian exchange student who spent the evening sitting alone eating Hershey kisses. In the photo I am slouching yet dwarfing him, and he clearly doesn't want to be touching my arm. I am wearing a dress that was, very literally, the only one that fit. That's all there is to say about it. I was saved by my 70 percent female high school class, where lots of girls had weird dates, and everyone hit the dance floor solo.

Dances are the battleground of tallhood. Here every possible tall-related issue comes out of the closet. First, there's the culture that calls for gaggles of girls and mobs of boys to hover around each other in separate corners, and you can't hear the conversation from eight inches above. And then there's the issue of not being asked to dance or, if you are so lucky, the supreme unease of sticking out on the dance floor in such a way that others might see you.

I skipped numerous winter and spring formals in high school and college, as well as my junior prom, because I didn't have a long enough dress, and shopping for my 6'3" V-shaped body was hell. When I did find one, it was never pretty, so I didn't feel pretty, which led to additional awkwardness and more dance-skipping. And then I had the minor issue of finding a date. Boys are the main currency of high school, and I was broke. (See the aforementioned arm-flapping incident.)

Tall teen dating follows a predictable track. As a general rule, tall boys start off their dating careers with average-to-short girls, both because it's socially desirable to date someone who is popular and average, and because many boys haven't yet identified their preferences. Tall girls start dating in late high school or early college; very tall girls usually take an extra year or two, waiting for boys to mature enough to handle them. Amy Sacco, forty, a 6'1"

Manhattan nightclub owner and social butterfly, is a good example. "You know, my mom said, 'Don't worry, you'll have a boyfriend in high school.' Then she said, 'Don't worry, you'll have one in college.' I didn't. I never had a boyfriend until I got to New York. It was hard to get a date to the prom. A guy told me that he really wanted to take me to the prom, but he took another girl because she was shorter." Sacco's first longtime boyfriend was one of the most famous chefs in New York, and the week I interviewed her, she got engaged.

At the same time older men come calling early. In high school I worked as a lifeguard at the Holiday Inn. Fourteen stories of hotel windows looked down at me, not unlike working in a fishbowl. Older men would come down and sit next to me and ask various inappropriate questions. I was a sitting duck, unable to leave the pool unattended. Only later did I realize that they thought I was twenty-four.

The Tall Fairy didn't come tap me on the head on my nineteenth birthday and give me a rockin' tall life. But I did begin to learn tall management. There's an art to it: I learned how to spot dates who would be comfortable with my height, what to wear to a party, whether to do heels, how to dance (or not dance), how to be the center of attention (or not), how to turn around and glare (an angry glare from a tall defuses many a situation.) Any one of these incidents would once have turned me into a wounded piece of pubescence.

That sense of outsiderness that was so devastating at age fifteen is now a lingering blessing in adulthood. Rob Bruintjes, a 7'4" Dutchman, is an unofficial adviser to tall teens and fields many calls from stressed-out kids. "I tell them that a lot of people are really boring. It's true. It's much better to be a little different."

Throughout my interviews, adults repeated the same clichés, genuinely hoping that teens would hear them:

It gets better. Great, in fact.

My twenties were much easier.

My thirties were awesome. Now I LOVE it.

I would like to tell adolescents that it will be better.

The dating is a numbers game. The numbers get so much better.

Now I kinda wish I were taller. Like megatall.

But perhaps the best part of growing up is the awareness that, actually, it's not about you and never was. I didn't realize until my twenties that all the little comments that I once found so upsetting, that I was *so* positive were bull's-eye commentaries on my height, body, and subsequent doomed future, never had anything to do with me. They were only a reflection of someone else's perception of tallness. Now, when I meet someone who seems uncomfortable around me, I understand that it's a statement of how *they* feel about themselves. I'm just standing there. Tall is, objectively speaking, gorgeous. It just is. Remember that.

CHAPTER 7

Sports
Long Limbs, Big Paychecks

"When I run, I'm like an egg whisk. There's absolutely no action above the knee."

—Alan Herbert, 7'2"

At summer camp one year, I ran into the woods after a tennis ball and found myself cornered by a bearded stranger beneath some fir trees. I thought I was about to be kidnapped. He squeezed my upper arm, then looked down at my legs. He identified himself as the local tennis coach. This happened a lot: The high school basketball coach found me in the Cinnamon Toast Crunch aisle and announced that I was destined to be a center. At a school fair a woman hurled a white ball at me (think fast!) and then asked if I'd considered playing volleyball. I might as well have had *athlete* tattooed on my forehead.

Sports are the hub of the tall experience—whether that means a lifetime of sports, or a lifetime of saying, "No, I don't play basketball." I've never met a tall person who made it through adolescence without at least a brief run at basketball, football, track, or swimming. As Jason Collins, the 6'11" Minnesota Timberwolves center, put it, "Everyone I know who is tall played a sport. Everyone." Including his twin, Utah Jazz's Jarron Collins.

The 29.9 million talls who aren't professional athletes are also in the game. "The reason I got started in basketball was because of the comment, 'You *must* play basketball,'" says Ben Butler, 6'8", now a Web site security administrator. "It was literally easier to play basketball than explain why not."

Basketball, for the record, is not as tall a sport as people think. A handful of centers are supertall—particularly Yao Ming, 7'6", the product of 6'2" and 6'10" parents who were married by a Chinese state program to create athletes. But if you look at team rosters, football and volleyball teams average members nearly as tall, and many swimmers and field athletes are only inches behind. Basketball is not so much the tall sport as the *tall umbrella sport.* Pretty much any tall body type—thin, thick, muscular, lanky—with good reflexes can excel. Many NBA and WNBA rosters feature two same-height players, one hundred pounds apart.

I was nudged to try every sport in which tallness could possibly be a benefit. I proved incompetent at basketball, ballet, tennis, bowling, and track. I was so bad at synchronized swimming that my mother made me quit. (You have to be really bad for your mother to make you quit a wholesome activity that involves extended time with you silenced, head under water.) But competitive swimming seemed to go okay. By eighth grade I was nationally ranked. I won some big races and developed something resembling confidence.

Swimming is an oasis for tall people—teams average around the 80th percentile for height. I was still the tallest girl on my team, but my best friends were a 5'9" girl and a 6'4" guy. I genuinely considered myself to be just a few inches taller than average. I swam with fifty lanky swimmers who did the same practice-school-practice-homework-sleep grind that I did every day, which made me feel spectacularly unspecial. Which is exactly how a 6'2" fourteen-year-old wants to feel.

The whole thing provided me with a cloak of normality. In my world, tall kids with big shoulders became typical. "Sometimes I have these moments when I go out in public, and I get kind of depressed about how short the general public is," says Caryn Davies,

6'4", a 2008 Olympic gold medalist rower on the U.S national team. "The team makes me comfortable. It's nice to wear heels and look people in the eye. I like hanging out with them."

I sat at the swimmers' table during high school lunch periods, a socially acceptable place where people sprayed each other with water bottles, and the height issue slipped into the background. As I inched my way from junior to senior nationals, the people on the pool deck got taller. Though I was hyper self-conscious at school, I was never remotely self-conscious on a pool deck, because there my long arms and legs had something to *do*—I had some sort of *use* for all that tallness. It was a valued tool. As Gabrielle Reece, the 6'3" beach volleyball player puts it, "Volleyball gave me a reason for being this big, big girl. It anchored me at a time in my life when I needed it."

I liked being tall because I had a *reason* to be tall. "Sometimes I wonder if I weren't an athlete how I would feel about being tall," muses Davies. "And I think I would feel a lot differently. Because in the average real world, I would be this anomaly. I would feel that there's no purpose for being that tall and not necessarily any reason to be proud of it."

Why Does Everyone Think We're Good at Sports?: A History

Sports are a recent endeavor for talls. Broadly speaking, pro athletics are an activity of the idle and healthy, a group that, socioeconomically speaking, often happens to be tall (see chapter 2)—and also a group that simply didn't exist en masse until the mid-1900s. A glance through the Union Army troop enlistment records clarifies why: mid-Atlantic troops averaged 5'6", with numerous health problems—vision loss, hernias, gout, the works. They were not exactly a group with energy to spare for a leisurely game of hoops. The gilded gates of elite preparatory schools have always held tall athletes, but they were an exception; elsewhere, most of the same bodies that today's sports fans drool over were considered unremarkable and sent to long hours at labor, desk, or military jobs. Tall athletes are a creation of modern health care, labor laws, and, in the case of tall American women, 1972's Title IX.

Even then, sports weren't considered a tall empire. Well into the 1980s, basketball point guards and football defenders were relatively short. Height was certainly adulated, but at nowhere near today's fever pitch. Today's NBA and WNBA games are perhaps the only place in the world where people are introduced with their height *before* the name: *And at 6'2", a New York Liberty center from Wisconsin, Janel McCarville!*

The widespread concept that talls are inherently amazing athletes, which I call the Charming Myth of Tall Athletic Perfection!, cropped up during the Regan years, largely introduced by an artificial source: sports apparel companies. It began when the sneaker industry started offering major advertising contracts to athletes with big feet, ultimately plastering people like Shaq and Michael Jordan, 6'6", on billboards around the world, often airborne and dunking, in shots emphasizing vertical height. Why? Because vertical height is easy to depict on film. Their goal was to sell athletic gear, but the advertisements inadvertently served as billboards for tall athletic bodies. Gatorade's "Be Like Mike" ads, featuring a tall guy (Jordan) outjumping other tall guys, landed worldwide in 1991, sealing the deal. Fifteen years and billions of dollars of advertising later, the idea was solidified: talls are good at sports.

Tall women were another story. In the early 1990s the women's sportswear market was in a slump. The Jane Fonda spandex era had passed, but companies needed millions of women to buy tracksuits. No woman anywhere wanted to wear a tracksuit; this was the age of shoulder pads and feathered hair. It was a marketing challenge. As Lori Smith, then Nike's sports marketing manager, told *Outside* magazine, "Men want to be like Mike. Women see Jackie

Joyner-Kersee, and think, 'She's terrific. I admire her tremendously. Do I want to be like her? No.' "

But the men's campaigns were so successful that apparel executives decided to try to create similar icons out of female athletes, carefully choosing tall women with long limbs that would play well in advertising photography, like Gabrielle Reece and, yes, Jackie Joyner-Kersee, 5'10". The ads went out of their way to present women athletes as feminine—sometimes they're just standing there, not doing a sport. As Reece put it, "For a woman athlete, it's tricky sometimes. A male athlete can just slam-dunk above the rim and that's that—he's a hero. If you're a woman, you've got to do the sexy thing. It's reality." The tall effect was further magnified by the standard Photoshop practice of lengthening the female models' shins. (If you look closely at ads, you'll see that many shins are double-length for a visually pleasing effect.) The net effect was female athletes posted on billboards around the world looking extremely tall and willowy. The association stuck. Visually, tall became shorthand for "good at sports."

But of course it isn't that simple. Talls have more muscle mass overall, and they are therefore objectively stronger. And tall bodies also have the advantage of sheer intimidation power, which comes in handy in positions like power forward in basketball and hitter in volleyball, or any sport that requires charging at an opponent. But the idea that talls are natural athletes is overblown. It's a tall tale.

Tall bodies are actually ill suited for numerous athletic endeavors. The same long arms that are good for swimming are a nightmare in the weight room. The crux of the issue is leverage. Long limbs allow the body to exert more force with less effort. Imagine trying to lift a couch with a two-foot crowbar—you probably couldn't do it. But if the crowbar were six feet long, you could move the couch with just a slight lean. As a general rule, any activity that involves generating force from the abdomen through a long lever arm, like pitching or swimming, works well for talls. And pretty much any activity that involves supporting weight far from the core is tall torture, because the lever is essentially being used against itself. This is what happens when you lie on your back and try to hold your feet off the floor—your feet are now dead weight three-plus feet from the core. You're making the core fight the lever. Short people can hold their legs up all day. When I told this to Davies, the 6'4" rower, she whooped. "Yeah! I do think that I have to work harder. And I notice I work harder lifting weights because I have to move them farther."

Another factor is in play: Taller people are much less strong relative to their body weight. Taller bodies can carry more muscle mass, but the extra muscle never eclipses the increased body weight. This is why I sweat profusely in yoga class, while the strong short people in the room are dryly, calmly supporting themselves on one arm. Yoga would be a very different activity if yogis were six-footers. This fact explains the lack of dominant 6'5" gymnasts in the world.

This was a repeating theme of my athletic days: I was either really good or really bad at various athletic exercises. As a swimmer, we did an hour of daily calisthenics, usually twenty to thirty minutes of the aforementioned leg lift torture, followed by some squats (also harder per inch and pound) and then some push-ups. When I was twelve, my coach got down on the floor with me for remedial push-up lessons. "You lower yourself down! Then you push back up! What's so hard?" It wasn't a comprehension problem.

"Push-ups are harder for tall people, absolutely," says Pat Sexton, Ph.D., the director of athletic training at Minnesota State. "For someone who has very long arms to do a bench press, they have to generate more force because they have a longer resistance arm and farther to move the weight. The extra leverage is a disadvantage." Sweet justice.

Talls have four other athletic nonstrengths that are worth being aware of:

- *We have slow tempo.* Our rate of turnover is roughly a third slower, because our limbs are traveling over a greater distance. Every time I take a swimming stroke, my fingers travel 33 percent farther than the fingers of a 5'5" teammate (16.2 inches versus 11.75 inches). Unless an athlete has a lot of fast twitch muscle, this can be a deadly hurdle for sprinters. This is precisely why people think talls lumber along—visually, we're moving slower.

- *We're tippers.* "The taller someone is, the higher their center of gravity is over their base," says Sexton. "If their center moves outside their base of support, they tip over." The center of gravity is roughly behind the belly button. This is relevant in any sport where there's a premium on staying vertical, like football or ice hockey or gymnastics: talls have a disadvantage. It's much harder to tip a short stocky person over, because their center of gravity is so low. A tall person with a wide base, like Andre the Giant, is unmovable.

- *We're slow to get moving.* Starting motion takes energy, and the bigger the person, the more energy is needed to build momentum. I experience this every time I get off the couch. But in sports it matters when the starting gun goes off at a race, or when making a switchback on a ski trail.

- *We get injured.* Talls are prone to certain impact injuries. "A blow to the outside of the knee [is worse] when the lower leg is long," says J. C. Andersen, Ph.D., a University of Tampa athletic programming director. "It takes a lot less force to rupture a ligament on someone who's 6'10" than someone who's 5'4". A similar situation applies to snapping a bone—it's much easier to snap a long yardstick than a short yardstick. Such injuries are particularly common during growth spurts, when tendons are pulling on their attachments. "The weakest link in the chain is what's going to break," says Richard Shoulberg, a two-time Olympic swimming coach. "The supporting muscles and tendons are all serving an interlocking purpose. People make the mistake of just working the main muscle, say the tricep or bicep, and making that really strong. But the forearm and fingers also need to be really strong." Sports trainer rooms are always populated with disproportionately large bodies, and I suspect it's because when a coach is staring at a 6'5" linebacker, he might not be thinking about strengthening tiny knee ligaments and tendons.

Beyond these weaknesses, however, the tall body is all athletic asset: It has longer reach, extra power, and superior leverage. These three factors combine to create a supreme fourth advantage: the fudge factor. In some scenarios, tall athletes have so much physical advantage that they can get away with fudging—with having less skill. For instance, Shaq can't shoot free throws—the ball often doesn't go through the hoop. "You've probably heard of basketball players who, in terms of talent, if you took a foot away, wouldn't be playing college ball," says Sexton. "But they're there because height gives them an advantage." Shaq can hold his position like no one else on the court, and he uses his height to grab rebounds after he misses. But the flawlessness required of shorter pro athletes isn't as necessary. The fudge factor has fueled many a tall career.

Talls and Sports: A Love Match?

"When I was in eighth grade, my parents sent me to basketball camp, and it was one of the most traumatic experiences of my life," says Dennis Kwan, twenty-seven, a 6'8" Los Angeles photographer. "I was uncoordinated and pudgy, and we had to play with our shirts off, and it was really traumatic. I don't think I told anyone. Seriously, you're the first person I've ever talked to about it." Tales of forced tall athleticism are commonplace because not all tall people have either the mentality or the physical skill for athletics. In fact, just like the general population, the majority don't. The question is whether all those talls who are funneled into sports by default actually want athletic careers?

Tall expectations are particularly intense in inner-city neighborhoods, where a sports scholarship is a ticket to a better life. The message is clear: Play basketball. Or football. Or track. "It's almost as if it's a waste if they don't utilize their height," muses social worker Nitara Wiggan, 5'11". The result is that many talls end up in long-term sports careers that they're not all that excited about.

"I played in college and on the national team and in Europe," a 6'5", thirty-six-year-old former professional basketball player told me. "I was channeled into it because I was tall, but I didn't really have the heart for it. I didn't eat, sleep, and dream basketball like you have to do if you want to be really good. When I quit, I quit for good. I haven't picked up a ball since." Her thoughts were echoed by others throughout my interviews: Lots of talls love their sports, but for every person who raved about athletics, another was ambivalent. Height is good for sports, but willingness is better.

I had a similar experience. As a swimmer, I was never really into racing. Truth be told, when I stood up on those racing blocks, I really didn't care if the girl next to me beat me or not. I'd rather read a book. Which is unfortunate for someone who is training five hours a day in a program that produces Olympians. But I was a sixteen-year-old senior national-level swimmer with a single parent, and it was clear that I would spend the next three years paddling toward a college scholarship, and the ensuing four years swimming out said scholarship. My tall body was a commodity, on lease to sports. In the grand scheme of things, it wasn't a hardship. I would eat well, get enough sleep, steer clear of the leg-breaking risks of skiing and ice skating, and whirl my long arms over my head roughly eight million times. On the one hand I felt stuck, but the benefits were numerous: discipline, college, my best friends, a use for my height, and self-confidence. And frankly, I was so accustomed to the lifestyle that I didn't know what to do with myself when not swimming. What would I do with *five* extra hours a day?

While speaking to hundreds of talls, I caught on to a trend: the talls who stick with sports they don't love usually have something to escape. "Basketball was something I utilized to get out of my hometown and see the world," the former pro told me. "I left this podunk Canada town, where being tall wasn't cool, and I found a lot of people who thought I was amazing. And I got by on hard work." Which is quite possible when you have the perfect body for a sport.

When I cashed in on the lease, I was well along the path to the cosmopolitan life I craved. Mission accomplished.

At the end of the game, sports are a jackpot for athletic-minded talls and an obstacle course for those who get ensnared. And above all, they are a uniquely available escape hatch, to be utilized as needed.

CHAPTER 8

On the Job, Counting Greenbacks

I wanted to know *why* tall people are so successful in the workplace? As we know from chapter 1, tall people bring home a lot more bacon than short people, to the tune of $789 more per inch per year. They also dominate the workplace, and always have, as explained in the wonderfully titled 1915 book *The Executive and His Control of Men.* It outlines research dating back to 1900 showing that bishops are taller than preachers, and sales managers are taller than salesmen. Ditto with lawyers, teachers, and railroad employees. The trend has not changed. The literature on this topic is an exercise in repetition: tall people, male and female, do very well at work, in terms of paycheck, hiring, and rank.

But *why?* What's going on each day at work that makes human resources departments worldwide roll over and toss plump jobs and paychecks to talls? I spoke to economists, sociologists, and psychologists to piece together a roadmap for the tall career.

The Tall Career Road Map

The Job Interview. The conquering begins at the job interview. Numerous studies show that hirers look favorably—perhaps a little too favorably—on talls. When two salesmen candidates, at 5'5" and 6'0", present equivalent résumés, a whopping 72 percent of recruiters hire the taller applicant, and only one percent hire the shorter. (The rest don't hire either.) The same is true for school principals and secretaries. As a rule of thumb, 70 percent of employers choose the taller applicant.

This is not to say that job-interviewing while tall is always a slam dunk. Recently I met with the editor in chief of a major magazine. The meeting was a slow-motion train wreck. From the introductory handshake, I felt that I was physically overpowering him, which was the last thing I wanted to do. I could feel my career at that magazine slowly evaporating. I limped home and told my super tall boyfriend. "Is this editor, by chance, much shorter than you?" Yes. "And were you being you?" Yes. "Well, there's your problem." Val Ackerman, 5'10", the head of USA Basketball, describes the kind of unease I felt. "It translates into funny body language, a feeling of tension and discomfort sometimes. Some men are fine, but I'm not convinced that men are totally at ease with taller women. It kind of makes you just want to find a chair."

That funny feeling is legitimate, the body's way of signaling a body power imbalance in your favor. "An eye cast down is a powerful behavior," says San Diego State University communications professor Peter Andersen. "An eye cast up is always a less powerful behavior. When I interact with a man who is 6'6", I feel very weird and less powerful, because the position of my eyes is almost feminine and in a more submissive position of facing upward." This submissive feeling is not what you want to unleash in your interviewer. It's quite easy for an employer to come away with a vague impression that a tall interviewee is too domineering, or for an interviewee to set off a chain reaction of discomfort, as with my editor. Luckily, upper-level employees—aka the people doing the hiring—are more likely to be tall.

Co-worker Relations. By and large, tall people get hired, and the rise continues. Once on the job, that same downward eyecast is invaluable. Because of that eye gaze, tall workers are instinctively perceived to have authority and confidence. And co-workers are aware of it. "What's interesting about height is that people are very good at gauging it," the economist Sir Roderick Floud told me. "One or two inches is actually very obvious." Tall women in particular, at first glance, are perceived as more intelligent, affluent, assertive, and ambitious than short women. The positive expectations begin before the work has even begun: tall police officers' new supervisors expect them to have fewer complaints and disciplinary problems, and to engender better morale. We *begin* in the power position and build from there.

Timothy Judge and Daniel Cable, the researchers who found the $789 in extra pay per inch, looked at seventy-one workplace studies to determine why tall people succeed at work. They knew that tall people are a bit smarter (chapter 1), but talls succeed far beyond their IQ boost. Why? They found two main social reasons for tall workplace success. First, talls are highly respected by co-workers and bosses. Well-esteemed workers are more likely to thrive due to social support. They have more helpful colleagues, get better assignments, are more easily forgiven mistakes, and receive more rewards and bonuses, to name a few.

Job Performance. Second, talls are perceived as better workers. "The perception seems to exist that taller individuals are somehow more capable, able, or competent," wrote one researcher. Nowhere is this more obvious than in job reviews. One study looked at longtime bosses' job reviews of seventy-eight women. The bosses heavily favored the taller women, considering them better managers, even when their work was comparable to that of shorter candidates.

Judge and Cable tried to parse whether tall people objectively perform better. It's quite hard to measure job performance—a tall salesman may make more sales, but the boss might also be giving him better leads. They concluded that talls are *not* actually any better at their jobs than other workers. Tall people are certainly competent at their jobs, but they are rewarded disproportionately. With promotions.

Tall Promotions. "A person's height has significant and direct effect on promotion and work," writes psychologist Marjaana Lindeman. "The taller the person, the shorter the time in which an individual advances from the lowest to higher levels in the hierarchy." These aren't just any promotions, but promotions that track directly to leadership roles. A study of accounting firms found that tall accountants were more likely than any other group—including highly qualified and attractive accountants—to be tapped to become partners. This is reflected in income studies. Tall income per inch ticks slightly upward toward the end of the career, topping the $789 per inch, presumably as talls step into their final leadership jobs.

Welcome to the Executive Suite. The tall job ladder often leads to the executive suite. American CEOs are the true hub of tall power, controlling most of the country's wealth. Among the CEOs of the fifty largest U.S. corporations, 29 percent are over 6'3"—a distinction shared by a mere 2 percent of U.S. men. The CEOs of the Fortune 500 are marginally less tall, averaging 6'0", or three inches above the national average. Thirty percent are over 6'2"—as compared to just 3.9 percent of American men. And roughly 58 percent of Fortune 500 CEOs are over 6'0", while only 14.5 percent of American men are.

Noncorporate leaders are also extremely tall. Examples abound: A thirty-year study of a West Point class showed that the tallest quarter dominated the military, claiming 42 percent of the class's generals.

The few CEOs who are short are tall in spirit. I recently watched Jack Welch, the 5'7" former CEO and chairman of General Electric, give a speech to an adoring crowd. The most frequent crowd comment: "[Gasp!] I didn't know he was so small!" I asked him about his height. "I beat the odds," he said. "I never noticed I wasn't a reasonable height." His wife, Suzy Welch, interjected. "Jack actually thinks he's very tall." Of the few other discernibly short CEOs, like Ross Perot, 5'5", and Warren Buffett, roughly 5'8", most created their own companies, since climbing the ranks is statistically nearly impossible without height.

In summary, pretty much none of talls' job success is their own doing. Beyond basic job competence, it's not really about us. Tall as-

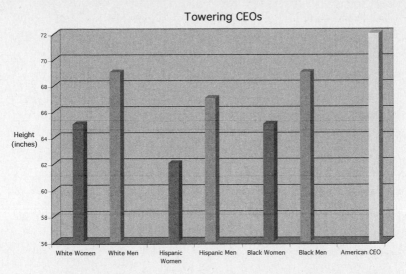

Towering CEOs

SOURCE: Adapted from the unpublished survey of Fortune 50 CEOs by Richard Fineberg, professor of international political economy at the University of California at San Diego, 2005. Based on data from NHANES.

cension is a matter of perceptions and actions by colleagues, who are often shorter. Much of tall worklife is about *how others perceive us*. It's just a series of simultaneous, positive perceptions by co-workers, replacing the job ladder with a veritable escalator.

Ninja Tall Cubicle Psychology

Since talls are so likely to become, *ahem*, bigwigs, I called up psychologists and sociologists to see if some sociological cause might be at play behind the numerous statistical studies we just read about. They described a subtle dance of body language that, throughout a tall career, propels a worker up the escalator. Let's imagine the career of Colin the Associate, a youngish employee at a big firm.

From the beginning, the body language of Colin's co-workers relate to him as a leader. "Research shows that taller people are given bigger personal spaces," says Northeastern University social psychologist Judy Hall. "Whether it's a primordial fear or a way to avoid craning necks is unclear." This means that Colin's co-workers give him one or two feet of extra physical space—which is similar to the personal space people give a boss. Close friends hold conversations eighteen inches apart, friends two to three feet apart, and bosses and employees four feet apart. Colin naturally falls into four-foot realm, which means that co-workers' body language relates to Colin as the professional leader. In turn, Colin plays the role of leader.

The whole office is instinctively aware of Colin's activities. One morning he walks into a meeting. Everyone at the table is evolutionarily primed to pay attention to him, because thousands of years ago, his entrance would have represented either a physical threat or protection, says Kory Floyd, the evolutionary psychologist. Colin is also at a great advantage because his presence incites a measurable physical response in his co-workers. "It wouldn't necessarily be a stress response, but perhaps an increase in pupil dilation, and increased visual acuity and attentiveness," says Floyd. "And perhaps increased cognitive resources would be spent on noticing and paying attention to this person." It's instantaneous—no one at the meeting can pinpoint why they're aware of Colin, and if asked, they'd likely say they enjoyed something he said. But really he's just tall, and so people automatically take notice of who he is and what he's doing.

Miles Patterson, a University of Missouri psychologist, compares the phenomenon to the effect of someone wearing a clown suit. "Tall people are just more distinct. If someone walked into a business meeting with a clown suit on, everyone would turn and look. Everything he did would get greater weight." It seems like an odd analogy, but the point is that clowns are striking and memorable. And so is Colin, who is trying to battle it out among thirty other associates. The evolutionary attentiveness paid to him means that Colin's good work is more likely to register with the boss. It's a double-edged sword, in that if he messes up, everyone will notice. But an ambitious worker will have an enormous advantage.

Another tall advantage on Colin's side is that he has more professional wiggle room to screw up and get away with it. According to University of Arizona nonverbal communication psychologist Judee Burgoon, "One of the things we know about height is that it allows a tall person to commit more social violations and have them interpreted to their advantage," says Burgoon. "Whether he is trying to win a date or close a deal, he has more latitude to commit a violation, and still have good consequences." Colin can mess up an account or inadvertently say something off color, and the gaffe will likely be overlooked. He gets a particular free pass on the same in-your-face behaviors that make a shorter person come off as bullying and domineering—he can yell, or make demands, or make an outrageous party toast, and he is likely pull it off.

These are prime workplace perks. "When you're outside the norm, you attract a lot of attention, and I think you can use that to your advantage," says Burgoon. "You're considered knowledgeable, poised, and attractive. The demeanor you carry can be used to your desired effect."

Politicians: Tall People at Podiums

No employees use that effect more than do American politicians. Politics make a good arena for studying height in the workplace, because each election is essentially a politician's attempt to get hired or promoted, and we can quantify the success in votes.

When voters hit the polls, they usually give the tall guy the job. As the *Washington Post* puts it, "the best measure of electability is the distance from the bottom of a candidate's calloused heels to the top of his or her well-coifed head." Height increases in importance with the stature of the job. In the last thirty-one presidential elections, the tall candidate has won the popular vote twenty-six times, or roughly 87 percent. Those odds are astounding—nearly nine to one. The exceptions are Jimmy Carter and George W. Bush, both of whom are shorter than the candidates they defeated (Gerald Ford and John Kerry).

The next job rung down, senators, are also quite tall. In 1866 senators averaged 5'10.5", quite tall for that time. Modern American male senators average 6'0", and more than half of American governors top 6'0"; the average governor is 3.5 inches (a full standard deviation) above the national average. Rare is the political campaign event at which the candidate doesn't stand head and shoulders above the crowd. Among senators, the taller candidate wins roughly 75 percent of the time.

But it's the U.S. presidents who really tower above the populace. Over the last half century, the average president has measured in at 6'1", the 88th percentile for men. The notable exception was James Madison, who claimed to be 5'4" (though his tiny furniture suggests he was even shorter). His wife, Dolley, was substantially taller. The chances of becoming president rise by 80 percent for a candidate over 6'0". Below is a chart of the lofty difference between average height and presidential height.

The failed presidential candidates are much shorter than the winning candidates, averaging a diminutive 5'9.5", which is 3.5 inches shorter. Height is so important to the job that a man under 5'11" might as well not bother running for president. Only one president in the last five decades was below 5'11.5", and that was Jimmy Carter (5'9"), who lucked out by challenging Gerald Ford (6'0"), who was facing public hatred for pardoning President Nixon.

In the 13 percent of cases when the shorter candidate becomes president, the popular vote usually favors the taller candidate, such as in 2000, when Al Gore (6'1") won by a margin of over half a million votes and an intervening Supreme Court decision elected the shorter candidate. John Kerry (6'4") remains the great exception: an extremely tall candidate who lost the popular vote.

Perhaps his folly was a failure to emphasize *looking* tall rather than actually *being* tall. George W. Bush's campaign managers

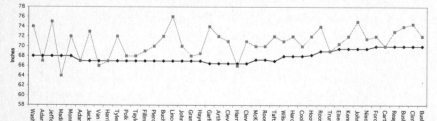

Heights of Presidents

SOURCE: Adapted from Andrew Postlewaite, et. al., "The Effect of Adolescent Experience on Labor Market Outcomes: The Case of Height," *PIER Working Paper* 03-036, December 3, 2003, 4.

YEAR	LOSER	HEIGHT	PRESIDENT	HEIGHT
1888	Harrison	5'6"	Cleveland	5'11"
1892	Harrison	5'6"	Cleveland	5'11"
1896	Bryan	5'10"	McKinley	5'10"
1900	Bryan	5'10"	McKinley	5'10"
1904	Parker	5'9"	Roosevelt	5'10"
1908	Bryan	5'10"	Taft	6'0"
1912	Roosevelt	5'10"	Wilson	5'11"
1916	Hughes	5'10"	Wilson	5'11"
1920	Cox	5'10"	Harding	6'0"
1924	Davis	5'9.5"	Coolidge	5'10"
1928	Smith	5'11"	Hoover	6'0"
1932	Hoover	6'0"	Roosevelt	6'2"
1936	Landon	5'11"	Roosevelt	6'2"
1940	Willkie	6'2"	Roosevelt	6'2"
1944	Dewey	5'8"	Roosevelt	6'2"
1948	Dewey	5'8"	Truman	5'9"
1952	Stevenson	5'10"	Eisenhower	5'10.5"
1956	Stevenson	5'10"	Eisenhower	5'10.5"
1960	Nixon	5'11"	Kennedy	6'0"
1964	Goldwater	6'0"	Johnson	6'3.5"
1968	McGovern	6'1"	Nixon	5'11.5"
1972	Humphrey	6'0"	Nixon	5'11.5"
1976	Ford	6'0"	Carter	5'9.5"
1980	Carter	5'9.5"	Reagan	6'1"
1984	Mondale	5'11"	Reagan	6'1"
1988	Dukakis	5'8.5"	Bush	6'2"
1992	Bush	6'2"	Clinton	6'2"
1996	Dole	6'1"	Clinton	6'2"

(continued)

YEAR	LOSER	HEIGHT	PRESIDENT	HEIGHT
2000	Gore	6'1"	Bush	5'11.5"
2004	Kerry	6'4"	Bush	5'11.5"

SOURCE: Adapted from the research of Richard E. Feinberg, professor of political economics at the University of California at San Diego, and former special assistant to President Clinton.

were quite adept at making him appear roughly Kerry's height in the debates—certainly, nowhere near five inches shorter. Campaigns want to maximize the positive associations that come with height, and they will do everything they can to enhance it or to create even the illusion of tallness. Campaign managers commonly adjust debate podiums to make their candidate appear taller, and male candidates frequently don man heels (see Bush's cowboy boots). Managers are also well practiced at having photographers stand below stage level, or wait outside on stairs, so that heights are obscured in the ensuing photographs. (Contrary to the popular impression, politicians don't spend an inordinate amount of time coming out of buildings with steps.)

In the 2008 election, the campaign of John McCain, 5'7", was masterful at never allowing photographers to capture him on level ground with Barack Obama, 6'1"; the campaign was particularly attuned to keeping the candidate far, far away from Michelle Obama, 5'11".

And padding the inches is standard practice. Bill Clinton claimed to be 6'2.5" during both his campaigns against Bob Dole and George Bush (both of whom claimed to be 6'2" even), only to have the White House doctor downgrade his height to 6'2" once he was safely in office. George W. Bush listed his height as 6'0" during his presidential campaign; the White House has since lowered him to 5'11". The gap between 5'11" and 6'0" is pivotal in popular imagination, much like the European gap between 188 cm (6'2") and 190 cm (6'3").

The vast majority of voters never meet their candidate, so the height battle is played out in photographs and on televisions.

Warren Harding, 6'0", pioneered the gold standard of *looking* tall; he entered the White House in 1920 with limited intellect, after a handler decided that his tall figure and broad shoulders "looked presidential." The advent of modern televised image handling was best exemplified in the 1960 election. John F. Kennedy (6'0") was within an inch of Nixon (5'11"). But Nixon slouched and had a short neck, a round face, and a bulbous nose, while Kennedy stood tall, with perfect posture. He looked taller. After the election a young psychologist named Harold Kassarjian asked thousands of voters about the candidates' height. The results were published in the *Journal of Psychology*. Nixon supporters swore up and down that Nixon was a touch taller than Kennedy, while Kennedy supporters were sure that he dwarfed Nixon by at least three inches. Kassarjian's study is still considered the preeminent research on the topic, showing that when political leadership jobs are on the line, height is in the eye of the hirers—the voters.

Where Tall Workers Make Their Money

The thirty million U.S. talls who do not reside in presidential, CEO, or congressional seats tend to cluster in certain corners of the working world. Mainly the high-paying corners. "The evidence indicates that taller people tend to sort into higher-paying occupations," says Princeton economist Christina Paxson. "There are a few exceptions—policemen, firefighters. And that may be because there's an advantage to height in those jobs." In other words, tall people are likely to enter professions that pay a bit more, like law and medicine, rather than publishing or public service. (And once there, they'll earn more than their shorter co-workers.)

Talls are also more likely to end up in socially oriented positions, like sales or publicity, where height and appearance are important. There, talls tend to make more than their $789-per-inch premium, capitalizing on their social advantages. In jobs where one's height is not seen, like computer programming or writing, talls often don't make the full $789 per inch.

Madame Tussaud's Wax Museum in Manhattan seconds as a 3D visual display of the pop culture industries in which talls dominate. I visited along with tourist throngs paying $26 each to look at wax. A 6'6" security guard whisked me through a side door, and when I told him that security is a tall industry, he grinned: the odds of a man working in security increase by 10.4 percent per inch, and 7 percent for women.

He opened another door, and I was face to face with wax Luciano Pavarotti, 6'0.5". Opera singing is a veritable tall club, where the proportionally larger cardiovascular systems are appreciated. "On average, the smaller the singer, the lighter and less powerful the voice," says 6'2" opera singer Brittany Hines-Hill. "The size of the body contributes immensely. Smaller lungs take in less air, producing a smaller sound." With the exception of a few roles that require particular vocal agility and lightness, opera is a tall art form. "Big people sing big operas with other big people," summarizes Hines-Hill.

I was expecting the wax museum to feature accomplished tall people, but the Hollywood room was jarringly petite. It was arranged like an opening-night party, and the actors were so short that there seemed to be something wrong with them. It's now clear that when Rocky Balboa, 5'8.5", declared victory atop the Philadelphia Museum of Art steps, he was excited mainly because he could see. It's easier to list the exceptions: Harrison Ford (6'0"), Morgan Freeman (6'1"), Donald Trump (6'2"), Angelina Jolie (5'8"), Julia Roberts (5'9"). Since all celebrities lie about their heights, the museum examines paparazzi shots and tailor records (or if applicable, casket orders), to determine accurate heights. But Tussaud's is also short-friendly, placing most women in four-inch heels, and men either in chairs (Bill Gates, 5'10") or leaning on a chair (Steven Spielberg, 5'7"). I was baffled by the numerous examples of rich, powerful shorties, most of whom have enormous heads: James Dean (5'7.5"), Nathan Lane (5'5"), Matthew Broderick (5'8"), Frank Sinatra (5'7"), Fred Astaire (5'9") and Ginger Rogers (5'4"). I paused to note that I am taller than boot-wearing Superman and the same size as Frankenstein. *I am taller than Superman.*

Burt Reynolds (a debatable 5'9") once cracked to the *New York Times*, "Lady, there's not an actor in the world who's six foot." There are, actually, a few, and they're likely to be at the top of their profession, in this case, the Oscars.

The Oscar-winning men and women average three inches above

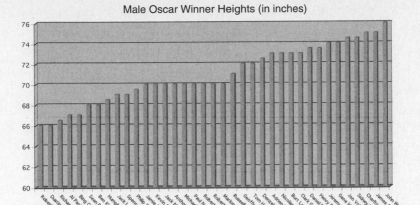

the average American. But the rest of Hollywood is teeming with short people. This appears to be an exception to the well-established rules of tall workplace dominance, but it's not: The people in charge in Hollywood—the producers and studio owners and directors and financiers—are tall. Though many actors grow famous, they are the lemmings of the industry, because their employment still depends on some tall person hiring them.

Outside the Hollywood room, the heights shoot up, particularly among Tussaud's collection of the miscellaneous famous, the singu-

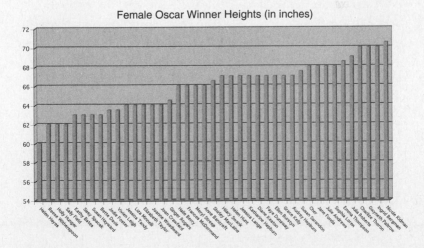

SOURCE: "Schott's Oscars Miscellany," *Vanity Fair*, March 2006.

lar ones who paved their own paths: Maya Angelou (6'0"), Princess Diana (5'10", 6'1" in heels), the enormous-headed Billy Graham (6'2"), Ernest Hemingway (6'0.5"), Annie Leibovitz (5'11.5"). What they all have in common is a knack for talking people into things. Height is, in a word, *convincing.*

Take Amy Sacco, 6'1", one of the few female owners in Manhattan's rough-and-tumble nightclub world. She told me that she's largely oblivious to her height on the job and doesn't view her long legs as being helpful to catering arrangements and phone calls. But others in her professional world are quite conscious of her height and aware of how it helps procure investors and celebrity patrons. "You can tell she has confidence, which is very attractive," said Chris Rovzar, editor of *New York* magazine. "She's a tall blonde and she's really cool. She wears heels a lot, which is bold."

The matriarch of this model is Julia Child, who was 6'2". Her big-boned frame appeared on television at a time when few women were that tall, and female height wasn't considered an asset for anything, let alone performance cooking. Yet in 1962 she became, at age fifty, a national sensation, filling the screen with her large head. Her great skill (besides cooking) was capitalizing on her height in an activity where it wasn't obviously relevant.

Russ Morash was Child's PBS producer for four decades. Television is usually the great equalizer of height. Everyone looks average. But if you watch *The French Chef*, you'll see that Child dwarfs her kitchen. She's awkward in her too-small space, and all her movements seem exaggerated. The counters hit her at midthigh, she hunches over surfaces, and utensils look tiny in her hands. The Smithsonian has a photo of her cooking on a French stovetop that reaches just above her knee. "We didn't have time for Hollywood niceties," laughs Morash. "Whatever it is, if it looks tall, chances are it was tall." Morash took to hiring tall cameramen who could shoot Child at eye level. This was back before ceiling cameras, so to get in-the-pan shots, a cameraman would stand on a very big box behind Child, holding the camera over her shoulder. She looks semiridiculous, her sneakers peeking into view.

Yet it's almost *because* Child's physicality so overwhelmed the frame that she's so relatable, regularly banging into things and dropping food. In her later shows when she was too old to harness her body, her earlier tall talents are more visible. "It became a problem when she was very old, sort of leaning on guests," says Morash. She looks much more imposing, propping herself up on countertops, slumping on Emeril Lagasse in 2000, inadvertently highlighting what a convincing asset her height once was. Her earlier shows are an advertisement for using the body to convince, comically looking down on bad-cooking guests in later shows, and exclaiming in a big, unabashed-tall-person voice. Perhaps that's why she is still in syndication. Because tall is memorable. Her height *conveys* confidence and cool, the ultimate workplace assets—to be deployed as needed.

$$\overset{\rule{1em}{0.4pt}}{\underset{\rule{1em}{0.4pt}}{\$}}$$

A Word on the Costs of Height

We are resource guzzlers. "It's a matter of physiology," says the anthropologist Barry Bogin. "Bigger individuals have more of everything in terms of body parts, meaning more bone, more muscle, and more fat than someone who's shorter. So they need more of everything to keep that alive and metabolically active. That's expensive." Yep, we have the double-price clothes, the 35 percent more food, the premium airline seats, the extra large towels, the high-ceilinged homes, and the extra provisions—a third more shower gel and lotion and what have you. But mostly it's the food. Sometimes I eat a fourth meal, which adds up.

I searched for a per-inch formula for the cost of tall life, to mirror our per-inch formula for tall income ($789 more per inch per year). I came up empty-handed with economists, so I ran an experiment on my own expenses. To get a rough estimate, I compared my last year of expenses to those of my friends. I found that height costs roughly $230 per inch per year, much of it in food and clothing. My basic necessities were 10 percent more expensive; for those who prefer well-fitted clothes, airline seats, and furniture, 25 percent more expensive. My figures are nothing more than a ballpark estimate, but they would reduce our $789 per-inch-per-year height premium to $559 per inch per year. It's still hefty, but muted.

Thus you can imagine my dismay when I read a tongue-in-cheek 2007 paper by two Harvard economists, Gregory Mankiw (6'2") and Matthew Weinzierl, suggesting that tall Americans pay a tax surcharge because talls consistently make more money. This, they argue, would be a fair way for the government to redistribute the roughly 14 percent of all income that is funneled toward talls. Under their proposed scheme, if two men made $50,000 a year, a 6'1" man would pay $6,011 in tall tax, while his 5'9" peer would pay only $1,446.

Note that the negative numbers are a tax *credit* for short people—a 5'9" man earning $40,000 per year would receive a $3,169 check from the government, just for being 5'9".

I called University of Pennsylvania economist Andrew Postlewaite to discuss this concept. He said it's based on the fact that ideally taxes would be based on talent and ability. "You could tax talent, and transfer money to the less able people to eliminate the misdistribution of raw talent," says Postlewaite. "But you can't see ability, so you tax income. If you found that height consistently gives an advantage in the workplace, then this would be similar to taxing ability."

Mankiw and Weinzierl seem aware of the wrath that their proposal invokes. "Most people recoil," they write. "And that reaction is precisely what makes the policy so intriguing . . . Many readers will find the idea of a height tax absurd, whereas some will find it merely highly unconventional." *Intriguing* and *absurd*. Yes, bilking tall people would tend to have that response.

This is far from the first Tall Tax proposal. Economists seem seduced by the height-income connection and tempted to redistribute the tall share. But they never account for the higher tax bracket that individual talls often already land in, and they certainly don't include the $230 per inch in extra cost of living. My tall sensibilities are offended. We are somewhat protected, however, by the fact that six-footers control Congress. Were the idea ever to escape the academic tower, our people on the Hill would never vote to tax themselves.

If your taxable income is closest to…	And you are – Short (69 inches or less)	Medium (70-72 inches)	Tall (73 inches or more)
	Your tax is –		
5,000	-22,671	-20,521	-20,112
10,000	-19,110	-16,715	-16,364
15,000	-16,078	-13,460	-13,035
20,000	-13,219	-10,384	-9,933
25,000	-10,551	-7,533	-7,031
30,000	-7,961	-4,850	-4,288
35,000	-5,516	-2,241	-1,639
40,000	-3,169	360	892
45,000	-848	2,953	3,453
50,000	1,446	5,478	6,011
55,000	3,634	7,782	8,403
60,000	5,844	10,080	10,822
65,000	8,900	12,387	13,801
70,000	11,964	14,862	16,779
75,000	15,297	18,185	19,758
80,000	18,655	21,540	22,751
85,000	22,012	24,895	25,855
90,000	25,246	28,251	28,958
95,000	28,159	31,387	32,065
100,000	31,071	34,172	35,191

If your taxable income is closest to…	And you are – Short (69 inches or less)	Medium (70-72 inches)	Tall (73 inches or more)
	Your tax is –		
105,000	33,983	36,957	38,317
110,000	36,895	39,742	41,444
115,000	39,808	42,527	44,570
120,000	42,720	45,312	47,696
125,000	45,632	48,098	50,823
130,000	48,544	50,883	53,602
135,000	51,333	53,668	55,973
140,000	53,334	56,288	58,344
145,000	55,335	58,388	60,715
150,000	57,337	60,488	63,086
155,000	59,251	62,526	65,457
160,000	60,742	64,545	67,662
165,000	62,232	66,564	69,705
170,000	63,722	68,583	71,748
175,000	65,213	70,602	73,791
180,000	66,703	72,621	75,827
185,000	68,193	74,640	77,770
190,000	n/a	76,659	79,713
195,000	n/a	78,678	81,657
200,000	n/a	80,697	83,600

SOURCE: N. Gregory Mankiw, Matthew Weinzierl, "The Optimal Taxation of Height," working paper, April 13, 2007. For a women's estimate, subtract five inches.

PART III

Tall Science

CHAPTER 9

Genes, Hormones, and Luck
Why You Are Tall

For the first six years of my life, I told everyone—"everyone" being my goldfish Bert and Ernie, before Bert's tragic encounter with the plastic castle—that I was tall because "my fat grew upward." I drew this conclusion because I had more height and less chub than my friends. My first-grade teacher gently suggested that no, perhaps I was tall because I ate lots of nutritious food. My mother promptly debunked this theory, informing me that I "had the tall gene." And for the next twenty years that's what I told people. It sounded reasonable.

There's no such thing as the tall gene. I learned this from pediatric endocrinologist Ron Rosenfeld, in his office at the Packard Foundation, down the road from his old haunt Stanford. I visited him because I thought that an international growth authority who titles his journal papers "A Tale of Two Centimeters" and "A SHOX to the System" would be good at explaining how tallness happens. He didn't disappoint.

"Growth is very, very complex," says Rosenfeld. "Dozens and dozens of genes feed into height, and you have to get a cluster of genes that will push you toward the tall side. Somebody who is

113

5'11" has more tall genes than short genes. Somebody who's 6'4" has even more tall genes."

Let's say you have a bowl of jelly beans, and the green and blue jelly beans represent tall genes. You scoop up eighty jelly beans, most of which are blue and green—and boom, you've got a tall person. Other families' bowls might have more red and yellow and magenta jelly beans, and they're less tall. This is why so many siblings vary in height: Their family carries some tall and some not-so-tall genes. Tallness is, literally, winning the genetic lottery.

The function of the individual jelly beans in producing height is still a mystery. One blue jelly bean likely controls how much growth hormone is produced, and another how the body responds to that growth hormone. But the height genes haven't yet been identified in humans. The very first height gene was identified in 2007, called HMGA2—and it controls a mere half-centimeter of height, or 0.3 percent. Which is to say that we have a long wait before we will have a full list. In dogs, however, the gene responsible for the difference in size between, say, miniature poodles and German shepherds was identified in 2007. It controls the release of a growth hormone called insulin-like growth factor (IGF-1).

We do know what happens once our genes are determined. The key player is human growth hormone (HGH). Despite its name, HGH isn't really what makes us grow (that would be too easy). HGH travels through the bloodstream, periodically stimulating the ends of bones and other tissues in the body to grow, but it is mainly a mailman: HGH's big delivery is to brush by an array of body tissues, stimulating them to produce IGF-1. The IGF-1 then travels around the bloodstream and stimulates the growth plates at the ends of the bones, causing the bones to grow.

So, what makes tall kids particularly tall? They don't necessarily have more HGH or IGF-1 than shorter children. What's unique is that talls are typically more *responsive* to IGF-1. "Tall people get more bang for their buck at the IGF-I level," says pediatric endocrinologist Naomi Neufeld. "A normal child should grow two to two and a half inches per year. I had kids with a 6'4" dad and 5'8" mom, and they were growing three and a half inches per year. So they're probably doing twice as much cellular replication and growth at the growth plate from IGF-1." The exception is children who are very tall, around the 99th percentile, who usually do have slightly higher levels of IGF-1 and sometimes higher levels of HGH. It's hard to measure growth hormone levels because they are largely pulsed into the body at night, and are affected by sleep, food, exercise, and season, but we do know that tall kids pump them out more often, and that growth is a springtime thing, when kids grow three times faster than during winter.

Rosenfeld summarized why I'm tall: "Either you produced more growth hormone, *or* you produced more IGF-1, *or* your receptors are more sensitive to it, *or* you're producing more of other growth factors—epidermal growth factor, vascular growth factor, there are dozens." In other words, I had a lot of blue and green jelly beans.

Height is much less fated than people think. About 20 percent of height differences—nearly a foot—are the result of environmental exposures, and three in particular: mother's pregnancy, childhood nutrition, and disease. The other 80 percent is genetic, though in poor regions, where heights often vary widely, height can be closer to 40 percent environmentally caused. We understand the environmental side of height much more because of the extensive research on height in relation to starvation and war. Conveniently, the same regimes that starve people also tend to be meticulous recordkeepers. During the Dutch Hunger Winter of 1944 to 1945 the Nazis starved the civilian population on 800 calories a day; similar records are available from child survivors of concentration camps.

Height starts at the beginning. The very, very beginning. You know the early days of pregnancy, before women even know they're pregnant? They're more important than you feared. Scientists hypothesize that a person's body size and organ size are determined starting shortly after conception, putting babies on a growth curve that will last their entire lives. As epidemiologist David Barker says, "Imagine you're some dieting British girl, and you've gotten pregnant by mistake, and the egg is working down the fallopian tube, having been fertilized, and these life-changing decisions are being made. And they're being made in response to nutrition." British Dieting Girl is not having a super tall child; nor is anyone who skips prenatal care or smokes. In Sweden, which has perhaps the best planned parenting and prenatal system in the world, babies are the heaviest in the world, averaging 7.7 pounds for girls and 8.0 pounds for boys. They're also the second tallest people in the world.

Once a baby is born, dads like to run around pointing out how big and healthy their kid is. Actually, newborn size has almost no correlation with adult height—two-thirds of their size is a direct function of the mother's size and health. But within weeks babies get on their own size track, and hop onto their own growth curve by months nine to thirteen. At age thirteen months a healthy child's height percentile is a crystal ball of the future, roughly the same as her adult percentile.

Once kids are safely upright, you can think of them as car engines. The car needs enough gas (nutrition) both to keep the engine running (basic metabolic function) and to move forward (growth). If the gas is watered down (malnutrition), or the engine is chugging (disease), the car will eventually stop moving forward. Disease takes a particularly sharp five-to-eight-inch bite out of height, particularly during early childhood. A kid with a common cold stops growing for a few days; a serious ailment, like dysentery or cancer, can stop growth altogether. "Children who are devoting energy to fighting off pathogens have few reserves left to expend on growth," writes ecologist Rebecca Sear. Thus, immunizations are key to height. Kids who are sick or malnourished will make up some of the lost growth later ("catch up growth"), growing well into their late teens.

The tallest adults are the ones who had the most childhood and adolescent growth *before* puberty started; puberty typically tacks on a standard nine inches, and then the game's over. "The children who are going to be the biggest adults are those who are tall by age one or two, and have a relatively late puberty," says Rosenfeld. Once in the three-year puberty growth spurt, the average kid grows 2.75 inches the first year, 3.5 inches the second, and 2.75 inches the third, or a bit more if they're very tall.

Will My Children Be Tall?

I'm often asked whether it's possible to predict a kid's height. Short answer: No. But you can make some educated guesses.

Currently the best doctors can do to predict a baby's adult height is employ this two-step formula:

Step 1. $Z = (\text{Mom inches} + \text{Dad inches}) \times 1.27$

Step 2. $(45.99 + 0.78Z) / 2.54 = \text{Boy future height (inches)}$
            $(37.85 + 0.75Z) / 2.54 = \text{Girl future height (inches)}$

The trouble is that this is a ballpark figure that assumes the parents grew up healthy and are themselves at their maximum height potential. Further educated guesses can be made based on the following factors, each of which can affect a kid's height by an inch or two; all of them together constitute the difference between being tall and not being tall.

Siblings. Kids from small families grow about an inch taller than those from large families. This is true regardless of income and social class, because a body can't grow well while fighting off nine siblings' cold viruses. Growth expert James Tanner also hypothesizes that children in large families can get lost in the shuffle and miss out on food and health care. A 2007 study found that on average, each younger sibling is shorter than their older sibling, particularly those who have older brothers, supporting the idea that boys are demanding on parents. This rule doesn't apply to the developing world, where big agricultural families have more working arms, and children grow taller.

Cash. Worldwide, children in the middle and upper classes are taller. Height is remarkably sensitive even to slight economic shifts. "Quite small differences in income can make a significant difference," says health economist Sir Roderick Floud. "The best example is a UK study that compared the height of children according to whether parents were employed or unemployed. Those receiving unemployment pay weren't destitute, and yet the children of the unemployed were significantly shorter at age two." By age five, the children were an inch shorter and never gained it back.

Stress. Stressed-out children stop producing growth hormone. When the stress disappears, the growth hormone returns. "When parents take children from abusive parents into adoptive homes, one of the first things they do is grow," says Floud. One study of students under the tutelage of a strict, mildly sadistic teacher found that they grew minimally. And yes, boarding school kids grow more during holiday time at home than during term time.

Chemicals. Exposure to toxins is one of the easiest ways to stunt a child. Children exposed to cigarette smoke grow less, as do children exposed to lead products. Exhaust, smoke, pollutants, and excessive household chemicals can also cause shortness. This area is minimally researched, due to the ethical glitch of knowingly poisoning children in the name of science. But children growing up in severely polluted areas, like the Love Canal, are notably shorter.

Noise Pollution. Shhhhhh—excessive noise stunts children. Medical anthropologist Lawrence Schell has found that children who live under a flight path are shorter; kids who grow up on a noisy street or next to a cranking factory can also be shorter.

Food. The fat kids at the playground are always two to four inches taller. "Make them obese," jokes Neufeld. "They'll make more IGF-1, and that's what's driving growth, so they become taller." As one doctor's manual explains, "Obesity and growth are so characteristic that the child with obesity and short stature should always be evaluated." In other words, overfeeding and height go hand in hand. The ramifications of childhood obesity (diabetes, shorter life span) are not worth the extra inches, but fat kids who thin out by age eight or so wind up a little taller.

Exercise. Exercise stimulates growth plates, by putting pressure on bone cells, forcing them to specialize and create new cells. Too much pressure, however, damages the growth plates, which are soft and fragile. "When you're growing rapidly, all these cells are turning over and the growth plates are a very slippery place," says Neufeld. "The muscle is tight. So if you're putting a lot of tension on them, you can actually cause the growth plate to slip, fracture, and then not grow." The rule of thumb is that lifting one's own body weight (in push-ups, pull-ups, etc.) is fine at any age, and kids over fifteen can lift weights.

Though it's nice to know what factors make children tall, much of the above information comes from historians and economists, not scientists. The "exercise good, siblings bad" summary lacks the scientific accuracy that helicopter parents would like. Scientists are working on ways to test indicators in the blood to track a child's height in real time. The idea is to look for indications of growth as they're produced so that doctors would be able to easily identify, say, a boy with the genetic potential to be 6'6" who is tracking toward 6'1". These are the children who are not currently identified as malnourished or otherwise troubled.

This strategy is a big detour around an explanation of tall genomics, which is not coming anytime soon—the dozens or hundreds of tall genes will take decades to unravel. Looking for height indicators is much like predicting heart disease: No one fully understands the genetics behind heart disease and cholesterol, but we know that cholesterol is the indicator of heart disease. "If you knew how tall a child should be, you could compare their height to that and learn if there was something wrong," says economist Richard Steckel.

Tall-related research is particularly slow because there's a dearth of it. Shortness is heavily studied, largely funded by the two billion dollar pharmaceutical industry for growth hormone. The reason? "Probably because most people perceive short stature as more of a disadvantage," says Steven Rosenthal, an endocrinologist at the University of California at San Francisco. "Lab work gets done if there's funding to pay for it. The National Institutes of Health are funding somewhere around ten percent of applications. They're looking for clinical relevance."

Ron Rosenfeld is also the CEO of a company called ProteoGenix, which aims to find protein indicators that will predict future height. Rosenfeld's company is one of the many looking at things from the short side, seeking a molecular basis for short stature. The company is under contract with Eli Lilly Pharmaceuticals to help identify very short children who might want growth hormone. Ideally, a leggy seven-year-old's blood could be tested, her height predicted, and a personalized treatment given to maximize her health and height—perhaps her body needs a lot of iodine to grow to its full height potential. When she's sick, doctors would be able to quickly gauge which treatments she responded best to, which would, in the long run, lower her sick time and increase her height.

In the far future, doctors will be able to test a baby's genome for tall genes; then the parents will know their child's maximum height potential before birth. And in the far, far future, genetic modification of height will be possible. "That's a long way down the road, but it's theoretically doable," says Rosenfeld. One could insert or remove, for example, a gene for extra growth hormone. A doctor at a prenatal clinic might say, "This fetus is a girl whose maximum height potential is 5'11".

The mother would say, "I would really like my daughter to be 6'2". Is that possible?"

"We could alter the IGF-1 receptors to be a bit more receptive to IGF-1."

"Done."

CHAPTER 10

Tall Health
Why Does Everyone Think We're Going to Die?

Our society has an unspoken (and sometimes spoken) assumption that very tall people have health problems. How can the heart *possibly pump blood up so high?* Tall people *can't possibly live that long.* Don't they, like, *hit their heads and keel over?* Never mind that some of the larger animals out there (whales, elephants) stick around for seventy-plus years.

Such myths are believed even by people who study height. A well-known auxologist told me, "Well, people taller than around 6'6" would have a lower life expectation because the pump doesn't work." Another said, "You die because of being too big. It's the additional weight on the vertebrae, the additional pumping of the heart, and so forth." A third (who really should have known better) mused, "I think really tall people have cardiovascular issues. It's architecture. You need higher blood pressure, and high blood pressure is very hard on arteries."

Not true! Much of the misinformation derives from the fact that what little tall research there is often ends up in highly specialized journals, leaving height experts unaware of published research in other specialties. I went on an epic search to gather information on our risk of mortality, heart disease, and cancer. Which is to say that I heard esteemed medical experts across the country say, "Tall people, huh? That's a good question." Tall people, huh? Here's the answer.

Cancer

Here the news is not uplifting. Tall people, particularly men, get cancer. I was astonished to learn this, though maybe I shouldn't have been: cancer is a disease of growth. Tumor growth. And what do tall bodies and their hormones foster? Growth. Tall women are somewhat spared—their cancer rates are in line with the rest of the population, except for breast and colorectal cancer: Women above 5'7" have a 110 percent higher risk of breast cancer and a 60 percent higher risk of colorectal cancer than women below 5'3". But the cancer rates of very tall women have never been studied, and there's speculation that cancer might correlate directly with height, which would explain why men have more cancer than women.

Very tall men host at least 30 percent more cancer than short men, and up to 100 percent higher levels of a slew of cancers, even after controlling for smoking, obesity, and income. The numbers vary significantly from study to study and cancer to cancer, but they consistently show elevated tall risk. This said, don't be too alarmed—the chance of getting any individual cancer is rather low. A 2006 study that followed 18,403 London men for thirty-five years found the cancer rates in those between 5'7" and 6'3" shown on the chart on page 123.

There's a pattern here: Talls are at no higher risk for smoking-related cancers, like lung and pancreatic cancer. Tall cancers are cancers where sex hormones play a role—namely breast and prostate cancer. An 84th percentile child has a 129 percent higher chance of dying from a sex-hormone-related cancer than an average child, and a 97th percentile child a 252 percent higher chance. The chance generally doubles for the very tall.

The upshot of hosting so much cancer is that talls are, for once, of great interest to researchers (hallelujah), so much so that the *British Medical Journal* devoted a 1998 issue to *why* talls get so

Tall Male Cancer Rates

TYPE OF CANCER	INCREASED RISK PER 2 INCHES OF HEIGHT UP TO 6'3"
Leukemia	9%
Rectal	0%
Kidney	20%
Brain	15%
Liver	5%
Skin	36%
Lung	0%
Stomach	−8%
Lymphoma	7%
Pancreas	3%
Esophagus	−1%
Prostate	7%–27%
Colon	3%–25%

much cancer. What's different about tall bodies? There are two theories, both of which center on exposure to the hormones estrogen and IGF-1.

I call the first the **Tall Eating Theory**. Tall teens and adults differ from others in that they eat 20 to 40 percent more food.

Most larger talls need roughly three thousand calories per day. Older and flabbier people need less; athletes burn up to five thousand calories. Tall people weigh more, which means they need roughly the following daily caloric intake, accurate by 10 percent in either direction:

Tall Caloric Intake, Compared to a 120-Pound Person

WEIGHT (LBS.)	EXTRA CALORIES PER DAY	EXTRA CALORIES PER WEEK	EXTRA CALORIES PER YEAR	EXTRA CALORIES PER 60 YEARS	EQUIVALENT LIFETIME SERVINGS OF ICE CREAM
140	300	2,100	109,500	6.5 million	18,771
160	600	4,200	219,000	1.3 billion	37,543
180	900	6,300	328,500	2.0 billion	56,314
200	1,200	8,400	438,000	2.6 billion	75,086
220	1,500	10,500	547,500	3.3 billion	93,857
260	2,100	14,700	766,500	4.6 billion	131,400
300	2,700	18,900	985,500	5.9 billion	168,943

* Ice cream=350-calorie serving, a generous tall-person serving of three scoops with sprinkles.

This eating surplus is supposed to be the biggest bonus of tall-dom. But perhaps it is not. Numerous observational studies in both animals and humans connect high calorie consumption to cancer, particularly breast and colon cancer, regardless of whether that eating leads to extra height or to obesity. As a review in the *British Medical Journal* put it, "Excess energy intake has negative consequences with regard to several major cancers." Human studies have shown cancer rates to be lower in those who were starved during wars, and rodent studies (including a major 2003 paper in *Science*) show that rodents fed a nutrient-heavy, low-calorie diet live longer with minimal cancers. You have probably heard of Restricted Calorie eating, a cult movement that follows a hyper-limited diet, largely based on this and other animal longevity studies.

Many scientists point to IGF-1 as the culprit. The more you eat, the more your IGF-1 levels spike. High IGF-1 levels in humans are associated with increased risk of several cancers; as mentioned earlier, some talls, particularly talls around the 99th percentile, have high levels of IGF-1. IGF-1 encourages growth and cell replication, both in healthy tissues and in tumors. The question is whether the IGF *causes* the cancer or is a secondary factor. "Many cancers don't become cancers as a result of IGF, but their growth and spread is potentiated by IGF," says Steve Rosenthal, the UCSF endocrinologist whose research looks at this relationship. New cancer treatments involve disabling the IGF-I receptors.

Estrogen is another hazard under the Tall Eating Theory. People who eat a lot are exposed to more estrogen in foods. Animal-derived foods—like beef, chicken, and especially milk—have been connected to breast, ovarian, and uterine cancers because they contain high estradiol levels. (Meat, milk, and eggs have always contained estradiol, testosterone, and other sex hormones, but the levels have gone up as producers treat animals with growth promoters.) Who drinks copious amount of milk? Growing tall people. Much as with IGF, it is unclear whether the estrogen causes the cancer or facilitates its growth after it appears.

No one is suggesting that talls should eat any less. As of now, the data indicate only that eating more than one's energy requirements is not a brilliant idea.

The second tall cancer theory, which I call the **Tall Puberty Theory,** holds that talls have more exposure to adult levels of sex hormones. Researchers have found that two groups of adults have high rates of sex-hormone-related cancers: adults who were tall as fourteen-year-olds, and early maturers who end up average-size. What do these two groups have in common? Higher and longer exposure to adult levels of sex hormones. Think about prostate cancer. Tall men have more estrogen exposure while they are growing, plus a high intake of estrogen through their food, plus extended exposure due to their longer lives. Older tall men are more likely to be diagnosed with late-stage prostate cancer. Similarly, a 2001 *British Journal of Cancer* study found that girls who are taller and leaner between the ages of seven and fifteen have an increased chance of breast cancer.

The Tall Eating Theory and the Tall Puberty Theory may be simultaneously at play, potentially along with a third hypothesis, the **More Cells Theory**. The more cells one has, particularly organ stem cells, the more opportunities one has for cancer. The take-home message is that tall people, especially those with a history of cancer in their families, need to be particularly vigilant about cancer screenings and risks.

Heart Disease

Tall hearts work just fine. Straight-talking exercise cardiologist Ben Levine, from the University of Texas, is quite sure of this. "The circulatory system adapts to the load placed on it," he says. "The hearts of elephants and blue whales work pretty damn well, and giraffes don't faint, so at end of the day size doesn't seem to be a problem." The bigger the body, the bigger the heart. An average heart is the size of a fist, and a tall person's is, well, the size of a tall-person fist.

Our slightly slower heartbeat (think hummingbird versus elephant) might also be a longevity bonus. "Lower heart rates have always been shown to correlate with longevity," says Hartford, Connecticut, cardiologist Paul Thompson. "A bigger, stronger heart doesn't need to beat as often." A 5'0" person might have a heart rate of seventy beats per minute, but a 6'6" person with a heart rate of fifty-five beats per minute would still pump substantially more blood per minute. This is the rule of thumb throughout the animal kingdom.

Part of the myth of tall heart problems derives from laypeople assuming that the heart *straiiiiiins* itself to force blood up so high through all those extra blood vessels, which *must* require astronomical blood pressure. In actuality, it's short people, particularly short women, who have statistically higher rates of heart disease. "If you're just tall, that's not fat," says cardiologist Thompson. "Fat is not metabolically active tissue, so the resistance to pumping blood through fat is greater. If you're tall, that's muscle, and it's not providing more resistance." The human body has roughly sixty thousand miles of blood vessels. A few extra inches of height are a nonissue. But waistline *is* an issue. Doctors will often tell you that men and women with waists greater than forty inches and thirty-five inches, respectively, have more heart attacks. You should ignore them, because tall people have bigger waists. The key is that waist measurement (in inches) should be less than half of height.

<hr>

A Word on Arthritis and Tall Folk

Osteoarthritis is a disease of talls, because it is linked to weight. And who weighs a lot? Tall people. "Because of the mechanics of the hips, back, and knees, every pound of weight gain is magnified in its negative effect fivefold and has a tremendously negative impact upon the mechanics and inflammatory nature of the joints," says rheumatologist Stephen Paget. Heavier bodies also have a higher risk of developing any inflammatory disease, such as rheumatoid arthritis and psoriatic arthritis.

<hr>

Tall people's blood pressure is the same as anyone else's. Blood pressure is based on the *difference* between upward and downward pressure. Imagine the blood going from heart to head (lots of pressure) and back down from head to heart (little pressure). If a tall person has a higher gradient going up, it's exactly reversed coming down, and the overall gradient (up vs. down) is the same. "Height could minorly affect blood pressure," says Thompson, "but so many other things are more powerful, like genes and diet." Similarly, giraffes don't have particularly high blood pressure. It's 260/180, double ours, even though giraffes are three times as tall as we are.

One caveat about tall heart health. Tall people may be a bit more prone to fainting, due to the distance from their hearts to their eyes. Blacking out happens when not enough blood gets up to the retina, and fainting happens when not enough blood gets up to the medulla (brainstem). Both blackouts and fainting are more likely, physiologically speaking, when long-necked tall folks stand up quickly.

I have a theory that the myth of tall ill health was widely proliferated by the passing of the best-known giant in history. Robert Pershing Wadlow, aka the Alton Giant, grew to 8'11" and 438 pounds, the tallest man on record. His hands measured 12.75 inches from wrist to middle finger. He was a successful used shoe salesman. (Who wouldn't buy shoes from the world's tallest man, for the pure benefit of telling people about it?) He toured the country with the Ringling Brothers Circus in the late 1930s, before dying in 1940 at age twenty-two. The cause: shoe trouble—a blister infection from an ankle brace. A dozen pallbearers carried his 10'9" coffin, the largest on record, at a funeral that was a national sensation. More than forty thousand people attended (the sign-in book is still at the Alton Museum of History and Art in Alton, Illinois). All aspects of the event—Wadlow's gigantism, his height, his foot infection, his passing, his enormous funeral—were statistical flukes of gargantuan proportions. Yet photos were splashed across newspapers worldwide, and Wadlow's death served as millions of people's first introduction to super height. In the back of the book, I've included an appendix of growth disorders to clear up the confusion once and for all: 95 percent of even super tall people do not have a disorder. Gigantism is a one-in-three-million phenomenon. Tallness is, broadly speaking, synonymous with excellent health and a good long life.

CHAPTER 11

Tall Treatments
Sixty Years of Height-Reduction Pills

I made my first appearance in an endocrinology department when I was three. Sedated by a lollipop, I trooped in behind my mother and let a grandmotherly endocrinologist named Dr. Kauger measure my height and limbs, test my reflexes, and look at my hand X-rays to determine my "bone age." This became an annual occurrence. As I got older, she would glance under my clothes for indications of womanhood, none of which appeared on her watch.

Then Dr. Kauger would heavily land in her chair, take her pencil to my growth chart, and look up to confirm what I already knew: I was going to be friggin' tall. "Well over six foot, dear," was the phrase. I thought that all kids had endocrinologists.

I didn't know that I was in Dr. Kauger's office to be considered for height-stunting treatments. The concept is to skip the last couple years of growth by administering horse-size doses of estrogen, which propel a girl into early puberty, and close the growth plates. It works like this. Growth plates (also called epiphyses) are the cartilage gaps at both ends of the bones, where cartilage is produced to become new bone. Estrogen matures the cartilage and closes the gap (epiphyseal fusion), stopping growth forever. Estrogen height-reduction treatment is common in Europe and an underground treatment here, which has been prescribed to many tens of thousands of girls, if not more. A similar testosterone treatment works for boys.

For eleven years, my mother and I repeated the autumn trip to Dr. Kauger. My growth chart was the central attraction. I peered over Dr. Kauger's shoulder, looking into the future. At one appointment my mom stepped into the hallway to talk to Dr. Kauger. I picked up my pink graph and with my finger traced my curve to its end: 6'5". *Wayyyy* above all the other growth curves.

The pill discussion was first broached when I was eight. My grasp of the concept of estrogen was weak, and no medical risks were mentioned. As a second grader, my main concern was that the treatments not affect my burgeoning swimming career. I remember asking whether the treatments would make my limbs shorter, because long arms and legs are important in swimming.

You have only until age eleven to make the decision, because the pills must be started a couple years before puberty. I pondered: I wanted to be tall for swimming, so I figured that if I wasn't happy being 6'5" when I was twenty or so, I could have the leg-sawing surgery where they cut your shins to make you shorter. And that was that. Employing my fullest decision-making skills, I decided to forgo treatment.

I could thank the nineteenth-century Belgian mathematician Adolphe Quetelet for the fact that I was sitting in Dr. Kauger's office, well aware that I was a late maturer on the 99th percentile who might be 6'5". In 1831 kids' final heights were as much of a surprise as the kids themselves. Quetelet discovered that human height continuums fit bell curves, which were at the time used only for astronomy. He then plotted thousands' of children's heights to create the first growth curve—a feat of prediction that was, at the time, on par with fortune telling.

My fate was sealed soon afterward in the late 1800s, when the father of eugenics, Francis Galton, coined the term *percentile*, at about the same time that the first national height and weight standards appeared. From then on everyone knew if their kid was in the 15th or the 99th percentile, and how much to worry. Galton's percentiles

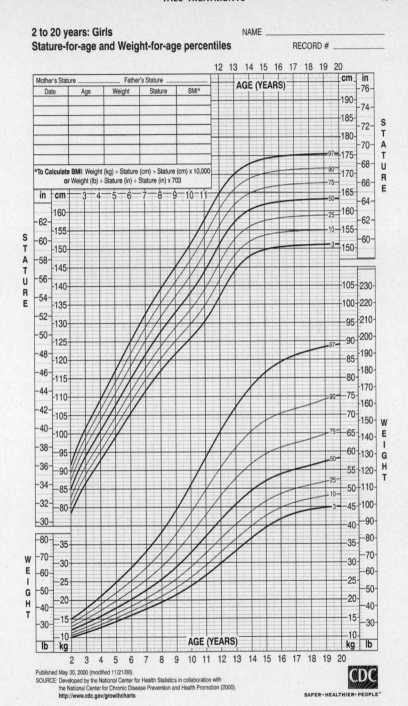

2 to 20 years: Girls
Stature-for-age and Weight-for-age percentiles

NAME _____

RECORD # _____

The Angst Chart. Providing fifteen years warning
that you might be kinda tall since 1895.

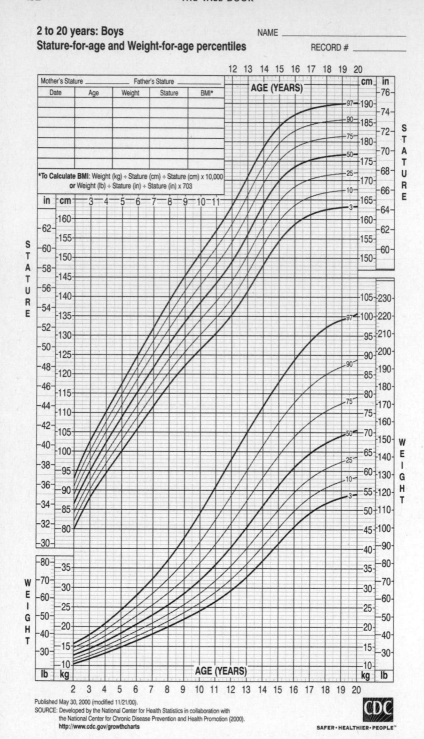

A boys growth chart

inadvertently defined *tall*, *very tall*, and (as height treatments suggest) *too tall*.

Melvin Grumbach is the grand poobah of endocrinologists and the ideal person to explain the history of estrogen treatments. He has run the pediatric endocrine program at UCSF since 1966, and he invited me to his office. He's a deep-voiced, nearly bald man in round glasses who makes you wish he was your grandfather.

The concept of treating tall girls arose in the 1940s, when doctors noticed that girls who went through early puberty also stopped growing quickly, and they surmised that estrogen must be the cause. A decade later, a Texas doctor named J. W. Goldziehr began experimental treatments on girls predicted to reach at least 5'8", and he successfully treated fourteen of them. He published his work in 1956.

"Around the world there was a flurry of interest," says Grumbach. "I mean, in 1950 women were expected to marry and have babies. It was a very different setting. The idea was that this [tallness] was a social obstacle. The girls themselves felt very distressed and kind of disturbed, and their parents were concerned about social contacts and how she was going to find a tall guy." Australian, Swiss, Dutch, British, and American endocrinologists began treating tall girls who were predicted to reach 5'9" or over. A handful of doctors and clinics, particularly in Boston and Chicago, became known for the therapy, using variations of estrogen at three or more times the dosage given for girls without ovaries.

By the 1960s tall girls in the know saw endocrinologists as a matter of course. "In the 1950s and 1960s tall stature, especially in women and girls, was considered socially undesirable," says pediatrician and growth expert Ron Rosenfeld. "And those patients were seen fairly frequently by endocrinologists." My visits to Dr. Kauger were simply a rite of passage.

My mother had begun her visits in 1962, when she was ten, after my grandmother read a small newspaper item. She had grown three inches that year, making her 5'7" and prepubescent. This made my grandmother quite nervous. Who would marry a hulking six-foot-plus girl from Brooklyn? Like most little girls, my mother soaked up all her own mother's anxiety, and by fifth grade she was convinced that the pills *could solve all her problems*. For the next year and a half, she took an orange pill every morning and night. Her endocrinologist, who may have been named Dr. Pearlmother, had a bevy of male assistants who tracked her for signs of puberty. "There was no real explanation in terms of what was involved and what they were looking for. When some guy you don't know is pulling up your shirt and seeing what's going on under there, it's awful." She had a few migraines, presumably from the hormones, and went into express puberty, gaining thirty pounds in a year. And then treatment ended abruptly. "They did a hand X-ray, said my plates were closed, and that was it." She was 5'11.75", thrilled to have dodged the six-foot bullet.

She didn't talk about the experience with anyone. "Nobody knew," says my mom. "My brother didn't know. My best friend still doesn't know." (Don't worry, I told her.) It was hush-hush.

As the 1970s came around, the treatments grew more common, particularly in the Netherlands. "When I started, in 1975," says Jan-Maarten Wit, a semiretired endocrinologist at Leiden University Medical Center, "there were quite a number of adolescents, particularly females, who didn't want to be tall. They were rather eager to do something about it. I heard from colleagues in the United States that it was much less common there, because height was considered a positive quality." Wit's clinic treated girls with predicted heights over 5'10", preferably 6'0". "We explained that there is a form of therapy, and the advantages and disadvantages. Then it was up to the girl herself or her parents." Just under half chose to undergo treatment.

The treatments weren't wildly effective. Most regimens removed an estimated one to four inches from predicted height, decreasing, say, a 6'2" girl to 6'0". One study classified the treatments as "low effective." Side effects included a puberty that appeared seemingly overnight and progressed very quickly, with headaches, nausea, joint pain, cramps, an elevated risk of ovarian cysts, pigmented nipples, and a lot of weight gain. "The treatment's not a great treatment," says Rosenfeld. There is no standard dosage or outcome, and the whole thing is based on a height prediction off an X-ray—mine (6'5"), you might recall, was two inches high. Rosenfeld treated one girl in his career, a Marfan Syndrome patient projected at 6'9".

She ended up 6'3". But would she have really reached 6'9" without it? No one knows.

It wasn't just girls. In Europe starting in the 1960s, tall boys were treated with testosterone, particularly in Zurich, with testosterone dosages that were eight to ten times the typical early-adolescent amounts, and three to four times adult amounts. "We saw many fewer boys," says Wit. "We had a 6'6" minimum before we would discuss treatment, because the disadvantages of the therapy are more than for estrogen." Those disadvantages include intense acne, the possibility of liver problems, breast development, psychological concerns around hitting puberty while so young, and the ban on teen athletics because testosterone is considered doping. Patients temporarily surge in growth, then stop. Wit says that about 25 percent of the eligible male patients did the treatment, losing two or three inches each from predicted adult heights, though different studies find widely varying figures.

In 1977 height-reduction treatments hit critical mass, and U.S. doctors held a medical conference called Estrogen Treatment of the Young. Endocrinologists were extremely divided on the practice; Grumbach was among those staunchly opposed to treating healthy children and concerned about potential long-term side effects. He talked parents out of it. "We'd say, 'Well, there's volleyball, and there's lots of tall men out there, and who says you can't marry someone who's shorter than you?'" (Grumbach is short. And convincing.)

No one knew how common the treatments were, because estrogen is prescribed for numerous ailments, and treatments are not regulated in any country. In 1978, to get an estimate, Grumbach circulated a survey to 319 U.S. and European endocrinologists. He found that treatments were widespread: exactly half of the U.S. doctors and 83 percent of the European doctors were treating girls for tall stature.

But the procedure still fell under the radar of the media and general public. Even in the Netherlands, where treatment rates have always been the highest, the general public didn't (and still doesn't) know about them. Perhaps this is because those treated didn't exactly make themselves known. Take my mother: Her treatment was never registered anywhere, and she doesn't talk about it. Were her daughter not a tall author, no one would know.

Similar scenarios played out silently around the world. "I had several friends in the 1970s who were quietly put on hormone treatments by their parents," says Janet Merewether, 6'0", an Australian filmmaker. "One friend's father put her on hormones without informing her mother. She has essentially told no one, not even her mother. It's very repressed." Not exactly public fodder, perhaps because, as I experienced, you can't really tell all your friends. They have no idea what you're talking about.

The fall came swiftly, beginning in the early 1980s, when evidence of associated medical risks appeared. First came word that estrogen treatments place girls at a higher risk of thrombosis and pulmonary embolism, because estrogen encourages clotting. Then came news of mild risk for hypertension, liver disorders, and gallbladder disease. And then came statistics of depleted future fertility. "Patients' periods always start three months after treatment," says Dr. Wit, "so for that reason, we always thought that fertility would be normal." But it was not. A 2003 study of 1,423 Australians found that treated women had 40 percent lower chances of pregnancy from unprotected sex and doubly high rates of fertility treatments. (My mom: "Well, clearly we didn't have *that* problem.") The final blow was increased cancer risk. Ovarian, uterine, and breast cancers were connected to heavy estrogen exposure.

In the 1980s it also became clear that the whole rationale behind the treatment—that extremely tall people would have psychosocial problems—didn't stand up. "All these terrible psychological problems that tall girls and women are supposed to have, they're just not true," says Grumbach. "The psychological aspect really has fallen through the ice."

We think. "Extensive psychological investigation before or during height-reductive therapy has never been performed," write researchers. Regular tall folks have also never undergone psychological testing. The closest psychological studies are of short boys. In 2003 Eli Lilly ran studies to prove to the FDA that there were benefits to taking growth hormones. But they couldn't prove a psychological benefit for their own pill. Their words: "The data do not support treatment for short stature to improve psychological dysfunction."

The follow-up health studies were minimal for women, mainly a few questionnaires, and nonexistent for men, despite over thirty years of calls for follow-up research. As a 2002 study put it, "The risk of cancer in young women receiving estrogens remains uncertain. The possibility of increased risks of breast cancer points to the need for long-term follow-up."

The lack of research is the result of a lack of funding. "To a certain extent, pharmaceutical companies drive the research, and right now pharmaceutical companies are producing drugs to increase growth rather than decrease it," says Rosenfeld. "That's where the market is for them." There's also no registry of treated patients, so tracking down the many thousands of women like my mother would be quite an undertaking.

Child psychologist David Sandberg sums it up. "There's no evidence of increase of quality of life with treatment of stature, and there is plausible rationale to suspect that it may cause harm later in life."

Nonetheless treatments continue today. "Anything outside of the two standard deviation range [above the 97.7th percentile] is grist for the mill," says Rosenfeld. In a 2002 survey of 411 U.S. endocrinologists, 137 still offered height-reduction treatments, and 92 had treated girls recently. One doctor reported treating eleven to twenty in the previous five years. In the United States boys are rarely treated, because height is considered beneficial.

Treatments are much more common in Europe, a telling reflection of which bodies are accepted where. The former president of the Netherlands tall club told me in 2007 that 50 percent of very tall girls still request the treatment. Dutch doctors confirmed this. "Girls with 6'2" predicted heights would be routinely offered therapy in our country," says Dr. Wit. "But now if the height prediction is lower than 6'1", no doctors in the Netherlands will even discuss therapy." In Switzerland it's not unusual for 99th percentile boys and girls to be treated. Boys' treatments have evolved to use estradiol or testosterone enanthate, which can now be given in patch form. "There are no national databases on this kind of treatment," says Valerie Schwitzgebel, head pediatric endocrinologist at the Children's Hospital of Geneva. "It is rare, but done at each of the five university hospitals, in Geneva, Lausanne, Berne, Basel, and Zurich." The biggest evidence that treatment continues are the sizable clinical studies that periodically appear in medical journals. Recent publications include a study of five hundred girls from Norway, and another of eight hundred patients in Australia. A 2002 study out of Germany discussed the most successful treatment techniques for forty-one boy patients predicted at 6'8".

I found it quite hard to research this chapter, because U.S. doctors are reluctant to discuss the topic. Many declined to speak, as did multiple pharmaceutical companies. Grumbach was by far the most willing, perhaps because he personally initiated the movement to halt the treatments. Every single U.S. doctor I interviewed announced, unsolicited, that he had treated only a small number of patients and then justified the scenarios. "It wasn't that we wanted to make everyone tall or not so tall," says one endocrinologist. "There's a public hankering for perfect children. They want us to do everything we can." Treating healthy children is always ethically questionable in a profession that lives by the Hippocratic oath; it's now a legally dicey issue, because thousands upon thousands of formerly treated adults, mostly ages thirty to sixty, are wandering around at a known health risk.

How doctors phrase things, it seems, is extremely influential in whether patients take the treatment. In a 1991 study of 539 Norwegian girls, all were offered and *all* accepted; in a similar Finnish study of 87 girls, a third declined. Wit explained how he approaches the situation: "My own perspective is that if a girl is predicted 6'0"–6'2", I would discuss it in a sort of neutral way, and leave it up to the parents and child. But if the prediction is higher than 6'2", I would be a little less neutral. I would highlight the advantages more. I would accept that taller than 6'2.5", even in the Netherlands, would be unusually tall."

At the end of the day the decision is, essentially, left up to patients. "In general, the pediatric endocrinologist is not a very positive adviser," says Wit. "Our attitude is that we would not like to put them in treatment. If the adolescent is very unhappy and attributes problems to very tall height and is afraid of tall height in his future, we use that as an argument. But we do not advertise."

I was somewhat stunned to find that the alternatives to hormone height-reduction treatments are *expanding*. There's now a new surgical height-reduction treatment called epiphysiodesis (translation: growth-plate-o-desis). "It started maybe five years ago in the Netherlands, and is one of the accepted forms of therapy," says Dr. Wit. The surgery is actually a cousin of the leg-sawing surgery that my eleven-year-old brain dreamed up. (The leg-sawing operation does indeed exist but is unbearably painful, and commonly results in complications like two different size legs. It isn't performed in the United States.)

Epiphysiodesis is a more predictable treatment than hormones because, rather than playing chicken with puberty, it works by removing growth plates. "The growth plates of the femur and the tibia, above and below the knee, are surgically removed," says Stenvert Drop, a pediatric endocrinologist in the Netherlands. This effectively ends half of leg growth, leaving behind two growth plates in each leg, one above the ankle and one below the hip. The younger the patient, the more reduction. The risks are well known, because the procedure has been used for decades to treat children with differing leg lengths and can be performed by an orthopedic surgeon. The cornerstone study is from 2006, following fifteen boys, who had their height reduced by an estimated average of 2.75 inches. Another, with six boys, showed an average of 3.7 inches in height reduction. The literature is quite upbeat, finding no significant side effects and a proportionate lower body. No studies exist on girls. It seems that only boys undergo the surgery, perhaps because height predictions based on their bone age are known to be more imprecise, while girls are still offered pills.

Drop estimates that dozens of Dutch children have the surgery annually. "It's certainly done in Stockholm. They have a lot of these operations," says Wit. "There is a form done in Gröningen, and also sometimes here in Leiden." In America most of the doctors I mentioned it to hadn't heard of it. David Rimoin, a pediatrician at

Cedars-Sinai Medical Center, knew of it and said that any orthopedic surgeon could do the surgery, but he emphasized potential side effects. "You can end up with asymmetry and all sorts of problems," he said.

Other alternative treatments are also cropping up. Doctors have suggested that growth hormone suppression, a treatment used in gigantism, might also be effective, though the results vary widely. A similar tack involves somatostatin, a hormone that essentially stops growth hormone release from the pituitary. However, long-term studies have not been done. Others have suggested that instead of focusing on puberty, treatments might be more effective if they were attempted earlier, allowing puberty to proceed normally.

I find the proliferation of height-reduction treatments to be worrisome, because it was in Dr. Kauger's office that I learned I was "too tall." The seed was planted that something was awry about being a very tall girl, so much so that there was a longstanding treatment process to "correct" it. As one doctor put it, "How do you deliver the message *you're okay* between several visits to an endocrinologist to consider height predictions and hormone treatments?" Well, you don't.

The question is, *who* is being treated in the first place? A 2005 Australian study found that 82 percent of formerly treated women said a parent or doctor had pushed them into it. And all elective medical treatments of children are, really, treating the anxieties of mothers. Multiple doctors told me that treated children usually have parents who are not happy about being tall and therefore perceive society as being not tall-friendly. Height-reduction treatments are, at the end of the day, a litmus test of parents' tall experiences.

One German study blurts out the root of parental concerns: worry that unusual body size will compromise a child's chances of marrying. The pills were never really about making children psychologically happier adults, or giving them an easier time finding clothes, as doctors told themselves and their peers. Grumbach shakes his head at all the psychological justifications that fell through: "Really what was behind it all was social." The irony here is great: The treatment to facilitate girls getting married and having babies turned out to cause infertility.

It all seemed like a tragic tale until I came across Astrid Scholz, thirty-five. When she was 5'8" at age ten, her mother had her examined at a local university hospital in Cologne, Germany, where she was projected to reach 6'10". "I vividly remember the doctor asking me how tall I wanted to be. I picked 6'3", two inches taller than my mother. That was important to me for some reason, and miraculously, the dosage worked out perfectly. Perhaps because I got to own my height at an early age, I have never tried to hide it in any way, and feel very comfortable in my body." She loves her 6'3" height, she told me, because she chose it, and could not be happier with her treatment experience. She'd consider treatment options for her children.

We know that just under half of treated women regret the decision. And 60 percent, like my mother and Scholz, are satisfied. And we know that those who skip the treatment and grow tall and gorgeous are nearly universally (99.1 percent) happy with their decision. Me too.

PART IV

Tall Quandaries, Explained

CHAPTER 12

In a Box of One
Tall Psychology

*To be big and tall and spiritless would be worse than
being little and short and spiritless; somehow more of
a waste, like an uninhabited tenement building.*
—Helen Simpson

When I traveled through India, people regularly stopped me to tell
me that I have *great height*. In a public bathroom, a woman paused
next to the sink to say, "Wow, you have such *wonderful* height!" At
a coffee shop, it was *fantastic* height. Other adjectives included *terrific, excellent*, and *very grand*. Compare this to Manhattan, where
standard comments are "Wow, you're really tall" and occasionally
"Dude, you're like man-tall." Suffice it to say that (a) I really like
India, and (b) much of my psychological fortitude has been shaped
by years of responding to these comments.

I began to wonder whether there was a book out there on tall
psychology. Any tall person can tell you that height is a huge psychological force that deeply affects personality, self-esteem, and behavior. Yet in the psychology stacks of Columbia University, the

closest I found was heavy use of the word *analogous*. As in, height is *analogous* to beauty or freckles or curly hair or fatness; that psychologically speaking, it's just like any other physical trait. "The analogous research with physical attractiveness indicates that attractive people are more liked, get along better with others, and do benefit from that, so I would say that height probably does good things for self-confidence," says the psychologist Miles Patterson.

Given the void of tall psychology studies, I can tell you a bit about my own tall psychology: it's not analogous to beauty or freckles or fatness. I've sparred with all three, and tallness trumps them cold. Tallness is exceedingly visible, defining, and above all unalterable. There is no personal choice involved. It is the psychology of being on display as permanently different, and wandering through life responding to that difference in a public forum. How could a lifetime of being on view, of inspiring comment around the world, not have a deep effect?

I am not, for the record, the first person to suggest that tall psychology deserves attention. Sir Roderick Floud, perhaps the only height studies expert ever to be knighted, told me, "I've never been able to interest psychologists in height. It's a pity. I think psychologists ought to be more interested."

For me, the tall psychological difference took root in second grade. I was the tallest kid, male or female, in Mrs. Dempsey's 2–3 Class, and I was so different that I might as well have had superpowers. My gym class periodically played this game where we split into two teams, and one person from each team hid behind a sheet. Each team had to yell out adjectives describing that person until the other team guessed who it was. I was behind my sheet for approximately 1.4 seconds. Someone yelled "Tall!" and another kid yelled "Arianne!" For me, there was no hiding. Ever. My self-image was crystallized in that sheet game. I was so different that the basic intrigue of the sheet game didn't apply.

People who grow up feeling different tend to think a lot. John Updike, who grew up with severe psoriasis, chronicled his thoughts in "At War With My Skin." Replace *psoriasis* with *tallness*: "Psoriasis keeps you thinking. Self-examination is endless. You are forced to the mirror, again and again; psoriasis compels narcissism." He catches his reflection in numerous mirrors—shaving mirrors, rearview mirrors, car mirrors, some flattering, some not. He's always looking, thinking, reflecting. I stared at myself in every glass window I passed and compared myself to every tall woman on the sidewalk from ages seven to twenty. I was different, and constantly computing that.

Since everyone could see me, I had to decide early on whether I was going to bask in the spotlight or do everything I could to get out of it. This is the fundamental decision that all tall people have to make: to be seen or not to be seen. Psychologists call this "issue self-consciousness," and it can go either way. Dutch life coach Arjan Rooyens, 6'7", explains, "Tall people either learn to cope or they don't. They can play with it and have a good time, or hide. If you're tall, it's a fact of life."

As the tallest person anyone had ever seen at Elsmere Elementary, I decided, screw it: I might as well be tall and seen. I grew a big personality to fit my enormous body, one that mirrored back what seemed to be expected. "You expect certain personality attributes in a tall person," says Elizabeth Cline, 5'10", twenty-eight, a Manhattan editor with the sort of body presence that tells you she's in the room even when your back is turned. "It makes a huge difference in self-perception. When I got into middle and high school, people took me more seriously because I had a physical presence. Of course you're gonna develop a really strong personality to go along with that."

I quickly found that people were surprised when I opened my mouth and spoke with a soft voice, which is what comes out naturally. I felt compelled to speak with a firmer size-appropriate voice.

It was, frankly, easier to reflect back the expected traits. Why go against the grain? Why not just be a happy confident type, a loud-voiced leader? Why not just let my personality fill the room as much as my body does? If society's going to give you license to do your own thing, why not take it? That's what I did. I am convinced that my personality would be much smaller if I were 5'3". I'm not, by nature, a leader or a people person. Yet I frequently am the life of the party, because in a group everyone's looking at me anyway. After twenty years of this, it's become habit.

Not all talls make the decision to go with the flow. Lots of talls try to hide. Which isn't a great option. Hiding means conforming, and conforming means not drawing attention—which is impossible in a body that automatically draws attention. It can come off as impishness, or a lack of confidence. My mother is a hider—she prefers not to be seen and would meld with the wallpaper if she could. Hiding creates a clash between body (very visible), expectation (big and bold) and presentation (quiet and shrinking).

The troubles of hiding while tall are well-illustrated by Patrick Fitzgerald. He's forty-two, an alterna-rock singer with a quiet, wry personality that would better fit a skinny 5'9" guy. He started performing five years ago. He noticed that every time he got up on stage for an open mike night, audience members would yell out, *How tall are you?* So he decided to cut to the chase and introduce himself as SixSeven. (His true height, 6'6.75", doesn't have the same ring to it.) When he steps up to a microphone, the audience is not expecting a subdued performance. "They don't want me to be a regular person. Not only am I not, but they don't want me to be." At first he maintained his typical personality on stage. Then he realized that it was simply easier to do what people wanted. "On stage, I let it go more because that's what people want. I'm learning how to maximize my height instead of trying to blend. Even though it's not in my personality, that's what people want. People expect me to be a leader. They literally look up to me. They expect me to do things I don't necessarily do. And sometimes they're intimidated, regardless of what I do. I find things go smoother in all directions when I act the way people expect me to act, even though that's not the way I would act if I were on my own." He pauses. "For most of my life I have tried to blend in as much as possible.

I wish that I could be my own person separate of my height. But I think that they go hand in hand." They do.

Much of that early decision to bask in the attention or to shy away is intimately related to what's going on at home. I asked sixty tall people about their experiences, and a pattern quickly emerged: Talls who love their height, nearly without exception, grew up with a tall parent, sibling, or very close family friend who loved being tall. In every interview, happy talls inevitably mentioned their tall sister or their 6'5" uncle. Unhappy talls talked about feeling alienated and alone.

Take Jena Benton, 6'2". She's the shortest of four siblings. "I like to say we are a family of Redwoods," she says. "I never really thought about being tall, because I'm one of the shorter people in my family. It took my 6'8" dad visiting me at college for me to realize that I stand out in the world. You don't notice the difference when you're in the forest."

Numerous other examples emerged. Ben Butler, 6'8", had a 6'4" father and a 6'5" brother: "I don't think I noticed it that much. I always saw it as a positive," he says. Minnesota timber wolves center Jason Collins, 6'11", has a twin, Jarron, who plays for the Utah Jazz. "We were tall skinny kids in L.A., 5'3" in third grade," he says. "But I never really thought about it because I had a twin. We didn't have to deal with kids teasing us because there were two of us." Jen Weaver, 6'0", is shorter than the rest of her brood. "From my perspective, everyone else was kind of strangely short," she says. It's a self-image that stays on permanently.

The common factor here is that *they never thought about it*. Tall was completely normal and therefore a nonissue. Psychologists second this observation. "It has so much to do with whether people come from a tall family," says psychoanalyst Susie Orbach. "If the family is tall, children grow up with tallness as a quality that doesn't seem odd. Children have an imagination about who they're going to be, and if people around them are tall, they envision themselves that way."

It's the loners who tend to have problems, developing slouching and self-esteem problems that can take years to reverse. Alan, 7'2", who I met at Europatreffen, towered a full foot over his family. "I think it helps to know someone else who is tall, and I didn't," he says. "When you're a teen, you don't want advice. You want someone who has been there." Alan struggled with his height into his thirties. He remembers seeing the first person who was his size. "I saw a super tall guy in a soccer game make a tackle, and I thought, 'That's what I look like!' It was a key moment for me." He was twenty-six.

Orbach agrees that the lone trees have their work cut out for them. "I think that unless it's really well handled, being tall can feel awkward and odd and a bit freaky." Sure enough, in the analogous research, the short adults who are most comfortable with their height grow up with positive short role models.

Parents who want their tall children to love their bodies face a challenging situation on the home front. Children are extremely impressionable to positive body imagery, which can easily outweigh tall teasing at school. "I think if some stranger comes along and says, 'Your height is absolutely lovely and I love it,' it can transform it and become pleasurable," says Orbach. I am a rampant complimenter of tall teens.

At Europatreffen I met Angela Roberts, 5'10", the mother of an adult daughter, Sarah, who unexpectedly sprouted to 6'8". Tall parenting has a few quirks all its own. It begins with the constant feedings, the bumped and bruised home from kids banging into doorways, the presents spotted at the top of the closet long before Christmas, and the decade where legs fit into pants for no more than six months at a time.

Roberts is finely attuned to the battle of making a daughter confident where no role model exists. "I used to wear the highest heels possible when she was a teenager to make her feel more comfortable," she says. When kids did double-takes at Sarah, she made up positive statements. "I said, 'Look Sarah, if you wear a funny hat, people look twice too.' I was always coming out with these crap positive sayings."

Those crap positive sayings are important. Amazingly, adults still play their parents' pep talks in their heads thirty years later. "My mother always told me how stunning it was to be a tall woman," says Amy Sacco, 6'1". "She always had to reinforce my sense of self, that I was beautiful and not everyone could be so fortunate." Kim Blacklock, 6'7", repeats her 6'6" father's mantras: "There's nothing uglier than a tall person who slouches." "You're gorgeous." "You stand out and you're beautiful." And (my favorite), "If anything interesting goes down and you're within a five-mile radius, who's going to remember that you were there if you were slouching?"

When crap positive statements didn't suffice, Roberts worked with her daughter to invent positive coping strategies. The two practiced ice-breakers that she could use when meeting new kids, giving them an immediate topic of conversation other than height: *My name's Sarah. I like to do gymnastics. Do you?* They realized that when she gave her real height, it caused teasing, so she learned to fudge it, with jokes. And they found *uses* for Sarah's height, groups like swimming or debate club, where her long arms and formidable presence were appreciated. The unhappy talls I spoke to rarely had found a *use* for their height.

Children are intensely attuned to their parents' true feelings, no matter how much parents try to hide them. Talls repeatedly told me their parents' inner perspectives on height with precision. "My mom is 6'4", and she's much less comfortable with her height," says Weaver. "I think she'd want to be shorter. She's quiet and won't dance or do things that might draw attention to herself. For her, it's part of this unquenchable search to be less unfeminine. I would not perceive her in that way. But when you're a broad-shouldered woman at 6'4", you're not gonna be a wilting flower."

Though my mother went out of her way to never say anything negative about being tall, I was well aware that she dreamed of being "discernibly short." Ideally, 5'2". "There's no benefit to me in being tall," she told me recently. "It's not a positive. It's less of an issue now, but I still can't get clothes. I stand out in a crowd, and I like to blend into the background. I'm not happy about it; I'm resigned to it." I soaked up this attitude. She never talked about it, but I knew it was there. She is aware of the semiridiculousness of being so bothered by her height. "It's really too bad, because when you think about it, other things are so much more important. As all-consuming as it was, we're talking about a matter of inches. I mean, the world is a very big place. Yet a few inches, which are so insignificant, are my bugaboo."

Orbach suggests that parents just acknowledge the awkwardness. "It might be best to say, 'You know, I didn't grow up expecting to be tall, so this is a second opportunity for me, a chance for the two of us to get used to it.' Because if parents are tall and uncomfortable, then children will feel that part of being tall is to be out of sorts, to be peculiar in some way. So they will feel like they are ill-fitting in a profound sense."

During my teen phase of feeling profoundly ill-fitting, I blamed everything on my height. If a boy didn't like me, it was because I was too tall. If someone teased me, it was because I was too tall. I genuinely *believed* that my height was to blame for these events, well into my twenties. I was very consistent on this point: I hung all my problems on the Tall Hook. Particularly the dating ones.

Spending years on the Tall Hook has led me to come up with Hook Theory: the idea is that people hang most of their problems on hooks. If it's not the Tall Hook, it's the Parent Hook or the Money Hook or the Looks Hook. It's a way of explaining your problems to yourself. The Tall Hook makes a particularly convenient hook because you *are*, undeniably, tall. The amazing thing about Hook Theory is that when you are under its spell, you *really truly believe* that all your problems hang on that hook. I was completely positive that if I wasn't tall, my problems wouldn't exist. In reality, even if I were five inches shorter, I would still have the same a big pile of problems and would just shift them to another hook.

Some people spend their entire lives moving their baggage from one hook to the next. Which is ridiculous, given that we all come from veritable closets full of potential hooks—we're just focusing on one hook. It isn't just talls who do this. In the analogous research, a Dutch study of short adults found that those who had sought out growth therapy treatments "attributed major life problems to their short stature, like finding a partner, finding a job, and being respected. None of the [nontreated] members reported these problems, nor a strong relation between stature and day-to-day problems."

The consequences of teens utilizing the Tall Hook (and disliking tallness) are rather dire. Teenage girls who don't like their height run a high risk of being unhappy adults: a third experience serious depression at some point, and 11 percent are depressed within any given year. That's twice the depression rate in the general population. Researchers have concluded that it's extremely important to follow up with teens who are showing signs of disliking their bodies.

The trouble with the Tall Hook in particular is that it ends up perpetuating the problem. "If someone projects that awkwardness or weirdness, they may get negative feedback," says Orbach. Take Jasmin, a 6'1" sixteen-year-old from Ohio, who e-mailed me: "High school is the worst experience ever. I get ostracized just because I'm not like everyone else. Trying to fit in and enduring the teasing are hardest. It's high school evils times two. Nobody talks to me because I am a tall freak." Jasmin is probably walking through school in a slouch; the kids sense it and promptly tell her that she's too tall. So she slouches even more, and pulls out the Hip Drop. It's circular: she projects it, and the world reflects it right back, which makes her project it some more. I've been there. It's an ongoing wash cycle.

We know that blaming height for your problems is, practically speaking, a case of wrong attribution. Child psychologist David Sandberg once asked sixth through twelfth graders to rate the likability of everyone in their class, then to cast a class play including roles like "gets picked on," "good at sports," and "bad at sports." He found that children above the 95th percentile in height had just as many friends as other children and were just as likely as the other children to be associated with each of the twenty-eight roles. The only difference for tall kids was their low likelihood of getting the "looks younger" role.

I asked Orbach how she would handle a patient of any age who was unhappy about his or her height. She emphasized that tallness does not necessarily require therapy, but that if she did see a patient, the sessions would largely be a matter of disentangling problems from hooks. "I think I would acknowledge that they feel uncomfortable. But then I would try to help them figure out what else they're putting on the tallness. I'd try to untangle the discomfort with tallness, acknowledging the bits but also talking about other individual qualities." She would also discuss tall role models, as well as people and activities that appreciate height, and the pros and cons of being tall, with the goal of helping the patient relate to his or her body positively.

If any question lingers that height is a mind game, consider the fact that tall people rarely perceive themselves as, you know, tall. To wit:

> "I don't think of myself as tall. A lot of times I'll be walking down the street, and I'll think, *Wow, that person's really tall!* And then I get close to them and realize I'm the same height as the person."
>
> *Art Bradford, 6'4"*

> "In my head, I don't tower over anyone. I sometimes look at pictures where I'm standing six inches over everyone else and think, I don't remember them being that short."
>
> *Kelly Chapman, 6'3"*

> "When we see someone our own height, we're like, *Wow, that girl's tall!* And of course, I'm as tall or taller."
>
> *Patrick Fitzgerald, 6'7"*

> "A very tall woman walked into the clinic where I worked, and when she left, I said, 'Man! She was tall!' All my co-workers paused and looked at me. One of them said, 'Cheryl! She's the same height as you!' "
>
> *Cheryl Sosebee, 6'0"*

Next time you see a hulking guy lumbering down a street, remind yourself: *In his mind, he's petite.*

Similarly, pretty much everyone I spoke to, male or female, from 5'10" to 6'8", insisted that they are *right on the edge of reasonable height*:

"I'm 6'1", and I'm at the cut-off height. I don't know if I would feel as confident if I were 6'5"," says Sacco.

"I honestly wouldn't want to be any taller than 6'4". I'm right at the maximum height of what I'm happy with," says rower Caryn Davies.

"I think my height is the absolute limit," says 6'5" dominatrix Goddess Severa. "I think being tall is great, but I think it would be really difficult to be 6'6" or more, because people make so big a deal out of it."

"If I could pick, I would want to be 6'8", because the sizes just don't fit after that," says Ben Butler, 6'8".

And on and on. We can all relax, because on the inside the psychological difference between 6'0" and 6'7" is small, and talls, whether kinda tall or super tall, perceive themselves as about the same size. "I think one should just embrace their height and learn to sort of just revel in the tallness," says body image photographer George Pitts, 6'0". "Roll with it, instead of longing to be otherwise."

And enjoy the resulting psychological tall club, legitimized every time you pass another tall person and do the Tall Nod. Alan describes it as, "an acknowledgment. It's not like when you're jogging and you pass another jogger. More than that." Men are particular nodders. "There's a tall guy subcult," says Arjan Rooyens. "If you walk into a club and see a tall guy, there's a pretty good chance you'll talk to each other." Freckled people don't get an analagous subcult.

CHAPTER 13

Into the Bedroom
Where Tall Folk Produce More Tall Folk

"To be tall is to look down on the world and meet its eyes on your own terms."

—PHILLIP LOPATE, PORTRAIT OF MY BODY

Dating While Tall and Male

In early 2007 I was standing at a bar when a short woman I know, a well-known writer for the *New York Times Book Review*, wandered in with a very tall man. My blood pressure spiked. I have a confession: I *hate* it when tall men date much shorter women. Particularly when a super tall man, for whom a 5'10" woman would actually be relatively petite, dates a 5'2" woman. I pretended that it didn't bother me, but my inner monologue was shrieking something like *Poacher!!!*

Caryn Davies, the 6'4" rower, echoed my thoughts. "I get annoyed. And my brother is one of the perpetrators. He's 6'6" and marrying a short girl. She's very nice, but I don't think it's fair. I just don't get it. A long time ago I said that he couldn't bring home a girl under 5'10". He paid me no mind and dated only short girls."

He paid her no mind because he can. Tall men are the most romantically successful group on earth, bar none: more successful than rich people, accomplished people, and educated people, says Kory Floyd, the evolutionary psychologist. Men's attractiveness is directly connected to height, as is their likelihood of financial success, and therefore a romantic boon. "Women favor men who show signs of power, resources, and the ability to provide for them, and height is an indicator of that," says Floyd. "On average, a tall man is going to do better in his love life, finances, and pretty much every aspect of his life."

There is one man who collects statistical data on tall dating habits. I liked him immediately because his name is Bogus. As in Boguslaw Pawlowski, a Polish anthropologist. Pawlowski looked at coupling habits in Poland, Great Britain, Austria, and Germany and found that on average men are 8 percent taller (roughly five inches) than their partners. This is not surprising, because overall men and women's heights differ by about 8 percent.

A closer look at the statistics is more telling. Most people couple within their own height range—short couples are 8 percent apart, midsize couples are 8 percent apart. The exception is talls. "Very tall men are attractive to many women," says Pawlowski. "Since there are not very many tall women, they pick up women who are 12 to 15 percent shorter." (Note: There are, actually, just as many tall women as tall men.) Tall women, meanwhile, date men who are approximately the same size, 0 to 5 percent taller; extremely tall women go for men 0 to 2 percent taller. Tall men are kids in a candy store, dating whomever they want. The 12 to 15 percent difference over their partners is an average, meaning that a significant group of men are partnering with women 20 percent (one foot) shorter.

But if you ask individual men about this fact, they seem surprised. "I've never thought of it that way," says Patrick Fitzgerald, 6'7". "There aren't many women who are up to my height, but I'm attracted to all kinds of women, tall or short."

I told Ben Butler, 6'8", that men of his height are, statistically speaking, particularly lusted after by tall women. "For real? If that's true, then I probably missed a lot of signals. I would definitely say that a tall woman who isn't forward is at a real disadvantage. That's gonna mean a lot of missed opportunities." I've always assumed that tall men just know that Tall female + Taller male = Crush. They don't.

The 8 percent trend is further broken once a month by short women. When short women are ovulating or are seeking a short-term relationship (two scenarios that, in my experience, overlap heavily), they jump far outside their 8 percent range and poach tall men. This confirms everything tall women have been shaking their heads at for centuries. Pawlowski has an explanation. "The hypothesis is that when short women are choosing a short-term partner, it is not important whether this guy's gonna be a good father, so women look for cues of higher genetic quality." Tall men are seen as genetic quality. Tall ladies, grab your guns.

Tall men often find themselves sought after for another reason, the assumption that they have large penises. This is a myth—numerous studies have shown that penis size and height are not correlated—yet it's a particularly popular stereotype in the gay male community. The result is that many tall men are extremely sensitive about their penis size. At issue is the fact that tall men's bodies are so big that even penises that are well above average size don't look it—see Michelangelo's *David*. (Memo to men: The men in porn movies often have small frames. That's why their penises look so big in comparison to their narrow hips and thighs.) Tall women around the world have spent centuries assuring their tall partners that they're fine.

Tall men's dating success can be quantified through online dating research. A study of twenty-two thousand dating ads found that men who are 6'3" or 6'4" receive 65 percent more responses than 5'8" men. A 5'0" guy with the same photo as a 6'0" guy would need to make $325,000 more per year to attract as many responses. Even a 6'0" guy would need to make $43,000 more to match the success of a 6'4" guy.

With all these hot dates, tall men are more reproductively successful, regardless of education, because they are more likely to get married. Men at 6'2" have the highest marriage rates, though all talls have higher marriage rates than shorts. Once married, Pawlowski explains, men at every size have the same likelihood of having children. This seems to be true across the Western world—a British study found that rare is the tall man who does not have children or a number of long-term relationships. Extremely tall men above around 6'5" date a bit less and have fewer children, but they are still more successful on both counts than average-sized men. And tall fathers are sought even when the guy himself is not in the picture. The major sperm banks don't accept male donors under 5'10" and actively recruit donors over 6'1" to meet demand, paying them extra for their, *ahem*, efforts. Tall swimmers go on to fertilize the resulting thirty thousand annual U.S. births.

Dating While Tall and Female

Western culture has a way of getting confused over what femininity is—and for better or worse, tall women sit right at the crosshairs of that debate. Popular media images often define femininity as petiteness, or, more often, smaller-than-man-ness. It's a definition that's always in flux. Right as this book was going to press, a spate of wealthy, famous men married much taller women: Tom Cruise and Katie Holmes, Keith Urban and Nicole Kidman, Nicolas Sarkozy and Carla Bruni. Their photos were suddenly splashed across the media, and dating up looked like it could become trendy. But the trend shifts every few years, and has nothing, actually, to do with whether or not tall women are desireable. The important point is that, objectively speaking, tall women are burgeoning with sexuality. Male response to that is beyond our control and has nothing to do with us.

Statistically speaking, dating and sex are less common in Tall Woman World than in Tall Man World. The biological forces at play begin with the fact that unlike the case with men, height is not a decisive indicator of attractiveness in women. Women's beauty is based on facial characteristics and body shape. "Men favor women who show signs of youth and health, and height has no significant relationship to that, so there's no significant relationship between height and attractiveness for women," says Floyd. This doesn't mean that tallness is attractive or unattractive—it means it's neutral, not in the equation.

Dating research says all sorts of things that tall women don't want to hear. "We find that men typically avoid tall women," the researchers of the dating ad study wrote. "This is a relative effect, such that men do not want to meet women taller than themselves." In online dating ads, a 6'3" woman receives 42 percent fewer responses than a 5'5" woman, the "ideal" online female height. (I know, I know.) Pawlowski doesn't think this is news. "It's nothing very original," he says. "It's just the fact that if you have a woman at 5'9" or 5'11", there are fewer men who would like to make a couple with such a woman. Very tall women have a much bigger problem than tall men because they have a much smaller pool of partners." My feelings about Bogus plummeted.

Women up to 5'9" don't feel a squeeze on their dating pool; many women I spoke with above 5'11" attributed their singleness, at least partially, to a smaller dating pool. "I'm still single at thirty-three, and I think my height is a part of it. Not the whole part, mind you," says Jena Benton, 6'2". "A lot of guys find my height intimidating."

Comedian Kim Blacklock, 6'7", is more blunt about it. "Guys see us, and they go into reptilian brain. They go *competition*! I think it triggers fight or flight. They're such Neanderthals. And I'm like, *You dumbass*."

It comes down to a numbers game: Women at below the 50th percentile have the entire male population to choose from for taller mates, while a woman at 6'2", is looking at 3 percent of the population. And men, by the numbers, rarely date up. A study of 720 American couples based on bank account applications showed that only *one* couple featured a taller woman. Based on probability for their heights, there should have been fifteen such couples. (Keep in mind that these are self-reported heights, and men are known to round up.) Similar results came from the UK National Child Development Survey, in which only 484 of 12,989 marriages had a taller wife (3 percent). If paired at random, it should have been 1,111 (9 percent). In other words, very tall women are being left mateless.

This situation is borne out in lower birth rates for tall women. "It's not related to lower fertility," says Pawlowski. "The problem is their lower chances of finding a partner. It's the same as with very short guys. They are not limited by sperm quality or hormone level—they've got problems with finding a partner."

The British biologist Daniel Nettle followed women born in a single week in 1958 and traced their birth rates. Women who are

5'4" have an average of 1.2 children, 5'9" women average 0.8 children, and extremely tall women have 0.7 children. The graph of birth rate verses height is U-shaped: extremely tall and extremely short women are more likely to be childless. Interestingly, the women who have the most children are *below* average height, between 5'0" and 5'2". This detail is significant, because it means that the species is selectively making sure that the 8 percent difference between men and women remains (and grows a bit) over time.

This is not what evolutionary scientists were expecting to find. Mating patterns usually maximize reproduction, and tall women are a better bet for childbearing. "Tall women have wider pelvises than shorter women, which allow them to have easier births and higher-birth-weight babies, both factors that reduce infant and maternal mortality," writes evolutionary ecologist Rebecca Sear. Tall women also possess "the greater energy reserves that large females can devote to reproduction." Tall African women do indeed have more children than shorter women, averaging four children, while women below the 25th percentile average three. In populations that don't receive medical care, for every inch of mother's height, children's survival rate beyond five years increases by 5 percent. But these factors are ignored in Western mating, perhaps because child mortality rates are so low with modern medical care. It's worth noting that Western mating actually ignores many basic rules of evolution, with its high rates of singleness (not evolutionarily favored) and its tendency to mate for nonprocreative purposes (pointless).

So what's going on here? *Why* do men, particularly tall men, opt for shorter women, despite every reproductive-health reason not to? I asked men what's going on in their brains when they meet a tall woman. "One thing is the eye contact situation," says Doug Spear, a 5'8" physical therapist. "I generally do not like being dwarfed by a woman. I like to be powerful, and that's hard. If I'm talking to a girl who's, let's say, 6'2", I feel dwarfed and a bit awkward looking up. How do I keep myself comfortable and get her to feel comfortable too?" Another, Seth Phelps, 6'8", admitted to being scared. "Tall women are intimidating, even to tall guys. This boils down to culture placing very tall women on a pedestal of intimidation that they didn't create themselves."

My own additional theory is that most humans are more attractive when viewed from above. When men look down at me, they see eyes and lips and cleavage—all the universal cues of fertility. When most of the world looks up at me, they see nose hairs, chin rolls, and acne. Not surprisingly, most photography is shot from precisely the angle of, oh, a person 8 percent taller looking down on their model. "We shoot most people from above, because they look better," says photographer Chad Hunt.

Sear thinks men's spurning of tall women is purely cultural, part of that quagmire around defining femininity. "In the West men may be more concerned with social norms that require husbands to be taller than their wives," she writes, adding, "men choose relatively short women, perhaps so that they can appear to be dominant in the relationship."

Other indications suggest a cultural cause as well. For her documentary *Jabe Babe: A Heightened Life,* Australian director Janet Merewether, 6'0", studied how tall women have been portrayed in pop culture. "There's this idea that taller women tend to be partnerless or are deemed unmarriageable by society," she says. "I found that tall women have been represented in popular media fairly negatively back to the Nordic myths," which often portrayed tall women as ogresses.

Take the tale of the giantess Angrboda who gives birth to (oops!) three female monsters. The firstborn has the lower body of a rotting corpse. This is the good daughter. The second eats the sun. The third blows poison into the skies. None of the mother-daughter quartet is on any man's A-list for marriage. "There's definitely a link, on a mythical level, of tall women being unmaternal," says Merewether. "They're not blond and princesses." In modern times, the image doesn't improve much. Tall women came into media prominence in the 1950s, a direct outgrowth of Rosie the Riveter as well as a number of tall female entertainers. But at the same time, fictional tall women suddenly were portrayed as aggressive: *Attack of the 50 Foot Woman* (1958), *The Incredible Shrinking Man* (1957), and *Attack of the Puppet People* (1957). "Tall women are not shown as the Flexon Maiden," says Merewether. It's a viral association. I recently wrote a magazine article about tall clothing stores, and the male magazine editors titled it "Attack of the 6-Foot Women." Not surprisingly, when polled, men say they consider short women to be more "nurturing" than taller women, perhaps suggesting that they see shorter women as, you know, not scary.

Merewether was personally invested in her findings as a late-thirties single woman who wanted to be a mother. She looked for donors until she happened to fall into an affair and pregnancy at forty. "Why was I unpartnered at the last period of my fertility? The base is that society, or men, or whatever, deemed me not an acceptable mate. If you fall outside of those very restrictive physical statistics of acceptability, then perhaps being childless is your fate. And I wasn't willing to accept that. I thought, I'm tall, but I have a lot to offer! And if being tall isn't enough to be considered . . ." She trailed off.

Before you look for the nearest window, there is a silver lining here. Pawlowski found that in Los Angeles, men and women with less traditional and more liberal upbringings opt for smaller height differences between men and women, and are much more likely to enter couples where the woman is taller than the man. "The more liberal and modern they are, the more tolerant they are of similar heights," he says. So a word to the tall: head for a liberal town.

Tall women's dating and childbearing statistics are neither universal nor hard and fast. They're strictly a quirk of Western culture. In South Sudan, among the Dinka tribe and their sometimes-hostile sister tribe the Nuer, tall women are actively prized. It's a tall region. "I'm 5'10", and I'm one of the shortest," says Angelos Agok, a Dinka refugee now in Maryland. The Dinka and Nuer are so tall that anthropologists argue that there must be a biological reason. (I feel compelled to point out that maybe they're tall because of their ongoing preference for tall mates.)

Tall Dinka women are considered the cream of the dating crop. "In Dinka culture, boys like a woman if she's 6'0" or more," says Agok, who dreams of marrying a taller woman. "There's no doubt about it. They bring tall children."

And why are tall children favored? "When you're tall, people like you, especially when you cross the river," says Peter Gatkout, a Nuer man who also immigrated to Maryland. "Sometimes in Sudan there is no canoe. If you're walking on the bottom, you can take people who are shorter and don't know how to swim with you. Also, it will be very easy for you to control cows. Most cows have long horns, so if you are a taller person, you can control them. If you are a shorter person, you will get horned." Note to self: Add "rivers" and "cows" to your tall résumé.

Agok adds that tall women are good at reaching things. "In our society, people don't use elevators and ladders, so of course being tall helps with so many things. In any society you need to reach." In exchange for these skills, tall women end up with rich husbands. "The average [dowry] right now for shorter girls would be fifty to seventy cows," says Gatkout. "But a taller girl can go for eighty to one hundred cows, maybe one hundred and fifty cows." Note: Add "reach things" and "one hundred and fifty cows."

The Dinka and Nuer are far from exceptional. Many non-Western societies feature high rates of coupling and childbirth among tall women. In Gambia, it's not so much that men prefer tall women but that they find height irrelevant in partnering. A full 10 percent of women are taller than their husbands, the same as would happen through random partnering. Much of tall women's "greater reproductive success is entirely due to the physiological advantages," writes Sear, who looked at Gambian villages. Gambian tall men are also more popular, with more lifetime marriages than shorter men, though they have the same number of children. Sear chalks up tall popularity to the fact that height reflects good nutrition and the ability to fight disease.

Even within the United States tall women's dating prospects vary by region and ethnicity. "I think the black community has fewer issues with tallness in women," says photographer George Pitts, 6'0", the founding photography director of *Vibe* magazine, whose own photographs focus on cultural identity and body image. His wife is 5'11". "It's like the way heavier people say there's more to love—it's perceived like that. In general, some ethnic cultures are less objectifying about height issues and have fewer hang-ups about the different kinds of packages that we come in." The cultural difference is readily visible on any magazine rack, by flipping through the advertisements and editorial spreads. Black media tends to proliferate the image of a man being *enveloped* by a warm female body. Such images are rare in white media, which typically glorify a powerful male *dominating* a much smaller female. The trend is similar in pornography. Attraction, of course, is a personal preference, not a cultural one, but the media can have a broad impact.

I've also found that older men are more likely to date tall women, and psychologists concur. "I picture an older guy being more comfortable with a taller partner," says psychotherapist Ken Page, founder of Deeper Dating workshops. "Something about an older, more mature dynamic makes it work." In their youth, men tend to couple in accordance with what society expects (not tall women), while later couplings fit personal tastes (tall!).

In every culture numerous men are gaga about tall women. "There are a eons of men who appreciate tallness, and don't necessarily fetishize it, but aren't necessarily threatened by it," says Pitts. And Alan wants everyone to know that "tall women are exquisite. There should be more of them."

Height is pivotal in the dating imagination. If you ask children to tell you about their imagined future partner, they can tell you how tall he or she will be. It's a preference that changes, but many social assumptions and needs are wrapped up in partner height. Not surprisingly, when people choose mates, height is a decisive factor, the third most important following education level and age—meaning that in a room full of classmates, it's the number-one factor, prioritized over region and social status. Some of the preference is likely genetic: a Finnish study of 2,600 twins showed that twins tend to marry men of about the same height.

I thought that height preference might have a psychological root, so I spoke with three therapists, who gave theories to explain why people are drawn to their partners' heights.

1. *People gravitate toward the partner height they're socially programmed to believe is acceptable.*

   "People gravitate toward people who are similar, and they avoid dissimilar," says communications professor Michael Sunnafrank. "It doesn't mean that they're attracted to them, but they gravitate to them. In other words, when you look at it, the height link is there primarily because people believe it should be there."

2. *People choose partner heights that balance out the whole relationship.*

I call this the Theory of Complementariness. "We're often attracted to people who seemingly complement us," says Manhattan family therapist David Greenan, Ph.D. In each couple, individuals take up roles to counterbalance each other, like a shy partner balancing out a more gregarious partner. "Another complementarity is height. One person will be attracted to someone because their partner is big and strong, and the other partner is attracted because they can be the protector. Often it's not on a conscious level." Greenan says that height frequently balances out other similarities. "In same sex couples"—who are often more similar, given their shared gender—"you sometimes find more exacerbated differences in height," says Greenan. Relationships are, then, a balance of presence and personality.

3. *People are attracted to the expectations that go along with height.*

"Height is absolutely loaded with projection," says the psychotherapist and dating guru Ken Page. "Projections are your assumptions about another person based on what you see. We all have these projections about what rich or blond or tall or any other sort of trait means. And those projections are what attract us." The Freudian school of thought says that we project things based on our own issues. For example, if you look at a tall woman and think she's attractive or unattractive, that's more representative of your own feelings about yourself than about her.

In our interview Page turned the tables and had me answer questions to reveal my own assumptions about height.

Tall Dating Self-Inventory

1. How do you feel when you're with a partner taller than you? What about a shorter partner?
2. What is the height of your fantasy partner? Why?
3. What are your fantasies with this partner?
4. Picture your current partner or crush. What qualities have you projected onto him or her?
5. When you think about your own height, what associations do you make? Think about power, intimacy, attractiveness, and competence.
6. How do you feel when you're in public with someone who is 5'1"?
7. What happens when you meet a potential partner significantly shorter than you? How do you feel, and what issues arise in your mind?
8. When you see someone of your gender who looks like you walking in a crowd, what do you think?
9. When someone is much taller than your comfort range, what do you feel? Why?

My answers to these questions mushroomed into a full blown self-psychological profile. Our impressions of height are purely a reflection of our own psychology, chock full of assumptions, unmet needs, and desires.

Ladies Dating Down: Matches Made in Tall Hell

Dating statistics are depressing enough to make a tall woman move to Holland. I mentioned them when I visited the home of feminist sex expert Betty Dodson and her partner, Eric Amaranth. Dodson is a sexed-up seventy-seven-year-old grandma in yoga pants who talks at full volume with a lot of arm swinging. She immediately launched into a rant to knock some sense into tall girls. "Don't think that what you're going through is so unique to being tall. It can happen if you're short. It can happen if you're disabled. It can happen if you are gorgeous. How many beautiful women say that people never see the real them? Or the homely man who says nobody ever sees his inner beauty? It's the same thing. So don't think that your situation is unique or that you suffer alone. Don't wallow in it, and don't dwell too much on it. Just be proud. And in the meantime I'd be having a very passionate love affair with myself all the time, so it wouldn't really matter if they liked or disliked me. And the ones that I'm interested in will be interested in me, and then we can get together. And it doesn't matter how long it takes. We have a lot of time."

When I mentioned that I generally don't date down, Dodson blew her lid. It's ingrained at this point—I don't even *see* the

shorter men. When I'm standing in a room full of people, my brain automatically registers the two who are taller than me, and the rest aren't there. Often I scan the room, see zero options, and make it an asexual night. This experience is, I think, similar for people who date within an ethnicity. I've broken my rule and dated down more often as I've gotten older—I find that certain confident men exude the sense, from the moment I meet them, that they just don't care about height—but shorter men generally need to hurl themselves into my path before I notice them.

Dodson disagreed strongly with my ban on dating down. "Oh, *you're* prejudiced?" She exclaimed. "I mean, develop a sense of humor! It will help. Look over and say *God damn, we're a weird-looking couple.* And then shut it off!"

Dodson had me stand up next to Amaranth. He's around 6'0" and forty pounds lighter than me. We stood shoulder to shoulder. I politely pointed out that though Amaranth is a lovely guy, my rule of thumb on dating shorter men is that they must be able to lift me. Dodson rolled her eyes. "You're in your twenties. Don't worry about this too much. I went through a period in my early forties when I said, I want a guy who's my size. So I had a martial artist, and we were exactly the same height and we kind of looked alike. We had incredible sex. And I said, 'This is it! This is great!' And then he went away, and I had other people, and I lost track of 'my type.' So remember that 'my type' is not permanent."

She paused to take a sip of wine. "Try to deal with what's inside the person. You've got to be a democratic fuck."

I've decided that the failure of tall women to date down is at the crux of our poor dating and reproductive rates. We complain that tall men follow pointless social norms and date shorter women, but *we too* are following a social norm and only dating tall men. "I actually recently decided that I will not date people shorter than me," Davies told me. "I used to say it would be okay. But you know what? Back to the heels. I really like wearing heels, and I really like going dancing with someone my height, so I won't date anyone shorter than 6'4". I just won't do it." Tall women are essentially saying that we want to be deemed sexy but *only* by men in the top percentiles. It doesn't work that way. Advertising as sexy means advertising as sexy to everyone.

Cutting ourselves off from 85 percent of the dating pool has a rather extreme effect—our 40 percent lower childbearing rates. Katherine Janus runs a New York–area speed-dating group. "Now that I think about it, I can't recall unusually tall people or unusually short people attending. It's usually average height clientele," she says. "Dating is a numbers game, and if you open your heart and mind to all sorts of potentials, you're increasing your numbers." I told her that some tall people don't want to play a numbers game—they just want tall people. "I guess this proves the point that super tall people probably have a defeatist attitude going in."

A number of tall women e-mailed, while I was working on this book, to tell me about their happy marriages with shorter men. Dunrie Greiling, 6'2", thirty-six, is in her second long-term relationship with a shorter man, this one her husband. "I've never been with anyone taller, though I really longed for that for a long time. I wanted to feel smaller. I wanted something external to make me feel normal. I thought that only a small pool of guys was actually available to me, and invariably these tall guys went out with tiny girls. For a while I really resented it. There was no demand for me. Later on I heard that I'd been the object of a few crushes from slightly shorter men. I was oblivious. I feel sad when I think of that now. What a waste of time!" It's amazing that any tall babies are born at all.

Pawlowski actually endorses couples who are mismatched in height. "I like it from a biological point of view," he says. He mentions Rod Stewart (5'10" in man heels) and Penny Lancaster (6'1"), and Mick Jagger (5'10") and L'Wren Scott (6'3"). "There are some nice examples if you look at very affluent guys. It is very good for their children. His sons are going to be taller and therefore are going to have high reproductive success. It's also good for women, because their daughters will be shorter than she is, and therefore it can increase their reproductive success. So in fact, they both can win, biologically and romantically speaking."

CHAPTER 14

The Tall Fetish

fet·ish, n. *something, for example, a nonsexual part of the body, that arouses sexual excitement in some people*

The tall fetish. I lived in ignorance of the fact that tall female bodies can be fetishized until 2005, when I went on a date with a man who requested that I wear four-inch heels. I thought it was funny.

I bring this to your attention because I really, really would like to have been more informed about tall fetishes when, on our second date a week later, he asked me to stand on a step stool in my heels, so that I could "tower over him." I was now 6'11". I lasted on the step stool for ninety seconds, and then our relationship was over. I was somewhat shaken by this experience, not because I was scared (he was perfectly lovely) but because I didn't understand it. I couldn't comprehend what he was after.

Tall fetishes are, at their heart, about power dynamics. They're about a man who wants to be enveloped by a woman. "It's the immediate physical presence of a woman towering over him that

makes him feel so submissive and out of the realm of every day,"
says Goddess Severa, 6'5" and 180 pounds, the top tall dominatrix
in the country, and the best person to ask about these things. "It's
immediate, it's unusual, and it's their turn-on."

And it's fairly common. Janet Merewether looked into the origins of tall fetishes as part of her research for her film *Jabe Babe*.
She found that just after men returned home from World War II,
hints of tall fetishism began to appear in popular media. First came
mainstream characters, such as the protagonist of *Attack of the 50
Foot Woman* (1958), "Tall women are shown as sexually predatory
figures, seen as destroyers of men," says Merewether. "It's almost
like, around the fifties, a role is imposed on tall women by society." Around the same time, the first batches of tall fetish porn
appeared. It began as relatively tame stuff—tall women and men
enjoying themselves—and quickly progressed to tall women dominating men.

This was all mostly trivial for forty years. A man's chances of
meeting a very tall woman on the street were quite low, and
women weren't necessarily aware of the fetish. Then the Internet
boomed. Suddenly, rather than be limited to the one or two super
tall women in his town, a guy could log on and find millions of super tall women online. At the same time the fantasies depicted
online grew more extreme, moving further from the reality of the
typical tall woman. "What I found talking to Jabe," says Merewether,
referring to the 6'2" sometimes-dominatrix subject of her film, "is
that it's often men who cast tall women in this role as sexually dominant. But often they're just normal women, and maybe they just
want to be loved and cared for just like any woman. Tall women are
not necessarily nurtured as much as smaller women. Assumptions
are made about them because of their physicality, and they become
the objects of sexual fantasy. And they become sort of fetishized by
men who have these domination fantasies."

"It's inescapable that some people attribute an erotic association
with tall women," the photographer George Pitts told me. "I would
imagine that they would love the spectacle of a tall woman having
an orgasm before their eyes. I'm sure that would be a core observation. And with a powerfully built lover it must be rather spectacu-
lar to witness. There's the beauty of someone enjoying themselves,

and if you throw in the factor of height, you have a beautiful and provocative picture, something to appreciate."

I asked him why no one else talks about tall fetishes. "That's polite culture. We are all so very polite."

Psychologists are remarkably supportive of tall fetishists. "It has to do with early sexual fantasies," says therapist David Greenan, who deems fetishes perfectly healthy. "When we develop fetishes, we're talking about sense memory. It's an earliest feeling of being aroused and being sensual, and as we develop, those get labeled as fetishes. In adulthood he's trying to replicate those earliest experiences of arousal."

Men can frequently pinpoint the origins of the fetish to a single incident: an older girl wrestling him down, or a stepmother sitting on him and pinning him, or older girls teasing him and making him feel humiliated, but also excited. The experience becomes solidified as a primary source of adult arousal. Leg and foot fetishes have similar roots: a boy looks up at Mommy's nylons and shoes and gets a warm maternal feeling, which morphs over the years into a love of shoes or stockings or warm powerful legs.

Most men are happy to tell you in great detail how their fetish began—I've received a dozen unsolicited multipage e-mails recounting the story. "I think for me it goes back to grade school," a stranger named Tony, 6'2", e-mailed me. "Me and the tall girls always got stuck in the back for pictures and compared our heights every year. I began to have a physical appreciation for these tall beauties." Another man, Steve, 5'10", e-mailed, "It all started when I was about eleven years old. My father and I were coming out of church one Sunday when this woman walked past, and she was considerably taller than my father, who was 5'11". For some reason I got very excited, and from that day on I have loved tall women."

Even more common are homosexual versions of the same fetish. "Many gay men are attracted to a height differential," says psychotherapist Ken Page. "I know someone who plays around in sex clubs, and his fantasy is of tall men hugging him and picking him up. It's that thing of being taken care of, of being held in someone's arms."

But tall fetishes are a more pressing issue for straight women, because as we saw in chapter 13, tall women have a harder time finding partners yet also have a fan base of tall fetishists. It's a unique space to occupy: complaining about singleness, yet having lots of e-mail attesting to your desirability. Jena Benton, 6'2", thirty-three, put it well: "There are guys who are interested in you only because you're taller than them, and that's a giant turn-on. I tend to avoid them. I have a lot more qualities in my favor than just my height. But yeah, I'm single."

Greenan points out that nearly all falling in love is a matter of objectifying someone and projecting traits onto them. The issue is whether other personality and intelligence traits are equally respected. "Assuming that the guy has other redeeming qualities and his fetish is something that the other person can accommodate, it's fine. Pleasuring one's partner is part of being a partner. For how many centuries have women gone to sports games because their husband enjoys it?" Point taken. He says fetishes are fine as long as everyone feels comfortable and the pair isn't stuck in a dominant-submissive power dynamic outside the bedroom, because the submissive will inevitably rebel.

This seems all well and good, until I recall how immensely uncomfortable I was on that step stool, contemplating the twelve inches between my head and the ceiling.* The man only wanted to make out. But what bothered me is that the step-stool had nothing to do with me—he was projecting imagined sexuality onto me. I called up the sex expert Betty Dodson and told her the story. She leveled with me. "Some men see tall, and they make a lot of associations that have nothing to do with you. If some man came to me and said he'd like to be towered over—honey, that's professional sex. Tell 'im you're available and then give him your fee. That'll set him straight."

The majority of fetishists do indeed end up in the hands of professionals. It's a world that most tall women know little about, yet it overflows into tall ladies' bedrooms or job possibilities regularly.

---

* The step stool, by the way, was a completely pointless gift from my mother ("What if you need to reach something?"), and that has been its only use thus far.

Dominatrixing has always been a quick way for tall women to make money. I've been offered two dominatrix jobs, one at four hundred dollars an hour.

Goddess Severa was the best person to explain what's going on. She's a Californian and former Manhattanite with a Wall Street client base. She does not engage in sex acts with her clients, only play. Severa says she's hardwired to be dominant. "This is not a job for everyone, or even most." She was the little girl who tied up her friends for fun and always had an interest in power dynamics. "I love being tall because I've embraced it. Ever since I was a kid, I have always been stared at a lot. Just people *staring staring staring*. So I'm utilizing it in a way I enjoy. I found a lot of people who think I am a goddess."

Her clients tend to be lawyers and financial men, over age thirty with high-stress jobs. Severa is, more than anything, a role-player, and her job is remarkably creative. While the job is certainly in the realm of sex—a flip through her Web site's galleries leaves no question of that—it's less overtly sexual than you might think. The goal is to re-create a feeling of childhood arousal, and that's done by proximity, not by sex. It is more akin to a child's game of dress up, with a heavy dose of very-adult power dynamics. For the privilege of romping in her fantasy world, customers pay her many hundreds of dollars an hour.

What, exactly, does a man get in a session with Severa? It's basically a big game of make-believe. Perhaps the client—let's call him Miles—pretends that his aircraft just crash-landed outside. He peeks into the room and finds himself on a planet where women rule. Perhaps Severa is a queen giant. Miles walks in, and Severa, dressed in something tribal, welcomes Miles to the planet. She explains that on this planet, she can do whatever she wants with men, like carry them around or crush them with her fist.

Or perhaps Miles suddenly finds himself shrinking. He's sitting on the floor, and Severa's in platform heels, looking down at him like he's Thumbelina. Whatever the case, Miles tries to regain control, which is part of the game. "I ultimately have to win," says Severa. "That's the rule. I come out on top." Miles is not used to the role reversal, and it creates an immediate reaction. "That's why he loves it," says Severa. Miles is positively giddy. Severa's membership-only

Web site is a popular alternative for those who can afford it (three hundred dollars per year). She offers a dozen characters—Nature Goddess in the Grass, Friendly Amazonian, Business Babe, Whip-Wielding Discipliner of Average Joes Who Look Thrilled. Some clients simply want to stand next to her, comparing limb sizes. That's not her favorite. She prefers something more dynamic. "I find it a little boring if someone wants to stand there and do back-to-back height comparisons. I prefer to interact."

At Europatreffen I was introduced to the apt phrase *tall hawk*, which means a guy with a fetishized preference for tall women. Tall hawks are omnipresent in my world, always hovering just at the edges. They emerge in the form of an intense look from a subway rider or fellow moviegoer. I can best describe it as a head-to-toe-to-head scan, settling into a sustained invasive gaze.

No one ever talks about tall hawks. It's a world to which the general public is oblivious. Anyone with a rare trait (and some common ones) has fetishists, but to be tall is to be public, and to be public is to be an easy target, and to be an easy target is to receive e-mail like this one, the first of many I received while writing this book:

> *Hi! I am Lollo from Brasil who prefers women your height and taller and I don't think there is anything wrong about that. However I just wanted to know what size shoe you wear, like in men's size.*

The follow-up e-mail always include a predictable set of questions: Have I always been tall, or was there a sudden spurt? How tall was the tallest guy I have ever dated? Have I met a woman taller? Do I come from a tall family? And if we were to hit it off, would I mind his being shorter than me?

I wasn't sure what exactly Lollo—or Step Stool Man, for that matter—had in their heads about me. I started looking around online. I found it immediately. The contours of Tall Fetish World are easily demarcated online. It begins at Tallwomen.org, a high-traffic Web site started in 1998 by a German man named Joerg Estelmann, 5'8", who emphasizes that he does not like the term *fetish* but has a "preference for taller women, a general interest that includes caring for the woman and treating her accordingly." It's ostensibly a resource Web site for tall women, listing names and photographs of a few hundred of the tallest women in the world and shopping options, but it also functions as a default listserv of tall women for those who love them.

Next comes Kaikura.net. A marvel, it features fully clothed, normal-looking tall women from 6'1" to 6'11" doing run-of-the-mill activities like standing in front of buildings, posing in doorways, playing volleyball—and standing on step stools. The Web site signals the wealth of intense, nonovertly sexual tall fetishes out there. The women are paid eight hundred dollars for a daylong fully clothed photoshoot.

Outside the online world, there's Amazon Fest, an annual gathering of models ranging from 6'1" to 6'9", skinny to obese, in (where else) Las Vegas. It's a long weekend of parties, photo opportunities, and private photo sessions with the tall models whom the guests have been ogling online all year. The conference attracts a hundred or so men who are thrilled to be in the same room with the models, snapping photos and paying a hundred dollars for parties and hundreds more for photo sessions. It's sort of like a club for unabashed tall fetishists.

On the various message boards, I repeatedly came upon the most beautiful descriptions of tallness I've ever read, odes frighteningly close to descriptions of ancient Greeks describing their tall, voluptuous gods. The attraction takes on a form of goddess worship, even in colloquial conversation. As one put it, "There's something about being able to look up to your partner that is so magical, it's hard to put into words."

I was curious as to who frequents these sites, so I called up a few of the regulars. Most were surprisingly forthcoming about their feelings and happy to talk to me. The word *fetish* was not appreciated. "I am a 5'11" slim male who has always preferred taller women," says Steven, a forty-five-year-old writer. "Just as you weary of the comments and looks you get in public, I get the word *fetish*. To me that connotes something unnatural about something that is, to me, a preference, nothing more. I certainly would not want to be perceived as creepy because of that preference. I value women for more than their stature."

Tony described it differently: "Here's the thing: height turns me on. When I see a tall woman, I just have trouble keeping my eyes off her. I think it's the overall largeness that really gets me. When all of a sudden you are looking up, it's intimidating and sexy all at once. I can't explain it, that's just how I feel. I'm currently in my forties, but when I was a younger man, this would set off an erection, and it would be pretty embarrassing. I don't want to be trampled or have someone stand on a stool, though heels would be interesting. I just want to enjoy the physical beauty that height brings. Is that so wrong?"

The taboo adds to the thrill, the sense of deviance in sleeping with a body that the mainstream doesn't quite idealize. It's an act of rebellion. "I would have to say no on bringing it up in conversation at the gym," says Tony. "I have been busted a couple times checking out a tall female. Other guys say something like 'You like the tall ones, eh?' And sometimes they'll say 'So do I.' I think there may be more men who like tall women than you realize."

An acquaintance of mine had never seemed particularly interested in dating up until I mentioned this chapter in the book. He immediately told me about sleeping with a much taller, curvy woman. "It was voluptuousness, but tenfold. She was like lying on a soft couch. And you get to exalt in this voluptuous long body. And it's all yours, you know?" Well, that is much clearer than the step stool.

CHAPTER 15

Retail Therapy
Buying Off the Rack and Other Pipe Dreams

Talls created three-quarter-length sleeves. Didn't you know?

—JESSI WALTER, 6'0"

When I was in high school, "choosing an outfit" meant picking the eyeliner and earrings and scarves and nail polish that went with the men's pants. Magazine fashion spreads and terms like "in season" were irrelevant, because my shopping strategy was *If it fits, I own it.* I tugged at tops and bottoms, hoping no one looked too closely, and paired short sleeves with sandals whenever possible. I developed an addiction to tank tops, the only fitting article of clothing I could pull from the racks on boring shopping outings with friends. Fashion was a spectator sport.

Even worse than not having good clothes was the sense that other people didn't know *why* my wardrobe was weak. My uncle once told me that my jeans were too short. I wanted to say, "Uncle Rich, given that I'm working off the palate of the Champion sports outlet and the Levi's men's store of Albany, New York, I look fantastic." Instead, I just looked mortified.

The great irony of tall life is that clothing is more noticeable, because you're more noticeable. "If you're tall and poorly dressed, you draw more attention than if you're 5'2" and in the same suit," says San Diego State communications professor Peter Andersen. So most of us fall into a wardrobe of basics: classic jeans, blacks, and khakis. As Arjan Rooyens, 6'7", summarizes, "It's riskless fashion. That's what tall people wear." I have never, ever loaned clothing to a girlfriend because the requests to borrow riskless fashion don't come pouring in.

My life changed one Wednesday in Manhattan's Herald Square. I was walking around after work and wandered into the Tall Girl Shop. I look back on that Wednesday the way born-agains treat the day they found Jesus. I pulled on pair after pair of thirty-eight-inch inseam jeans, all of which fit. I uttered phrases like "Does this come in a smaller size?" and "Gosh, I need to hem these." I can still list precisely what I bought. Most talls can all tell you about their born-again day. In Germany I met a six-footer named Petra Baehr who told me in ecstatic terms about the first time she bought women's shoes—at age twenty. She detailed the pumps down to their lining. Ever since that fateful Wednesday, I'm like an addict on a binge at Tall Girl. I can drop seven hundred dollars in half an hour.

I wish we could end this section here: Super Tall Cinderella found her Super Size Slipper. But tall clothing stores are still few and far between, despite the fact that we're talking about 10 percent of all clothes purchased. There are forty-five million tall Americans who don't want to be naked, and the U.S. market for tall clothing is worth six billion dollars. Yet as Timberwolves center Jason Collins, 6'11", told me, "We travel so much, and it's hard finding big-and-tall shops in different cities. If I want dress shoes, the only place is Friedman's Big and Tall in Atlanta." He's not from Atlanta, nor has he ever lived in Atlanta. Tall clothing is nearly nonexistent in most cities, and when it is available, it's often expensive. After two decades of exiting the mall empty-handed, I wanted to understand the economic forces at play and see what can be done.

The most practical information I learned while working on this book came from one person: Linda Carlo, the executive vice president of the men's big and tall store Casual Male XL and a former executive of the plus-size store Lane Bryant, where some tall girls go when at a loss.

She introduced me to the term *fit size.* "Every company decides what they think their perfect customer would look like, makes that the fit size, and then sizes it up and down," she explained. For example, lets say there's a mainstream store called The Bap. And they choose a 5'4", size 6 woman as their perfect customer. They'll create a size 6 blouse, and then grade the patterns up and down into sizes 0 to 16. The closer you are to the fit size, the better that blouse will look on you.

The reason that blouse will never look quite right on a 6'2" frame is that tall clothing requires more reproportioning than just grading the pattern upward: tall clothes require longer zippers, larger collars, much lower shirt hems, and darts in different places. This is particularly obvious in designer stores. The bows and frills that look great on catwalk sample sizes look garish on size 16. (Sample sizes, usually 0 and 2, are often cut extra long for tall models but have no bearing on The Bap's fit size, which is aimed at not-tall Americans) When in doubt of the fit size, look at the size of the mannequins, or glance at the best-stocked sizes on the racks. You never want to be the largest size on the rack. Tall Girl is such a boon for me because I am the fit size.

The Bap makes money by turning over a rack of clothing as quickly as possible. Think of it as a restaurant. Imagine cordoning off a corner of a restaurant just for tall customers. It would be fun, but chances are those tables would often be empty. That's why The Bap doesn't carry size 14-long. Statistically, it's not going to sell as quickly. Instead, they increase their turnover by catering only to *their* shoppers, people in the core range around that size 6—say sizes 2 to 10—and not to the general population. In fact, The Bap probably only carries six or seven sizes of each item; if they can get away with it, they'll do four: S, M, L, and XL. It's a risk for them to stock twenty sizes, because they might be left with unsold inventory, particularly in women's fashion, which turns over every four months. Though lots of other retailers stock up on merchandise and simply dump the leftover inventory abroad, the clothing market is tricky because sizing is often different in each country. Which is a long way of saying that The Bap does not carry superlong inseam pants in your size. Their clothes are not cut for tall bodies, and they not only don't cater to talls, but see them as an economic risk.

Instead, take your business to a tall store. Men's tall stores are a little easier than tall women's stores for customers and retailers alike. Men's fashions are consistent—the same khakis can stay on the racks for years—so a tall men's store can safely invest in a couple dozen sizes. Take Casual Male XL's bestseller, the Harbor Bay Waist Relaxer. It comes in six colors, *forty-nine* sizes, and lasts forever. These are the pants you might wear yachting twenty years from now. As a result, stocking inventory is much less risky for tall male stores—and the stores are easier to run, more financially stable, and better stocked. The only downside for men is that "big" stores and "tall" stores have merged, and the fit size at big and tall stores is kinda big and kinda tall, which makes tall skinny clothing hard to find. (Amusingly, men are apparently sensitive about having "big and tall" on their shopping bags. Casual Male XL was once Casual Male Big and Tall, but they scrapped the name for this reason.)

Tall men's stores are also much more abundant than tall women's stores, by a factor of twentyfold. Many of the men's stores are corporate-owned, such as Casual Male XL which shares a corporate roof with three other tall stores: bigandtall.com, the upper-class Rochester Big & Tall, and luxury custom company Jared M., with its core base of basketball players. Together the conglomerate has five hundred stores and makes up around 10 percent of the men's tall market.

By contrast, there are only a hundred or so tall women's stores in the United States, most privately or individually owned, meant to clothe twenty-two million tall women. You see the problem. "Not as many people have done the tall women's thing," says Carlo. "It's hard to find beyond Tall Girl. My cousin is six feet tall, and she has a hard time." Tall women's clothing is a brutal business. Fashions change so quickly that a store that buys the wrong blouses for one season can bury the business in dead inventory. Most notably there's Tall Girl Shop with a few dozen stores; there's also an array of online tall shops, including Katclothing.com, Longelegantlegs.com, and Talllady.com. But the rest of the industry is in crisis: Tall Etc., a fifteen-year-old chain and catalog with eight stores in mostly midwestern cities, closed their stores in 2008; a few other chains have flamed and gone out over the decades, most notably Shelly's. "I'm aware of several other single operators about to close up," says Linda Gould, 5'9", the CEO of Tall Girl, "because it is increasingly difficult to meet the volume purchases that manufacturers require." Most women like to try clothes on before buying and end up at the "tall" lines of department stores, which usually stop at thirty-six-inch inseams and are designed to a much smaller fit size.

The sizing system also works against tall women. Women's clothing sizes evolved from dresses, which were never sized with much precision. Now those same sizes have flowed over into blouses and pants. Witness: A guy might pick out thirty-four-by-thirty-eight-inch men's pants. A woman hopes she's a size 8, but depending on the store and article of clothing, could be a 6, 10, or even 4 or 12. "In women's, you look at the rack and have to try everything on," says Carlo. "Guys are simpler." It also makes catalog ordering, a major force in tall men's retail, nearly impossible for women. This is why male tall stores account for $4.8 billion of the $6 billion tall clothing market. Which is particularly astounding given that women typically spend twice what men do on clothes.

The tall women's market is minuscule, making up just *one* percent of the $100 billion that women spend annually on clothing. Ironically, one reason tall women's stores flounder is that years of struggle have made tall women too adept at buying everything they can from general retailers. "We always said we were a trouser business. That's what they came to us for," says Judy Rich, founder of the UK's Long Tall Sally. And unlike the plus-size market, where customers spend more, tall women feel entitled to be able to spend the same amount that they would at The Bap. This is a challenge for tall stores, because it's a heck of a lot cheaper for The Bap to order one million T-shirts in S, M, L, and XL than it is for a tall store to order four hundred T-shirts in ML, LL, XLL, and XXLL. Sometimes tall stores dodge this problem by launching their own clothing labels. Tall Girl has the Neva label, which made the pants I wrote this book in. (Yes, I wore one pair, almost exclusively. Velvety dark pink sweatpants.) Or they can make deals with brand-name companies, such as Calvin Klein, which does a line of tallwear for Casual Male XL. But none of these options produce four-dollar T-shirts and twenty-dollar jeans. There still is no budget option for tall clothes. Tricky.

In a quirk typical of Tall World, the founding of tall women's clothing stores has been profoundly influential on the retail industry, much more than their small numbers would imply. In the 1960s the specialty market—plus-size, maternity, petite—was barely a blip on the retail market. If a shopper was outside the mean, she was out of luck. As every tall girl knows, when there's no store for your body, you feel like an outcast. It's one more way the world doesn't accommodate you. Adding to the tall angst was the industry term for tall clothing, *outsize*. Size *14-outsize*, anyone? The introduction of the simple word *tall* to women's clothing gave definition to a beautiful body shape.

Hazel Gould, 6'0", launched Tall Girl in 1959 because she had nothing to wear to the oil company where she worked. Her retail experience consisted of her day job as a Calgary geophysicist. "Had she had the standard retail background, she would've thought it an impossible task," says her daughter, Linda, the current CEO. Hazel Gould went down to local markets and asked if she could get their clothes in tall proportions. They said no. "A lot of my mother's success was her ability to make friends," says Linda Gould. "She had the ability to walk into a room, the vendor would say, 'No no no,' and an hour later say, 'We'll try it.'" She started out of a basement and immediately began mail orders to keep her numbers up. She capitalized on the fact that tall women didn't have other viable options. Through trial and error, she figured out tall women's tastes: tall women hate three-quarter-length sleeves and Capri pants, for example, since those are precisely what they're trying to escape.

A decade later, across the Atlantic, Judy Rich, 5'11", also couldn't find anything to wear to work in London. "I was a militant feminist

at the time, and I was irate that
I couldn't find clothes that fit
me," says Rich. Rich's retail
background consisted of "a
number of years on a charter
boat in the Virgin Islands." So
she too began by knocking on
doors in London's rag district,
asking people if they could cut
twenty shirts or trousers a little
longer in the limbs. She was
lucky that factory owners were
in the midst of a downswing. "I
thought they'd just add a couple inches to the sleeve," says
Rich. "I didn't know that they
would have to interrupt pro-

We should just switch to capes.

duction and make a whole new pattern. You probably couldn't do
what I did today, or at least you would have to go for bigger orders.
We started with a twenty-five-thousand-dollar investment. It was
scary."

Long Tall Sally sold high-end clothes, because that was all Rich
could get. The chain now has twenty-five stores, with a boutique
feel. They are trying a new strategy of infiltrating UK department
stores by paying commission for the space, a trend that will hope-
fully catch on here for women. The catchy name comes from the
Little Richard song popularized by the Beatles.

Both stores pulled in a third of their business from catalogs,
which set a precedent for the larger industry of catalog retail. The
age of opening one's mailbox to a pile of Victoria's Secret/J.Crew/
IKEA catalogs had not yet dawned. Catalogs continue to be pivotal
to specialty stores because there's no other way to advertise—
there's no magazine or TV show that talls specifically watch. I
asked Gould where she finds her shoppers. "Under crevices, behind rocks," she joked. The catalogs also serve the pivotal purpose
of telling the companies where their customers are and therefore
where to expand. It's a happy mailing list. After all, there's no

more enthusiastic customer than a tall woman being sold tall clothes.

There tends to be some confusion about the purpose of a tall store. Casual Male XL's annual report is quite blunt about what it sells: "Over 50 percent of the merchandise is basic or fashion-neutral items." *Basic and fashion-neutral.* This is what tall people wear. As a people, we do not get to express ourselves through our clothing. It's an economic reality. Sometimes I walk past hipster twenty-somethings in alternawear, and I think I would've been one of them if it didn't require hand-sewing my clothes. But it's not to be, because tall stores will never carry risqué fashion. Unlike The Bap, which attracts a specific niche (say, youngish casual people) and provides options for that lifestyle (hundreds of casually chic outfits), tall stores attract customers based on their height and weight. "At our store you might see a twelve-year-old kicking and screaming, and her mother and grandmother, and we have to cover up all three," says Susan Harrison, senior buyer for Tall Girl. Which is not to say that the clothes aren't cute—just basic.

The Manhattan Tall Girl Shop is a cult tourist attraction. I went one day as "research" for this book and spent $535. I met a 6'0" woman named Jamie Pliant. "I'm from Omaha. There's no clothes for tall people in Omaha." And sure enough, she was grinning with her stringbean mother, who watched over a gangly toddler in a stroller while Pliant carted away half the store. I also met Chanel Jackson, 6'2", who had taken the train in from the far end of Queens. "I'm slowly transitioning out of my men's jeans and sneakers collection," she told me.

Tall store shopping is something of a therapeutic experience. All the shoppers stand around and grin and talk to each other, thrilled to be partaking. It's normalizing: after years of stretching seams beluga-style, and hopelessly thumbing through the racks past hundreds of outfits that will never fit your body, to stand in Tall Girl and pull on outfit after outfit that fits is like being given a big hug by your 12L jacket. It's affirming. Your body is *so normal that someone took the time to make clothes for it.* Imagine that. "We fit around 5'9" up to 7'0"," chirped Crystal Morris, the 6'2" assistant manager, who hugs shoppers on the way out. She took the job for the discount and is arguably their best advertisement. "Whenever I see a tall woman on the street, I give her a card and tell her where she can shop."

I began my foray into tall retail rather frustrated with the retail world, but I came away sanguine because it is clear that the future of tall retail is firmly in the hands of tall people. The most important thing a tall consumer can do is support tall stores. Talls shouldn't be spending money at stores that don't have tall fit sizes, nor should they be squeezing into clothes that don't fit. If people buy tall clothes, stores will stock them; if stores order tall clothes, manufacturers will make them; if profit margins appear, investors will invest; if capital rolls in, stores will branch out into the thousands across the country. And happy tall people will roam the earth wearing fashionable, well-fitting tall clothing.

CHAPTER 16

The Fitting Manifesto

I always feel so hostile when I see a short person in the airplane emergency row. I mean, come on—their feet aren't even touching the floor. Why are they sitting there?

—GODDESS SEVERA

Want to watch a tall person get agitated? Lean over and whisper *airplane seats*. "Don't get me started!" exclaims Ben Butler, 6'8". "To get my legs to fit, I have to lift my knees up so they dig into the metal on the seat ahead, and my feet are off the floor. One time I was in a window seat in the back of the plane. The curve of the plane was so low that I had to spend the whole ride with my neck curved to the left." Obviously an appropriate seating arrangement for a paying customer.

Then lean over again and whisper *exit row*. "You hit my *biggest* problem!" shrieks Uwe Seyler, 6'9". "Who is sitting in these seats? Little old people or frequent flyer members!" He says *little old people* with such vengeance. He's in his late sixties.

The price of height.

Nothing brings out creativity like nine hours crunched in a seat. "I have an idea about this!" announced Jen Weaver, 6'0". "You know how they have that little stand that tells you if your carry-on luggage is too big?" Yes. That's where they usually take away my luggage. "I think there should be a small handrail that's about thirty-six inches tall, and in order for you to get an exit row seat, you have to straddle the railing." Perfect.

All transportation inherently requires putting varying sized bodies into a small, quickly moving cabin. It doesn't really matter which kind of cabin. Whether it's a car, bus, sailboat, or glider plane, talls are screwed. Which would be fine and good if airplanes and cars and sailboats were the only places where talls don't fit. But that's not the case. Tall people often don't fit on air, land, or sea. We are Nonfitters.

I am a Nonfitter. Perhaps you have seen me slouched on the subway, crouched in front of a public kiosk, or curled into a theater seat. Yes, I function, but *fitting* implies some quotient of physical comfort and, dare I say it, ergonomic posture. I don't fit. And neither do the top 15 percent of the population. Which is strange. We are a different size (a better size! an amazing size!), and yet the world does not accommodate us. Let's take a quick walk through the great accomplishments that the modern design world has bestowed upon tall people:

- *Theater and movie seats.* My knees are at my chin. "We're always trying to get in as many seats as possible," says Amy Donohue, 6'0", an affable architect with the Boora design firm. Talls have been reduced to thanking the fire code. "If there are more than fourteen seats across, we have to make deeper seats. The idea is that someone can pass in front of you."

- *Public toilets.* Fourteen inches high. Men miss, and women hoist themselves up by leaning on the toilet paper dispenser, which is not designed to support the weight of a leaning tall person. Designers create toilets at heights that small children can access. Yes—barely over one foot tall.

- *Bathroom stalls:* "I've been in some stalls where I have to sit diagonally, because if I sit straight, my knees hit the stall door," says Olympic gold medalist rower Caryn Davies, 6'4", of stalls that are a mere thirty-six to forty-two inches across. "That's pretty frustrating." Also, tall heads stick out above six-foot stall doors. The bathroom is a private place. Tall people deserve privacy too.

- *Chairs, seats, and couches.* I can't get up. Waiting rooms and libraries are filled with narrow seats fourteen inches from the floor. The soft, plush furniture that designers favor compounds the problem, due to sinkage. Tall person seating should be eighteen to twenty inches high, with a wider seat.

- *Exercise bikes.* Help. With the seat raised to its highest point, I teeter four feet above the ground. Even when I add a handlebar extension and foot brackets, it's very clear that the bike was not built for me. Taller riders require a longer frame, longer cranks (pedal arms), and our dignity.

- *Doorways.* "There's a point of my head that's been hit hundreds of times," says Chris Rovzar, 6'3". "Right behind my forehead, like three inches behind the hairline, there's a divot." Older doorways are typically 6'9" tall, and new ones are 7'0". This height isn't sufficient. A tall person walking through a doorway at the top of her stride—keep in mind the extra five inches from her shoes and the doorsill—will nail her head on the lintel (doorway top). Designers avoid eight-foot doors because of their cost. "In design, you're encouraged to go with the standard because it's cheaper," says Donohue.

- *Ceilings.* "I've been hit on the head by more ceiling fans than I can count," says Butler. "They're just high enough that they don't enter into my vision, but they've rung my bell pretty good." Eight feet is the minimum for an office; architects aim for ten-feet-plus in public spaces. As all tall people know, the trouble is not the ceiling, but the things that hang down from it. Butler too has a divot just behind his hairline.

- *Tables.* My life changed the first time I studied at a thirty-nine-inch library table. Shoulder hunching is not, actually, a natural part of using a table. They're rarely above thirty-three inches high. "That's the standard universal height that everyone in a wheelchair can use," says Donohue.

The tall life is plagued with other nonfitting products: too-short yoga mats, massage tables, train sleeper cars, golf clubs, and cubicles, head-squeezing baseball caps, chest-exposing shower stalls, and bath towels that force prioritization between the upper and lower regions. Talls are shockingly complacent about it all, somehow disoriented by years of being scrunched into pretzel-people. We are not pretzels.

The importance of fitting is not to be underestimated. As one short friend asked, "Is it really that much of a hardship to sit on a low toilet?" Yes. Her apartment's toilet is twelve inches off the ground. (I measured.) And it's not about the toilet. It's about an entire world of too-low toilets and benches and counters and ceilings, much of it funded by tax dollars. Tall people pay roughly 30 percent more taxes than do short people, due to their higher incomes (see chapter $), all for the pleasure of not fitting. The health risks of not fitting are well documented: chronic muscle and back problems, structural abnormalities from years of ducking or walking wrong, and abdominal organ crunching. We are actually *warping* our tall bodies. All of which makes it even harder to use the nonfitting items. "When you add in a back or neck problem, that three-foot water fountain really becomes a problem," says architect Abir Mullick, director of industrial design at Georgia Institute of Technology. Then there are the accidents from wrongly sized products, like chairs that collapse, or a large foot slipping off a too-thin ladder rung. (The Dutch have 2.5 million such accidents annually; the United States doesn't tally.)

I was jarred into action last year on the subway. I hopped a little too perkily while exiting and nailed my head on the 6'5" doorway. Ten people on the platform winced. I was woozy for a moment and had to grip the grimey rim of a trash can for support. Which is something you should never do in New York City.

Rather than my usual railing against the Fitting world, I thought that understanding the design and fitting issues at hand might help pose a solution. So I went on an epic search to find out, who designs this stuff? And what are they thinking?

Flying While Tall

Over the years I've developed a strategy for maximal airplane seating comfort: the Barefoot Splay-and-Stuff position. I take off my shoes for the extra inch, splay my legs open into my neighbor's leg space, and cram my feet below the center of the seat ahead. Since my feet consume the subseat space, I have to stuff my bags between my legs, strategically shielding them so the stewardess doesn't make me stow them. The food cart bruises my knee. If the person ahead reclines, I am literally *pinned to my seat*. This position is best described as "bearable for short flights."

The Barefoot Splay-and-Stuff is not the healthiest position. The American Heart Association calls it "economy-class syndrome," which they say risks deep vein thrombosis (when a leg blood clot travels to the lungs, causing pulmonary embolism). On some flights an embolism would improve the situation.

So who, exactly, is behind this seating plan? Not the airplane

Help me.

manufacturers—a common misconception. Airlines order planes, and manufacturers like Boeing and Airbus deliver them as empty shells. Airlines create seating, bathroom, and alley configurations as they choose. No safety regulations force them to create cramped seating configurations either. "There's nothing forbidding airlines from providing extra legroom seating," Bill Mosley, a spokesperson for the Department of Transportation, told me. "That's a misconception."

I called up Weber Aircraft, a seating manufacturer for major airlines. "It's really the choice of the airline of how closely they want to put two seats together," says Rakibul Islam, Weber's director of engineering. "If you're looking at U.S. domestic carriers, you're going to see some very close spacing."

When Islam and his engineers create a seat, they design it standing alone. So from his point of view, the seats fit most people. "When you are saying you don't fit, you are saying that with respect to knee and leg room." He is also largely focused on safety regulations, which among other things, require new seats to be nonflammable and able to survive a plane crash, yet be lightweight. Tall comfort is low on the priority list.

Yet Islam also says that engineers design seats to fit from the 5th percentile up to the 95th percentile, as well as toddlers. The male 95th percentile is a lean 6'2". Which means that seats are knowingly not designed for very tall people. Before the seat is ever on an airplane, the entire top 5 percent of customers have been cut out. Then the airlines install the seats so close together that the 85th to 95th percentiles no longer fit. Take another look at that Splay-and-Stuff image.

To their credit, airlines do realize that reclining is impossible for some. As a partial solution, designers have created seats where the seat bottom slides forward or drops down, creating the sensation of recline. "With two inches of recline, it can give the feeling of five inches," says Islam. Which would be lovely on tightly packed domestic flights—except, of course, that these seats are also 20 to 40 percent more expensive and appear primarily on international flights, where seats are more spacious to begin with.

Airlines say that seat squashing is a matter of dollars and cents. I did the math. If an airline adds an extra four inches of legroom, every tenth row of passengers disappears. On a midsize plane, that's a loss of eighteen to thirty-two passengers. But before you play the violins, the loss is just $30 per seat on the rest of the plane, a few percentage points of ticket cost, and much less than the daily fluctuations alone in ticket prices. It can be made up by otherwise shifting internal per-passenger costs. Airlines are actively choosing to squeeze in passengers and distract them with food and movies in hopes they don't notice.

It's no accident that talls don't fit well in airplanes. In an industry that measures dimensions to the micrometer, airlines know *exactly* what they're doing. As a general rule, airlines are not fans of people who weigh more, whether they're tall or fat. Extra body weight reduces their profits, to the tune of five hundred million dollars in fuel costs per year. They'd like us to pull our own weight. It's in airlines' best interest for the tallest 5 percent to be so intensely uncomfortable that they pay for first or economy-plus class, or just use an-

other airline. Which airlines encourage by making us as uncomfortable as physically possible. In practice, it's a discriminatory policy with an elegant economic grounding: *alienate talls, squish in
smalls.* What motivation do they have to amend the situation when
they profit more off of average sardine style seating?

I wanted to hear major airlines' explanations in their own
words. So I called them up. Delta, which has among the worst
legroom in the industry (usually thirty-one inches between seat-
backs), took three weeks of daily prodding to respond. The friendly
skies are not tall-friendly. They ignored most of my questions and
sent an e-mail suggesting that tall travelers opt for the exit row or
the bulkhead (which Delta typically blocks off until twenty-four
hours before flight and then gives to frequent flyers) or book business class. American Airlines, which also has a mediocre record
(usually thirty-two inches), made the same suggestions, albeit more
pleasantly. United Airlines (usually thirty-three inches) claimed
that I was requesting "proprietary" information and refused further response. After a bit more poking, they loosened up. United is
one of a few airlines to come up with a business approach for talls
by offering "economy plus" seating in the first few rows, with
thirty-four to thirty-five inches of legroom. Customers can up-
grade at the gate for $14 to $119. I am not a fan of tall people ever
paying extra—yes, we make more money, but airlines should be offering appropriate seating as a matter of course—but at least
there's an option. Islam sighed. "I've seen tall people, and I know
how they suffer. But as a passenger, there is really nothing much
you can do."

Oh, but there is. Tall clubs around the world have battled airlines
for years, valiantly attempting to find mutually agreeable solutions.
The femur (thighbone) has an over 90 percent correlation to
stature—a 10 percent increase in femur length increases height by
6 percent—which means that tall people are the only victims of
airplane legroom scrunching. The airlines were nonresponsive to
their complaints. So in 2000 the Tall Club of Silicon Valley tried
another tactic: they sued.

The club filed lawsuits in the state of California against a dozen major U.S. airlines, claiming that the airlines' failure to provide seats constituted unfair business practices. The suits didn't ask for money, or even new seating solutions. They just asked for airlines to "provide preferential seating to tall people, in exit rows and other seats with greater legroom, for anyone who self-identifies as being either 6'2" or having a buttock-to-knee measurement greater than 95 percent of the population."

The California state court took one look at the case and, in order to avoid a legal tangle with the numerous agencies that oversee airlines (Federal Aviation Administration, Department of Commerce, et al.), bumped it up to the Department of Transportation. This was a major loss for the tall club, because rather than arguing unfair business practices on a state level, they were now on federal domain and were forced to push for a federal regulation of special rights for tall people. The only similar federal regulation in existence guarantees disabled people airplane seating, and the wording is intensely narrow in its definition: "those with fused or immobilized legs, and those traveling with service animals."

The ensuing legal documents are deeply amusing. The tall club is furious that the state is preventing it from suing the airlines directly and is clearly aware that arguing tall discomfort in federal court is not a strong legal position; the Department of Transportation just can't fathom that it's being asked to create a *federal regulation* because *some tall people are uncomfortable.* The tall club hedges its bets by using nearly verbatim wording from the existing disability seating law and tries to point out that the change would not be expensive because the airlines could keep their current seating configurations.

I'll end the suspense: the Department of Transportation said no. (If you read the tone of their response, it was more like "Hell no.") The department bluntly dismissed the case, citing concern that a tall seating regulation would create "a regime in which certain individuals who are not members of a protected class would be entitled to special seating accommodations, but other individuals with equally compelling arguments, both disabled and nondisabled, would not." The department also thought that the costs of training staff and altering computer reservation systems, as well as losing favor among other groups who might like more space (the elderly and obese), would be mountainous.

The tall club complained, rightfully, that the legal proceedings had left them without a forum. They appealed to the state and lost. They hoped that the bickering would at least drum up some bad press, but airlines are inoculated against bad press about squished seating. It's sort of like saying that Bill Clinton was unfaithful—everyone knows. Shortly afterward the airlines gained a wave of public sympathy with their financial and fuel troubles. Which are conveniently also a smokescreen for their ongoing policy of screwing talls. Really, why should consumers accept service that is monstrously uncomfortable and includes proven health risks?

Lawyers say that talls have a potential golden parachute. The industries that best accommodate talls are those that have faced personal injury lawsuits. And economy-class syndrome (thrombosis) is a pretty serious injury. The legal snafu here is that in order to force airlines to change their ways, a group of talls who were denied comfortable seating and subsequently incapacitated by thrombosis would need to sue—and skip the private settlement that airlines often prefer. "It's much easier to get companies to hand over money than to change their ways," says a Manhattan lawyer who represents two major airlines. "The purpose of a class-action suit would be to create such a large expense"—both monstrous legal bills, and the risk of having to pay out an enormous settlement—"that they're forced to fix their policy." Class-action suits are also useful for the negative press that they stir up, thereby encouraging other airlines to change their policies. As of this publication, a few thrombosis cases are weaving their way through state courts, but none are large class-action suits.

Being In Public Space While Tall

Tall fitting is not much better on the ground. "Everything in public space can be a problem," says Johan Molenbroek, 6'2", a professor at Delft University of Technology in Holland. He has specialized in industrial design and anthropometry, the study of size, for thirty years. "Advertisements are too low. Dispensers are so low that you can't see them without bending. All the places where people sit are too low. And it's not only about height but related measurements like large fingers, which means that small buttons on phones can also be a problem. And very tall people might have to bend their heads in an elevator. I collect mismatches between products and tall people."

It's not hard to find the culprit. An architect I interviewed who designs stores and malls blurted out, "We don't really think about tall customers. We're not really designing for the extremes." Stores are an amalgam of all the different ways to be a Nonfitter in public space. For me, shopping is a course in Nonfitting: I regularly don't see store products, and I never know how much anything costs because I don't see the sign. Fixtures are placed for a 5'6" woman. I hunch a lot, which is a strict no-no in retail psychology. "You never want to put things too low," says Lois Mackenzie, a designer for the interiors of a top sports apparel retailer. "Psychologically, there's no kids' section because people don't see it, or don't like to reach down because it's uncomfortable." The entire store is my kids' section.

When designers do need to design for specific-size people, they work off of industry and government standards. "The standard might be something developed twenty years ago, perhaps to fit a population different from the intended users," says Mullick. "So designers don't know what consumer they're addressing, because they're addressing a standard. And they are not making a conscious attempt to ask whether the standard includes or excludes."

In America many of those standards come from the Americans with Disabilities Act (ADA). "I find what governs height is accessibility," says Donohue. "Clients and designers are really focused on making sure that people in wheelchairs can reach, so what happens is everything is lowered. Water fountains are low, countertops are low, and all working surfaces are low, because everybody has to be able to get to that." The ADA is a very necessary piece of legislation to allow the disabled an even playing field, and its standards should continue to be met. But in practice, designers tend to meet the requirements of the ADA rather than accommodate the bodies of *all* users. Take a simple item like the public bathroom mirror. ADA guidelines state that bathroom mirrors should begin 3'4" from the floor. Most designers hang a two-foot-long mirror, and the result is that I haven't seen my face in a public bathroom in years. A simple solution would be hang a four-foot-long mirror, or perhaps to hang two mirrors at different heights. Designers need to think in terms of the users, not the guideline.

The combination of government standards and large populations comes, to a head on the public bus. Manhattan bus seats make airplane seating look spacious. I blame this on a string of short mayors (Abe Beame was 5'0"; Mike Bloomberg is 5'7"). It's hard to know for sure who is responsible. I do know that I sit with my thighs at a forty-five-degree angle to my torso, with my knees three inches beyond the seat ahead. The seats are too low, and when I sit facing the aisle, my feet get tripped over.

The guy whose job is to create New York City bus specifications is Jerry Higgins, director of bus development. He decides how fast they go, the air conditioning, and the layout.

I like Higgins, because he's the only transportation engineer I spoke with who did not try to assure me that I fit. He designs buses to fit a broad definition of average. "The idea is to capture as much of the general population as possible, realizing that there's gonna be a basketball player on the bus. People in that range are probably not gonna be comfortably accommodated. The basketball

Tall head level

person is probably gonna hit their head, and the little person's feet won't hit the floor."

Higgins makes his seating designations based on a set of body standards from the Society of Automotive Engineers (SAE). "They're basically saying that a 95th percentile male [6'2"] and a 5th percentile female [4'11"] need to be accommodated," he says. So city buses, at base level, don't accommodate 10 percent of the population stature-wise, or 820,000 New York City riders. That's nearly half a million tall folk.

The SAE guidelines are quite enlightening, because they "define the worldwide human physical dimensions" used by the bus and car industries, as well as the construction, agriculture, and mining machinery markets. Their numbers, I found, come from the "Weight, Height and Selected Body Dimensions of Adults, United States, 1960–1962," based on a sample of 7,710 people who were measured between 1959 and 1962. Mean height has not changed in fifty years, so the height figures are still accurate. But Americans are significantly wider. "Americans are definitely fatter than those numbers would indicate," says Loughborough University anthropologist Barry Bogin. This explains why my bum, which is of absolutely reasonable tall proportion, barely fits on a bus seat.

The main show in the SAE book is a pair of diagrams of one sitting and one standing person. The measurements are intensely detailed, down to the fact that humans naturally slump (by −90mm) and that a winter hat can expand a human's head width (by +100mm). It amazes me that engineers adjust for winter hat head width but can't accommodate a 6'2" guy. So that you can measure yourself to see how you fit, the chart shows the minimum and maximum sizes engineers design for, in inches.

Most striking is the sheer numbers of people excluded by these standards. When the SAE standards were created, the U.S. population was 177 million. Now it's over 300 million. And while it might be vaguely acceptable to not design for the tallest 17 million Americans in the name of budget, it's distinctly no longer appropriate to cut out 34 million tax-paying tall Americans.

And the 5th-to-95th policy is less inclusive than it seems. There's

	SMALL (5TH PERCENTILE FEMALE)	MEDIUM	LARGE (95TH PERCENTILE MALE)	ARIANNE COHEN
Back of Calf to Back of Buttock (sitting)	16.1	18.0	19.9	23.2
Floor to Top of Knee (sitting)	19.5	21.9	24.1	24.8
Elbow to Fingertip	16.1	18.1	20.1	20.9
Shoulder to Fingertip	25.0	27.8	30.4	33.5
Seat to Head (sitting)	31.4	34.6	37.8	38.5
Standing Height	61.0	67.6	74.0	75.0
Arm Span	62.4	68.6	75.6	76.7

no such thing as a 70th percentile man or a 90th percentile woman. Both might have 70th percentile feet and 96th percentile hip width and therefore fall out of the rage. In fact, the more body dimensions are involved, the fewer people fit into the range. Molenbroek ran an experiment where he designed a workstation following the 5th-to-95th percentile policy, based on eight body dimensions, like height, leg length, and hip width. He found that when all eight body dimensions were included, *47 percent*, not 10 percent, of the population were excluded.

Being Tall in Private Space

Tall people weren't always Nonfitters. For thousands of years, design went like this: a customer trotted over to the chairmaker shop— or in the case of a weathly customer, the chairmaker trotted over to the customer—and they sat for a measuring. Then individual chairs were crafted. Tall families had tall tables and tall door frames, and if the mayor was tall, the town had tall benches. The needs of talls, particularly rich ones, were met. Calibrated rulers didn't yet exist, so designers used their own bodies as rulers, measuring length by pinky to wrist, or elbow to fingertips. "When people started to produce small series," writes Molenbroek, "they resorted to rules of thumb. For example, when buying a sock on the market, the circumference of the fist was used as a measure for the length of the sole." Tall doom came the moment that the guy doing the measurements and the producer became different people. If the designer had an average-size fist, which fit the sole of an average foot, he passed along those measurements to the producer, and suddenly tall people couldn't buy socks that fit. Mass production marked the end of any tall hopes of fitting.

Since then the default size that designers design for has been Average Young Healthy Male, a 50th-percentile body. This thoroughly explains my nightmare of trying to be a Fitter with female hips and breasts and a 99th percentile frame. It's a particularly misguided strategy because pretty much *no one* is a 50th-percentile male body. Molenbroek measured 350 students, and found that only *one* student had five body dimensions that fell within 12 percent of the 50th percentile. There's no hope for a 90th-percentile body to fit, let alone 99th percentile.

Yet many U.S. schools still teach various takes on this design strategy. "There are design schools which do egghole design, which means designing only for yourself, because you assume everyone has the same measurements," says Mullick. "Or designing for small people because they are the weakest. Or designing for average." Sigh.

Even in the age of technology, the best-intentioned designer has difficulty gauging customer size. Human beings do not come in sizes. Once we reach adult size, our weight and posture shift profoundly, as do our physical abilities (for example, the ability to rise from a chair). Sometimes whole populations shift in size within a generation, such as the Dutch, who have grown upward, and the Belgians, who have grown outward, adding further complication when designing an item that will stick around for a while.

"It's very sexy to do things that just look good," says Mullick. "But in the process they forget the users." One time I threw my back out getting off of a too soft, too low, too small, red chair. It was a gorgeous chair.

The industries that do bother designing to fit precise body ranges, such as producers of exercise equipment and office chairs, do so because dozens of body measurements are required. Standard procedure is to design for either the 10th-to-90th percentiles of the population, or the 5th-to-95th. Which is a blanket policy of excluding thirty million (or in the former case, sixty million) Americans. No wonder we're Nonfitters.

Not surprisingly, none of the companies I spoke with wanted to elaborate on what their "5th-to-95th percentile" meant. But Precor, the company that makes the elliptical exercise machine that I run on three times a week, was willing to talk to me about its design process. I told Jim Burrell, the head of research and innovation, that though I love the machine, the magazine rack is forty degrees below my line of vision, the stride is way too short, sometimes my knees slam into the front of the machine, and my natural hand level is four inches above the handgrips. I told him that I am, by the numbers, a 96th percentile male. "We tend to try and address the needs of what we call the 5th percentile female to 95th percentile male," he explained.

Like most tall-horrific items, the elliptical was, from its birth, not aimed at talls. The elliptical came about when an average-size runner developed an injury; her father filmed her running, traced her foot path, and built a machine. "If we look at the development of the elliptical, it wasn't developed to meet the needs of Shaq," says Burrell. It's popular because it has a low "perceived exertion" level, which means that I think I'm using less energy than I am, which is the hallmark of a much-loved machine. But I still don't fit. Home gym equipment is worse, designed to an even smaller consumer.

The elliptical is also a product that requires that you attach your body to it, which as a rule of thumb is bad news for talls. The official term is "dependent" machine, which means that moving one leg forces the other to move, as on an exercise bike. Whenever this happens, the stride range is limited by the hamstring length of short folk. An "independent" machine, like a treadmill, is much better for talls because leg movements are not chained to the machine. But even independent machines have their hazards. On treadmills I often feel I'm too close to the handrails. Burrell acknowledges this. "Though someone 6'4" can run on a longer treadmill, it's psychologically not always that comfortable." He suggests increasing the incline, which lengthens stride on most machines. This is why gyms are filled with tall people using free weights.

As Molenbroek explained in a four-hundred-page paper on the woes of design exclusion, designers are trained to focus on comfort, safety, and efficacy. Not on fitting. The culprit is "impracticable tabular data, incorrect information, and designers' ignorance." In other words, tall needs just aren't on designers' radar.

The Answer

Mullick was thrilled that I called him to talk tall. He is an outspoken proponent of universal design (also called "inclusive design"), which means design for all users. "Universal design says that there are people on the fringe, below the 10th percentile or above the 90th percentile, and they are being marginalized. It's not enough to design to 90 percent." We're being marginalized!

Universal design is more of a social movement than a design policy, popular only in countries with diverse populations and a government attuned to other sorts of social and economic marginalization. The arguments for universal design tend to use the same buzzwords as civil rights arguments—*marginalization, inclusion,* and *community*—and follow the same lines of logic as well: separate-but-equal is not okay, and neither is same-but-excluding. Providing fitting seats for only 80 percent of the community is on par with forcing some citizens to sit in the back of the bus.

Universal design is often wrongly confused with disability design. "A lot of universities want everyone to move along the same path, so that it's truly 'universal,'" says Donohue. "They really push it. They don't even want you to do switchback ramps at an entrance." Nor do they want two water fountains, or two tables. The result is that in practice, designers often produce one-size-fits-all products that are comfortable for almost no one. It's best illustrated by watching me fill out a deposit slip at my bank's thirty-two-inch counter.

There are four broad ways to size a product: one size fits all, adjustable, multiple sizes, or adjustable *and* multiple sizes. To get a sense of which approach tends to be the most successful for tall consumers, I made a chart of some of the products in my tall life and organized them by approach.

As you can see in the chart on page 206, the one size fits all approach is a total failure. Let's all say it together: *one size fits all does not fit talls.* Multisize products are actually quite successful from a design standpoint—the glitch is a logistical one, the manufacturer's failure to produce an XL size. Adjustable *and* multiple-size options often truly fulfill 1st-to-99th-percentile design.

Munich's subway system, the S-Bahn, is a perfect example of adjustable-and-multiple-size universal design. The trains are roughly seven feet tall, with a range of comfortable seating bench and chair options at different heights to fit every conceivable body type. The head rests are well-placed, and you are in no danger of brain damage from the handrails. Neither space nor cost is compromised, and the seat count is exactly the same as in the New York City subway. So it's quite possible. Remember the elliptical trainer? It's screaming for two sizes of adjustable machines. One could fit the 1st-to-65th percentile, the other the 45th-to-100th percentile. The problem would be solved. As for public furniture, I once saw a bus stop bench that had seats at three levels, one child-size. Brilliant. Yes, some days the tall seat will already be taken by another tall person. But that's better than relegating all tall people to a life of standing.

I didn't realize how uncomfortable I was until I stepped off the plane in the Netherlands, home of universal design. Suddenly I was comfortable. The water fountains were in two heights. The hotel check-in desk had a lower area and a higher area. My hotel bed was seven feet long. Seven feet! I took a picture. My friend's hotel

ONE SIZE FITS ALL	MULTIPLE SIZES	ADJUSTABLE	MULTIPLE SIZES AND ADJUSTABLE
Street furniture *Verdict*: **Doesn't fit**. Too low. Who knew that the mail pickup times are printed on the mailbox?	**School furniture** *Verdict*: **Doesn't fit**. The largest size is too small.	**Backpack** *Verdict*: **Fit!**	**Belt** *Verdict*: **Fit!**
Telephone booth *Verdict*: **Doesn't fit**. I often can't see the dial pad.	**Rolling suitcase** *Verdict*: **Doesn't fit**. The tallest handle is too low.	**Elliptical trainer** *Verdict*: **Doesn't Fit.** The highest adjustments are too small.	**Bicycle** *Verdict*: **Fit!**
ATM Machine *Verdict*: **Doesn't fit**. I have to duck for the computer screen to not be glared.	**Shoes** *Verdict*: **Doesn't Fit**. The biggest size is too small.	**Vacuum cleaner** *Verdict*: **Doesn't fit.** Back pain. The longest handle adjustment is too low.	**Refrigerator with movable shelving** *Verdict*: **Fit!**
Sunglasses *Verdict*: **Doesn't Fit**. The head-squeezing induces headaches.	**Clothing** *Verdict*: **Doesn't fit**. The biggest size is too small.	**Architect's lamp** *Verdict*: **Fit!**	**Office Chair** *Verdict*: **Fit!** The big-and-tall models are great.

had a bed extension. I took another picture. The corner pizza shop ("New York Pizza") had a couple small tables and a couple tall tables. I was too busy eating to take a picture.

I called up Molenbroek to figure out their secret. "We once had a very tall prime minister," he joked. Actually, they've had a few. Molenbroek turns the problem around: Americans don't seem to know that they're uncomfortable. It's an intriguing quirk in a culture of body hyperawareness. Americans buy air purifiers and flock to chiropractors and sleep clinics and yoga retreats in levels that Europeans find comical. Yet we have a total blank spot around the concept of fitting. "For Americans, the knowledge that their posture is bad and that there are better products is not there," says Molenbroek, who consults with U.S. companies. "Here parents and teachers tell kids how to sit and find something that fits."

I think the disconnect happens because Americans are peculiarly programmed to purchase mass-marketed household items. Mainstream big-box stores make their money by limiting their models, selling only one or two versions of each item. Tall is not one of the two options. Big-box stores are, by definition, not tall-friendly. Yet we buy our too-small porch furniture and too-low dressers there.

The Dutch love affair with universal design began when they found themselves towering over the rest of Europe, marginalized. The initial battlefield was unexpected: school chairs. The standard European school chair was seventeen inches off the ground— laughably low for the Netherlands' many six-foot-plus teenagers. The Dutch tried to talk Europe into offering chairs in multiple sizes. "It cost fifteen years and a lot of meetings," says Molenbroek. "But after our interference, kids had chair legs up to twenty-three inches. And we are most proud of a simple cardboard tool that shows you how long the legs are in seven colors, and you put it along a table to see which size chair you need." Molenbroek excitedly adds, "If kids are measured twice a year, it is satisfying to control the fit."

Molenbroek is right about Americans' denseness about fitting. I spent my last nine years in school not fitting the chairs. I had no idea there was another option. Molenbroek's specialty, the mix of body size and industrial design, does not, as far as I know, exist in the United States. "I don't know any schools that have a program in universal design," says Mullick. "They may have a course here and there."

The day I called Molenbroek, he was studying swimming pool fences as part of a committee that tests products to identify which bodies are excluded. He goes out of his way to teach his students to design for all. Each year in his opening lecture he invites two of the tallest and smallest people in the Netherlands, 7'4" and 4'2", to attend, to illustrate the troubles they have in daily life; the students' first assignment is to measure people who are not average. Eventually students are tasked with making items that people of all sizes will love to use. I like that: *love to use.* That's so different than *use because they have to.*

The Dutch didn't just wake up and hit their heads one day and decide to have a fitting revolution. The 7'4" man whom Molenbroek invites to his opening lecture each year is Rob Bruintjes, fifty-five, who is among the top-forty tallest people in the country (the tallest is 7'7"). Bruintjes weighs 352 pounds, and his shoe size is 17. Bruintjes would like to fit. In the mid-1980s and 1990s, he headed the three-thousand-person Netherlands Tall Club and began lobbying retailers, companies, manufacturers, and governments on universal design. At the time, the clothing industry had recently shifted manufacturing operations to Asia, and big barrels of clothing in one size were appearing in Dutch garment districts. (Hint: the one size was not tall.)

Bruintjes realized that his lobby would be stronger if he combined forces with other excluded groups. He invited clubs for short, overweight, and disabled people to join forces. But the tall club resisted being lumped with other groups, so Bruintjes left and founded Uniform.

Uniform is an umbrella group of two thousand Nonfitters, aiming to find design solutions that will work for everyone: "We deal with the 30 percent of the community who are less comfortable. They're bigger, taller, older or disabled." Bruintjes circulates a newsletter, *Tailor Made*, and visits European commissions and companies. "I just stand up, and they see what the problem is." His presentation is straightforward: he represents a large minority of the market that would be happy to spend millions on well-sized products. He begins with the obvious example of the chair he was just sitting in, usually a standard twenty inches high. (His chair is likely two to four inches taller than the one you're sitting in, if you live in America.) He explains that 16 percent of the population couldn't fit in that chair.

Much of his job is simply informing companies of their wrongs. "One of the stupid things I saw on a bus was a low-hanging screen right in the middle, for news and delays. So I made pictures of that to show them." He also passes along tall sizing standards and, if appropriate, suggests a solution, perhaps multiple sizes (as with Italian and French furniture) or adjustable (as with office furniture). Many manufacturers, it turns out, are quite friendly because they're thrilled to not be dealing with obesity lobbies. "The community responds in a nicer way to tall people," says Bruintjes. "They think that tall people are not to blame for being tall."

Bruintjes is well aware of what the Tall Club of Silicon Valley learned the hard way: no one cares about tall discomfort. But companies, builders, and designers do care about money. So Uniform stresses the sizable wallets of over 20 percent of the population, as well as the reduced public health expense and government savings of designing now for a Dutch population where the average male is expected to grow to 6'3.5" (heaven!). The net result: Dutch stores carry four standard furniture sizes, building codes require 8'6" ground-floor ceilings and 7'2" door frames, and train and elevator height minimums are 6'6". Bruintjes considers their biggest successes to be the design twists that help tall people without annoying others, like deeper stairs and longer bathtubs. If only he knew that the U.S. tub standard is five feet. His next focus will be amusement parks. "If you're over 6'6", they let you in, but sometimes you're not on the safe side," says Bruintjes. Yes, tall beheadings would be bad.

I imagine universal design to be like baking a cake. It's much easier to bake one pretty, tasty cake than a cake that fits the needs of diabetic, lactose-intolerant, and dieting customers. No one would ask the baker to create the perfect cake for everyone. But perhaps the baker would make more money if he made two different cakes. Or three or four.

The major barrier in tall-friendly design is, I think, competence. Universal design hasn't been widely adopted because, frankly, designing for everyone is hard. "It's very easy for a designer to not deal with a certain type of user," says Mullick. "It's very easy to do things that just look good. As soon as you deal with different bodies, it becomes very complicated."

It has not escaped my notice that the U.S. industries that design the widest variety of fitting products are those vulnerable to injury lawsuits. "There's a lot of litigation around workplace injuries, accidents, and whatnot, and that forced the standards to change," says Mullick. Big-and-tall office chairs, fully adjustable in myriad ways, have cropped up because workers sued companies and employers over back problems. Injury lawsuits are powerful.

But there are, I think, two better answers than litigation. One is Tall Consumerism. Tall people have no excuse to continue spending millions of dollars at companies that ignore our existence. Tall Consumerism is, I find, more a matter of *not* buying, and holding out for the perfect item. It's a campaign of positive reinforcement. As of this writing, JetBlue is by far the most tall-friendly airline—most of its flights have economy seating at a thirty-four-to-thirty-six-inch pitch. Its strategy is to attract the 15 percent of passengers who are discriminated against by other companies, which is fine by me. Tall consumers are fully in control of 15 percent of the market and should wield their power accordingly. Companies will get the message quickly.

The second answer is lobbying. Today one would be hard pressed to find a height lobbyist on Capitol Hill, because they don't exist in America. But individual lobbying is powerful, important, and in the e-mail age, very easy. In many cases what's needed is simply education. Higgins, the guy who orders the bus seats that stay in the New York City transport system for decades, said that I was the very first person to call him up to talk about height. He was genuinely surprised to hear that a 6'3" person couldn't fit into the seats. Jim Burrell, from Precor, hadn't heard requests for longer hand grips and a higher magazine holder until I called him. "If we start to get a tremendous number of requests for something, then we go in and do it," he says. "If people don't raise their hands, then we don't know." Universities don't know that their desks are too small unless someone tells them; the city doesn't know that its toilets are insanely low until someone takes an illustrative photo. "Designers are well meaning," says Mullick. "It's just that most have no clue who is buying their products."

We are. With this in mind, I am starting Think Tall at TallBook .com, where we'll contact companies, industry associations, and designers and let them know how their products could be more tall-friendly. And of course, we'll provide photographic evidence. The Dutch precedent is a strong one. Think Tall will demonstrate the issues at hand, discuss sizing standards, find solutions that work for everyone, and support manufacturers that are particularly tall friendly. Readers can visit TallBook.com to send in photos, join e-mail campaigns, and suggest companies and products that need to change. Nonfitters unite: we're going to become Fitters.

Acknowledgments

I often read authors' acknowledgment pages in the hope that they'll disclose the great secret of their literary acumen, or at least list a bunch of their famous friends. This is not that page. I have no famous friends.

Tall people are, however, famously friendly. I made that lovely discovery when I began this project, gripping a blank reporter's notebook with the line *Tall: Research!* scrawled across the first page. Hundreds of talls and not-so-talls from around the world were thrilled to talk tall, which made my job a delight.

Thank you to agent Judith Riven, who said, "Tall people . . . hmmm, I like that!" and to former Bloomsbury publisher Colin Dickerman, who said, "Tall people . . . I'll purchase that," and to editor extraordinaire Ben Adams, who said, "Tall people. I'll read about that over and over again on my vacation weekends." This book would look much shabbier without their efforts, as well as those of the tall graphics team. Illustrator Myra Gourley, who once again didn't blink when I mailed her stick-figure renditions of what the illustrations might look like, and right fully ignored them. And Beth Kleckner's *Excel*-lent graph skills astound.

When authors write books, everyone they know suffers a little. My college roommate Becky Mitchell dropped her Ph.D. studies on a moment's notice to plow through medical journals with me; Elizabeth Cline did a marathon early reading in exchange for salad; Bre Levy and Nancy Redd gamely provided eighteen months of tall phone support. Jennifer Price repeatedly made sure I got where I needed to go, when I needed to get there. This endeavor also required the extraordinary patience of one Alan Herbert, who around the clock happily fielded questions like "What did you last hit your head on?"

And thank you to my mother, Arline Cohen, who is, of course, where all the tallness began. She regularly reminds me that she is the reason I am tall, and has no qualms about threatening to take eight inches back. Thanks, Mom.

This project is a compilation of tall knowledge and as such contains the musings of roughly two hundred interviewees, to whom I am grateful. Among the many: Economist heavyweight John Komlos warmly invited me to his University of Munich office, and Barry Bogin and Richard Steckel spent hours helping me interpret data. The University of California at San Francisco endocrinology department welcomed me for a day, headed by endocrinologist extraordinaire Melvin Grumbach, the kind of guy who answers e-mail queries during family emergencies. The tall psyche was unleashed from the mind of Ken Page, who did an hourlong interview with me from his car in a commuter rail parking lot. Julia Child's longtime producer at PBS, Russ Morash, gave a lively interview, as did retired FBI criminal profiler Greg McCrary, most of which had nothing to do with height.

Thank you to Betty Dodson and Eric Amaranth for answering every possible question about tall sex that's ever occurred to me, then taking my follow-up calls when more occurred. Janet Merewether, director of the tall art house film *Jabe Babe: A Heightened Life*, chatted late into the Australian night with me, and Boguslaw Pawlowski took my call in Poland, repeatedly apologizing for his impeccable English. I struck gold in Stephen Hall's beautifully researched *Size Matters: How Height Affects the Health, Happiness and Success of Boys*, which provided ample early direction and is referenced throughout.

The world's premiere tall ambassador, Sandy Allen, America's tallest woman, welcomed me with a hug and spoke to me for hours a day after her discharge from the hospital. She passed away a few months later and will be deeply missed.

Last but not least, this book should open and close on the tall haven that is Europatreffen. I thank the organizers of Europatreffen 2007 for welcoming me with (very long) open arms, as well as the hundreds of participants who didn't mind my running behind them on their vacation with a reporter's notebook. Thank you all.

Appendix: Growth Disorders That You Probably Do Not Have

When I was eleven, a cardiologist glued sensors to my chest, gave me a waist pack, and sent me off to school. He was looking for signs of Marfan syndrome. I spent the day baring my belly to show everyone my heart monitor. I missed afternoon swim practice for an appointment with the ophthalmologist to check for detached eye lenses, another symptom. Swimming wasn't going well that year, and I wanted to quit. So I prayed that I had Marfan, a genetic mutation that—oops!—wouldn't allow me to swim anymore. I didn't have Marfan, and my swimming career extended another decade.

Since then I've been asked once a week whether I have "some sort of disorder." People seem to think that tall people commonly do. I don't, and neither do 95 percent of exceptionally tall people. "If a tall child comes in to see me, I will look at growth hormone production and a couple other conditions," says pediatrician Ron Rosenfeld. "But chronic diseases that come with tall stature are rare." He flipped open an enormous medical textbook. Of the hundred-page chapter on growth, three pages were on tallness. Dozens of pages outlined short ailments.

It's good that talls don't have many ailments, because few very tall kids are taken to the doctor—nine out of ten kids seen for growth problems are short kids. This said, super tall kids often get a medical workup at some point to make sure their growth is not a hormone abnormality. "I remember having hospital appointments when I was around twelve," says Belinda Nokia, a 6'7"

Brit. "I had absolutely no idea what was going on." In the next few pages we can all learn what's going on.

Tallness Disorders at a Glance

Tallness itself is never a disorder; it may be at most a symptom of something else gone awry. Studying tall disorders has brought me to an obvious conclusion: the number-one warning sign of a growth disorder is a kid who is way taller than siblings or parents. The chart below summarizes disorders associated with tallness. Most are quite rare. Once they are counted out, the kid in question is just tall. The next few pages summarize each disorder, in order of prevalence.

CHROMOSOMAL DISORDERS	ENDOCRINE DISORDERS	BONE OVERGROWTH SYNDROMES	DISORDERS WHERE TALLNESS IS THE OBVIOUS SYMPTOM	SECONDARY DISORDERS
Klinefelter Syndrome*	Gigantism/ Acromegaly	Sotos Syndrome	Marfan Syndrome* and Marfanoid	Precocious puberty*
XYY and XYYY Syndrome*	Hyperthyroidism/ Thyrotoxicosis	Weaver-Smith Syndrome	Estrogen Resistance or Inactivity	
	Beckwith-Wiedemann Syndrome		Homocystinuria	

*=relatively common

SOURCES: Stenvert L. S. Drop, et al., "Sex Steroid Treatment of Constitutionally Tall Stature," *Endocrine Reviews* 19, no. 5 (1998); and Dennis M. Styne, *Pediatric Endocrinology* (Philadelphia: Lippincott Williams & Wilkins, 2004), 78.

The Commons

XYY and XYYY Syndrome

I put this one first because it's often missed—I've dated two XYYs, neither of whom knew what I was talking about. Males with an extra Y-chromosomes grow into extremely tall, thin boys who may have severe acne and mild behavior and learning problems. The key signs: Boys who are much taller than siblings, with IQs ten to fifteen points lower than siblings or parents. One in a thousand boys has it, meaning five to ten are born in the United States daily. Most go undiagnosed.

Marfan Syndrome

Marfan Syndrome is the best known of the tall disorders due to a handful of high-profile deaths. In 1986 Volleyball Olympian Flo Hyman, 6'5", died at thirty-one during a televised game, and *Rent* creator Jonathan Larson, thirty-five, died in 1996 the day before the Broadway show opened. Other suspected Marfanites are Charles de Gaulle, Sergei Rachmaninoff, Abraham Lincoln, and Osama Bin Laden. All of them have the distinctive Marfan body: tall and lean, because all the "long" bones overgrow, leading to high-waistedness; an arm span longer than height, and arachnodactyly, which means spider fingers and toes. Not surprisingly, tall clubs have adopted Marfan as their fund-raising focus.

Marfan is a one-in-five-thousand disorder of the connective tissue, which one doctor described as like "having a house with a rotten frame." It's caused by mutations in the fibrillin-1 gene, which causes improper numbers and types of elastic fibers. Marfan parents run a 50 percent risk of passing it on, but a quarter of cases are spontaneous mutations. The pressing health risk is that the fibers in the aorta can stretch and tear (aortic dissection), causing instant death.

Sports are the worst possible hobby for an undiagnosed Marfan kid, which is why most tall, spindly kids are tested. Diagnosis is a confusing identification of possible symptoms: an obvious physique, a telltale protruding or pigeon-chested ribcage, a dislocated eye lens, a large aorta. A weakened dura membrane, which surrounds the brain (dural ectasia), will also win a Marfan diagnosis. Other connective tissue symptoms include double-jointed and hyperextendable joints (try pulling your thumb to your forearm), flat feet, a long head, and nearsightedness. To make things more confusing, two hundred similar connective tissue disorders involve mutations of related genes. Thus, various combinations of the non-life-threatening symptoms are sometimes diagnosed as "marfanoid."

In earlier decades Marfan patients lived carefully and died young. Now preimplantation embryo testing is possible, and the aorta can be replaced with an artificial tube. Recently the anti-cholesterol drug Losartan was found to reverse aortic stretching in animals; it is now in experimental trials.

Ehlers-Danlos Syndrome

Ehlers-Danlos is a Marfanoid syndrome that's just as common as Marfan, but physicians rarely know about it and instead diagnose individual joint problems. Its calling card is loose, hyperflexible joints, flat feet, and delicate, easy-bruising skin that doesn't heal well. Of the six varieties of Ehlers-Danlos, only one, the so-called vascular type, is life threatening, due to artery ruptures. In the other varieties, lifespan is normal, though children can't do sports.

Klinefelter Syndrome and XXY Syndrome

Klinefelter men are quite tall (75th percentile for height, regardless of parents) with effeminate wide hips, as a result of low testosterone levels. One in five hundred men have the extra X-chromosome. "This one is picked up earlier because kids don't hit puberty," says UCSF endocrinologist Robert Long. "We put them on male sex hormones, and they can have normal sex lives." The easiest way to spot this disorder in young boys is to look for high overall IQs but bombing scores on verbal and reading tests. It's also possible to be asymptomatic, or to be XXYY, XXXY or XXXXY. One in two hundred thousand girls has the related XXX syndrome—they are two to four inches taller than siblings, with similar symptoms.

Homocystinuria

This is another Marfanoid condition. It is like Marfan but involves mental retardation, seizures, and mental health problems. I mention it because the mental effects can be prevented by early treatment and diet, and many states require newborn testing. Patients are tall and very thin, with dislocated eye lenses, nearsightedness, and skeletal and joint problems. One in 250,000 babies are born with it. Both parents must be carriers.

Hyperthyroidism

Hyperthyroidism, or hyperactivity of the thyroid gland, is quite common, at one in one hundred. I list it here because sometimes children can quickly become lean and thin from the speeding up of vital functions; in documented cases kids are in the 97th to 100th percentiles, with healthy siblings at the 50th percentile. Hyperthyroidism has many possible causes, ranging from Graves' disease to tumors, and it results in shakiness with high blood pressure, high heart rate, and a whip-fast metabolism. It is very treatable.

Precocious Puberty

Precocious puberty is puberty at age nine or younger for girls and eleven or younger for boys. An early growth surge makes these kids extremely tall for a brief moment in time, and then they're finished growing forever. In my hometown, this award went to my neighbor who reached menarche in second grade, with the typical breast and pubic hair development. She came within an inch of taking my Tallest Girl at Elsmere Elementary crown, and then she finished off at 5'2". The experience can be psychologically difficult for girls who have a seventeen-year-old body at age eight. Half of cases are caused by a disorder, anything from a brain tumor to an ovarian tumor.

The Rare Birds

Weaver-Smith Syndrome

Weaver-Smith is a fascinating but exceedingly rare genetic disorder of 97th to 100th percentile adults with normal mental abilities. Babies are born quite large and continue growing, resulting in muscular elementary schoolers at teacher heights. Weaver babies have what doctors describe as a distinctive "hoarse low-pitched cry," as well as reflex problems, slow motor skills, foot deformities; and sometimes lagging mental development. Only four dozen cases have been reported since the mid-1970s, though it is often undiagnosed, or diagnosed by individual symptoms.

Sotos Syndrome (Cerebral Gigantism)

Sotos is a genetic mutation (one in thirteen thousand) of overgrowth. It starts out in newborns over the 90th percentile, who continue into very tall children with large hands and feet and easy-to-spot prominent foreheads, elephant ears, and slanted eyes. It proceeds into a genetic form of mental retardation that is often extremely mild. The diagnosis is often missed in children with general mental disability.

Estrogen Resistance or Inactivity

The discovery of this disorder is how endocrinologists learned about the specific actions of estrogen in growth. Estrogen closes the growth plates during puberty. In extremely rare cases, bodies either lack estrogen receptors or don't produce estrogen (usually due to lacking aromatase, which breaks down testosterone into estrogen), and growth continues indefinitely.

Beckwith-Wiedemann Syndrome

Beckwith-Wiedemann is a genetic mutation causing excessive IGF-2 production, producing extremely large newborns and toddlers who have overgrown organs and tongues. It's life-threatening, because the overgrown pancreas can cause blood sugar to plummet to fatal levels; there's also a high risk of developing tumors. At one in 13,700, Beckwith-Wiedemann is the most common of a number of similar disorders, some of which cause hyperinsulinism (when the pancreas secretes too much insulin), which can also result in tall children.

Gigantism and Acromegaly

Along with Marfan Syndrome, gigantism, the overproduction of human growth hormone, is the other well-known tall-person disease. The former and current tallest women in the world, Sandy Allen and Yao Defen, as well as the tallest man, Leonid Stadnyk, are all sufferers. Only three in one million have it, but they tend to be extremely visible.

Most people know gigantism as "that disease that André the Giant had." André dominated the WWF wrestling circuit for fifteen years, then turned in a stellar performance as Fezzik in my favorite movie, *The Princess Bride.* André was actually André R. Roussimoff, a Frenchman who made a career out of being tall. His fans thought he was both the tallest and the strongest man in the world, thanks to the wrestling foundation that kept billing him as such. He was 6'10", not remotely near the world's eight-footers, though he eventually topped four hundred pounds, largely owing to his ability to drink dozens of beers without significant effect. He opted not to treat the benign pituitary tumor causing his illness and died at age forty-seven in 1993 of congestive heart failure. Sandy Allen, who passed away at fifty-three, is the only known giant to make it to her fifties.

Gigantism (called acromegaly in adults) comes from a benign pituitary tumor (or in rare cases, a pancreas or lung tumor) that floods the body with hormone, causing excessive growth and a host of hormone-related problems—diabetes, heart disease, high blood pressure, infertility, arthritis, overgrown organs, and often a lack of sexual development. It's picked up in tall teenage girls by their lack of menstruation. Treatment is a tumor-removal surgery, which used to go through the brain or roof of the mouth but now can be done through the nose, and it is followed up with gamma knife radiation. Most untreated sufferers ultimately die of heart attacks. "Too much growth hormone weakens the heart and can cause it to fail," says cardiologist Paul Thompson. In adults, acromegaly (1 in 20,000) sometimes appears after the growth plates are closed, in which case there is no tallness, but cartilage continues to grow.

Notes

For those who are excited by words like "citation" and "bibliography," dig in.

Chapter 1. A Primer on the Tall Life

7   Four inches of height . . . Anne Case, Christina Paxson, "Stature and Status: Height, Ability and Labor Market Outcomes," *NBER Working Paper Series*, August 2006, 2.

7     $789 per inch per year . . . Timothy Judge, Daniel Cable, "The Effect of Physical Height on Workplace Success and Income: *Journal of Applied Psychology* 89, no. 3 (2004): 428–41. The four surveys are by the Great Britain National Childhood Development Study, the University of California at Berkeley, and the U.S. Department of Labor (2).

8   MBAs found a similar figure . . . Irene H. Frieze et al., "Perceived and Actual Discrimination in the Salaries of Male and Female Managers," *Journal of Applied Social Psychology* 20, no. 1 (1990): 46–67. Tall MBA graduates earned $570 more per inch per year than their shorter MBA peers. Which is comparatively higher than the $789 per inch, because all the MBAs have graduate degrees, which is not the case when studying tall salaries in the open market.

9     $170 billion is transferred . . . Andrew Postlewaite et al., "The Effect of Adolescent Experience on Labor Market Outcomes: The Case of Height," *PIER Working Paper* 03-036, December 3, 2003, 3.

9   The wage gap between black and white . . . Ibid., 1.

9   Average hourly wages . . . Gregory Mankiw, Matthew Weinzierl. "The Optimal Taxation of Height," Working Paper, April 13, 2007, 22.

9   Only 3 percent of white men . . . Of men ages 30 to 39, 98.1 percent are 6'3" or lower; U.S. Census Bureau, *Statistical Abstract of the United States 2003*, 140. Among white males, the figure is 96.5 percent. Gregory Mankiw, Matthew Weinzierl. "The Optimal Taxation of Height," Working Paper, April 13, 2007, 22.

10 A 2001 STUDY FROM THE MINNESOTA TWINS . . . Jere Behrman, Mark Rosenzweig, "The Returns to Increasing Body Weight," *PIER Working Paper* 01-052, 2001.

10 OTHER SMALL STUDIES FIND . . . Postlewaite et al., "Effect of Adolescent Experience," 2.

10 THE GENDER GAP STUBBORNLY STICKS . . . Case and Paxson, "Stature and Status," 21. Some studies find the gender pay gap as high as 30 percent.

10 TALLS HEALTHY BODIES ARE . . . Sara Stinson, "Growth Variation: Biological and Cultural Factors," in Sara Stinson et al., eds., *Human Biology: An Evolutionary and Biocultural Perspective* (New York: Wiley-Liss, 2000), 454.

10 COMPARATIVELY LARGE STORES OF ENERGY . . . Robert Fogel, *The Escape from Hunger and Premature Death, 1700–2100* (New York: Cambridge University Press, 2004), 218. Talls have comparatively higher body mass index readings.

11 BABIES OF TALL MOTHERS HAVE A HIGHER . . . Rebecca Sear et al., "Height, Marriage and Reproductive Success in Gambian Women," *Research in Economic Anthropology* 23 (2004): 203–24. See chapter 13.

11 TALL TRIBAL SUDANESE WOMEN ARE WORTH . . . Peter Gatkout, a Sudanese Nuer man, personal communication, May 2007.

11 PH.D.'S ARE JUST 1.5 INCHES TALLER . . . H. E. Meyer, R. Selmer, "Income, Educational Level and Body Height," *Annals of Human Biology* 26, no. 3 (May 1999): 219–27.

11 TALL CHILDREN FROM SHORT FAMILIES . . . Postlewaite et al., "Effect of Adolescent Experience," 2.

11 TALLS ARE ABOUT 10 PERCENT MORE . . . Case and Paxson, "Stature and Status," 29.

11 BEING TALL AS AN ADULT . . . Andrew Postlewaite, personal communication, May 2007.

12 IN 2006 PAXSON AND HER PRINCETON COLLEAGUE . . . Case and Paxson, "Stature and Status."

12 LARGE SWEDISH . . . STUD[Y] . . . T. Tuvemo et al., "Intellectual and Physical Performance and Morbidity in Relation to Height in a Cohort of 18-year-old Swedish Conscripts," *Hormone Research* 52, no. 4 (1999): 186–91. The Swedish study of 32,887 men found that the tallest men scored 19 percent better than shorter men in cognitive testing.

12 OF 76,111 DANISH MEN, THOSE OVER 6'3" . . . T. W. Teasdale, D. R. Owen, "Intelligence and Educational Level in Adult Males at the Extremes of Stature," *Human Biology* 63, no. 1 (1991): 19–30.

12–13 A HONOLULU STUDY FOUND THAT SHORT . . . Robert D. Abbott et al., "Height as a Marker of Childhood Development and Late-Life Cognitive Function," *Pediatrics* 102, no. 3 (September 1998): 602–09.

13 FOR EVERY STANDARD DEVIATION INCREASE . . . For the chart, I centered

the heights and IQs around the mean. A one-tenth standard deviation from the mean is roughly a 3.98 percent increase in IQ.

13   PAXSON AND CASE WERE BOMBARDED WITH E-MAILS . . . Mark Borden, "Shortchanged," *New Yorker*, October 2, 2006.

14   BY COMPARING TWINS REARED SEPARATELY . . . J. M. Sundet et al., "Resolving the Genetic and Environmental Sources of the Correlation Between Height and Intelligence," *Twin Research and Human Genetics* 8, no. 4 (August 2005): 307–11.

14   ENVIRONMENTS WHERE CHILDREN ARE WELL FED . . . A Finnish study of the academic achievement of 8,798 adult twin pairs concluded that taller twins succeed further in academia, primarily due to environmental upbringing (not genetics). K. Silventoinen et al., "Genetic and Environmental Contributions to the Association Between Body Height and Educational Attainment," *Behavior Genetics* 30, no. 6 (November 2000): 477–85.

14   LONG, FIVE-TO-TWELVE-MONTH-OLD BABIES . . . S. A. Rose, "Relation Between Physical Growth and Information Processing in Infants Born in India," *Child Development* 65, no. 3 (1994): 889–902.

14   THE REIGNING THEORY IS THAT . . . Abi Berger, "Commentary: Insulin-like Growth Factor and Cognitive Function," *British Medical Journal* 322, no. 7280 (January 27, 2001): 203.

14   CHILDREN IN THE 99TH PERCENTILE . . . M. Tauber et al., "Growth Hormone Secretion in Children and Adolescents with Familial Tall Stature," European Journal of Pediatrics 153 (no. 5) (May 1994): 311–16.

14   A WELL-KNOWN STUDY TRACKING 1.8 MILLION NORWEGIAN . . . H. T. Waaler, "Height, Weight and Mortality," *Acta Medica Scandinavica* 679 (1984): 1–56.

14   OTHER STUDIES ACROSS CENTURIES . . . K. Silventoinen et al., "Social Background, Adult Body Height and Health," *International Journal of Epidemiology* 28 (1999): 911–18; A. M. Peck, D. H. Vagero, "Adult Body Height, Self-Perceived Health and Mortality in the Swedish Population," *Journal of Epidemiology and Community Health* 43 (1989): 380–84; Pekka Jousilahti et al., "Relation of Adult Height to Cause-specific and Total Mortality," *American Journal of Epidemiology* 151, no. 11 (June 2000): 1112–20.

14   A STUDY OF UNION ARMY SOLDIER DEATHS . . . Fogel, *Escape from Hunger*, 25.

14   A 2003 STUDY THAT FOLLOWED 2 MILLION . . . Anders Engeland et al., "Height and Body Mass Index in Relation to Total Mortality," *Epidemiology* 14, no. 3 (May 2003): 293–99.

15   ARMY RECORDS TALK ABOUT . . . Gina Kolata, "So Big and Healthy Grandpa Wouldn't Even Know You," *New York Times*, July 30, 2007.

15   A 2000 FINNISH STUDY OF 31,999 PEOPLE . . . P. Jousilahti et al., "Relation of Adult Height to Cause-specific and Total Mortality."

15   THEIR RISK OF MORALITY IS 4 PERCENT LOWER . . . G. D. Batty et al., "Adult Height in Relation to Mortality from 14 Cancer Sites in Men in London," *Annals of Oncology* 17, no. 1 (2006): 157–66.

15   THE FIGURES ARE SIMILAR FOR WOMEN . . . Waaler and Jousilahti both
found similar tall female longevity. An excellent graph of men and
women's height, age and mortality risk is in Phyllis Eveleth and James
Tanner, *Worldwide Variation in Human Growth* (Cambridge, U.K.: Cambridge University Press, 1990), p. 209. You can plot the mortality risk of
you and everyone you know.

16   TALLS ALSO HAVE SUBSTANTIALLY LOWER RATES . . . G. D. Smith et al.,
"Height and Risk of Death Among Men and Women," *Journal of Epidemiological Community Health* 54 (2000): 98–103.

16   WEALTH IS A STRONG PREDICTOR . . . Marco Sunder, economics Ph.D.
candidate under John Komlos at the University of Munich, personal
communication, May 2007.

16   MEN AT 6'3" HAVE THE FEWEST . . . R. Fogel et al., "Secular Trends in the
Distribution of Chronic Conditions and Disabilities at Young Adult and
Late Ages, 1860–1988," *NBER Summer Institute* (Cambridge, Mass.,
1993).

16   THE 2003 STUDY OF 2 MILLION NORWEGIANS . . . Engeland et al., "Height
and Body Mass Index in Relation to Total Mortality."

16   A SEPARATE STUDY FOUND THAT . . . Silventoinen et al., "Social Background, Adult Body Height, and Health."

17   IT'S GOOD TO BE TALL . . . John Komlos, personal communication, May
2007.

17   AN INTRIGUING THEORY EXPLAINING . . . Steven Rosenthal, endocrinologist at the University of California at San Francisco, personal communication, February 2007.

17   FLIES AND MICE WITH LOW LEVELS OF IGF-I . . . Valter Longo, Caleb Finch,
"Evolutionary Medicine: From Dwarf Model Systems to Healthy Centenarians?" *Science* 299, no. (5611) (February 2003): 1342–46.

17   THE 1999 STUDY OF 32,887 SWEDISH MEN . . . Tuvemo et al., "Intellectual
and Physical Performance and Morbidity."

18   IF THE WOMAN IS TALLER . . . Aaron Boyson et al., "Height as Power in
Women," *North American Journal of Psychology* 1, no. 1 (1999): 109–14.

18   WHEN CHILDREN AS YOUNG AS THREE ARE SHOWN . . . Joann Montepare,
"The Impact of Variations in Height on Young Children's Impressions of
Men and Women," *Journal of Nonverbal Behavior* 19, no. 1 (Spring 1995):
31–47.

18   ONLY 15 PERCENT OF WOMEN ARE TALLER THAN MEN . . . Stinson, "Growth
Variation."

18   ASSISTANT PROFESSORS ARE 1.24 INCHES ABOVE . . . Wayne E. Hensley,
"Height As a Measure of Success in Academe," *Psychology* 30, no. 1
(1993): 40–46.

Chapter 2. Tall People Around the World

21 MISERY PRODUCES SHORT PEOPLE . . . Quoted in Burkhard Bilger, "The Height Gap," *New Yorker*, April 5, 2004, 38–44.

22 APPROXIMATELY 37,000 AMERICANS DIAGNOSED . . . National Cancer Institute, "Pancreatic Cancer Treatment," www.cancer.gov/cancertopics/pdq/treatment/pancreatic/healthprofessional.

23 CAMBODIANS ARE EXTREMELY SHORT . . . Cambodian National Institute of Public Health and National Institute of Statistics, *Cambodia Demographic Health Survey 2005* (December 2006), 184.

24 IF EVERYONE IN THE WORLD GREW UP . . . Though the overall heights would be the same, body proportions would continue to differ among ethnicities. Africans, particularly sub-Saharan Africans, have 4 percent longer legs than Europeans. Asians have the shortest arms and legs, roughly 7 percent and 10 percent shorter than Europeans and Americans, respectively. Stinson, "Growth Variation." 437 in Sara Stinson et al., eds., *Human Biology: An Evolutionary and Biocultural Perspective* (New York: Wiley-Liss, 2000).

24 A FEW RARE, EXCEPTIONAL GROUPS ARE GENETICALLY DESTINED . . . Sara Stinson, "Growth Variation: Biological and Cultural Factors," Ibid., 426.

25 TALL PEOPLE ARE SHORTHAND FOR THRIVING Richard Steckel, Roderick Floud, *Health And Welfare During Industrialization* (Chicago: University of Chicago Press 1997), 4.

26 THE UNITED NATIONS USES [HEIGHT] TO MONITOR . . . Bilger, "Height Gap."

27 SEVENTY PERCENT OF DOCTOR'S OFFICE . . . T. H. Lipman et al., "A Multi-Centre Randomised Controlled Trial of an Intervention to Improve the Accuracy of Linear Growth Measurement," *Archives of Disease in Childhood* 89 (2004): 342–46.

27 THE NATIONAL INSTITUTES OF HEALTH HELD A WHOLE . . . Phyllis B. Eveleth, James M. Tanner, *Worldwide Variation in Human Growth* (Cambridge: Cambridge University Press, 1991), 22.

27 DOCTORS ARE TRAINED TO MEASURE THREE . . . Dennis M. Styne, *Pediatric Endocrinology* (Philadelphia: Lippincott Williams & Wilkins, 2004), 49.

27 THE MOST ACCURATE HEIGHT MEASUREMENT . . . H. Zhang et. al., "The Use of Knee Height to Estimate Maximum Stature in Elderly Chinese," *Journal of Nutritional Health and Aging* 2, no. 2 (1998): 84–87.

27 BUT ONLY ACADEMICS KNOW THIS . . . W.C. Chumlea et al., "Stature Prediction Equations for Elderly Non-Hispanic White, Non-Hispanic Black and Mexican-American Persons Developed from NHANES III Data," *Journal of the American Dietetic Association* 98, no. 2 (1998): 137–42.

27 DURING THE DAY PEOPLE LOSE 1 TO 2 PERCENT . . . A. R. Tyrrell et al., "Circadian Variation in Stature, and the Effects of Spinal Loading," *Spine* 10, no. 2 (1985): 161–64.

27 THE AVERAGE PERSON ALSO LOSES A HALF-INCH . . . J. R. McPherson et al., "Stature Change with Aging in Black Americans," *Journal of Gerontology* 33, no. 1 (1978): 20–25.

28 DUTCH HEIGHT EXPERT HANS VAN WIERINGEN . . . Bilger, "Height Gap."

28 IN 1865 DUTCH ARMY RECRUITS . . . Stenvert L. S. Drop et al., "Steroid Treatment of Constitutionally Tall Stature," *Endocrine Reviews* 19, no. 5 (1998): 540–58.

28 MAMMALS IN COLD CLIMATES TEND TO BE . . . These are the tenets of Allen's Rule (limbs) and Bergmann's Rule (trunk), cornerstones of zoology.

28 A 2000 DUTCH STUDY OF EUROPEAN HEIGHTS . . . A. E. Cavelaars et al., "Persistent Variations in Average Height Between Countries and Between Socioeconomic Groups," *Annals of Human Biology* 27, no. 4 (2000): 407–21.

30 AMERICANS STOPPED GROWING IN THE 1950S . . . John Komlos, Benjamin E. Lauderdale, "The Mysterious Stagnation and Relative Decline of American Heights in the Second Half of the 20th Century," *Annals of Human Biology* 43, no. 2 (2007): 206–15.

30 TODAY THE AVERAGE U.S. MAN . . . Cynthia L. Ogden et al., "Mean Body Weight, Height and Body Mass Index, United States 1960–2002," *Advance Data* 347(October 27, 2004): 10.

31 TALLS ARE FOUND WHEREVER CHILDHOOD . . . Barry Bogin, personal communication, March 2007.

31 OUR LIFE EXPECTANCY RANKING, 28th. Bilger "Height Gap."

31 WE'RE ALSO MALNOURISHED Komlos, Lauderdale, "Mysterious Stagnation and Relative Decline."

31 TWO-THIRDS OF U.S. CHILDREN ARE DEFICIENT . . . J. Komlos, Marieluise Baur, "From the Tallest to (One of) the Fattest," *Economics and Human Biology* 2, no. 1 (2004): 57–74.

31 A RECENT UNICEF REPORT RANKED THE UNITED STATES . . . Paul Krugman, "America Comes Up Short," *New York Times*, June 15, 2007.

32 THE GOVERNMENT MEASURES . . . National Institute of Public Health and National Insititute of Statistics, *Cambodia Demographic Health Survey 2005*, (December 2006), 184.

32 A QUARTER OF WOMEN ARE 4'10" . . . D. De Walque, "The Socio-Demographic Legacy of the Khmer Rouge Period in Cambodia," *Population Studies* 60, no. 2 (2006): 228.

32 THOSE WHO WERE YOUNG TEENS DURING THE WAR . . . Ibid., 223–31.

33 AT BIRTH EACH BABY, BASED ON A SIX YEAR ROTATION . . . Each baby also gets an "animal," such as a tiger or rat, and also a "material," such as wood or iron, which predict future accomplishments and temperament. But let's not confuse things.

Chapter 3. The Birth of Tall People

35 OUR PREDECESSORS, FIVE MILLION YEARS AGO . . . "Chimp-sized Hominid Walked Upright On Two Legs Six Million Years Ago," *ScienceDaily* (September 3, 2004), www.sciencedaily.com/releases/2004/09/040903085349.htm; and R. L. Stauffer et al., "Human and Ape

Molecular Clocks and Constraints on Paleontological Hypotheses,"
Journal of Heredity 92, no. 6 (2001): 469–74.

36   IN THE PROCESS OF FOOLING THE BIG CATS . . . This is posited by Darwin in
The Descent of Man.

36   SPECIES GROW UNTIL THEY EITHER . . . Joel Kingsolver and David Pfennig,
"Individual-level Selection as a Cause of Cope's Rule of Phyletic Size Increase," *Evolution* 58 (2004): 1608–12. Cope's Rule is the brainchild of
nineteenth century paleontologist Edward Drinker Cope. The idea was
discredited for a while, but is now back in vogue following recent fossil
studies. See Carl Zimmer, " 'Bigger is Better' View of Evolution Gains
Credence," *New York Times*, December 28, 2004.

36   THE TALL HUNTER-GATHERERS WHO COULD ADEPTLY . . . Barry Bogin, personal communication, May 2007.

37   EXPERTS HYPOTHESIZE THAT WOMEN . . . Ron Rosenfeld, pediatric endocrinologist, personal communication, February 2007.

37   TALLS BITE THE DUST Rebecca Sear et al., "Height, Marriage and Reproductive Success in Gambian Women," *Research in Economic Anthropology* 23 (2004): 203–24.

37   THE CRO-MAGNON PEOPLE . . . Barry Bogin, personal communication,
May 2007.

38   MALE CHEYENNE INDIANS WHO . . . Bilger, "Height Gap." Based on the
work of Franz Boas. See Stephen S. Hall, *Size Matters* (Boston: Houghton
Mifflin, 2006), 294.

38   GENERAL CUSTER'S CAVALRY . . . Scott Carson, University of Texas historical economist, personal communication, July 2007.

38   MORE RECENT STUDIES OF THE INDUSTRIALIZATION . . . John Komlos,
"Shrinking in a Growing Economy? The Mystery of Physical Stature
during the Industrial Revolution," *Journal of Economic History* 58, no. 3
(1998): 779–802.

38   WHEN GOODS SUDDENLY BECOME CHEAPER . . . Ibid; and Timothy Cuff, *The
Hidden Cost of Economic Development* (Aldershot, U.K., and Burlington,
Vt.: Ashgate, 2005).

38   CAESAR AND TACITUS . . . Hall, *Size Matters*, 14.

38   KING SAUL GOT HIS JOB . . . 1 Samuel 9:2.

38   AS ECONOMIST ROBERT FOGEL SAYS . . . Bilger, "Height Gap."

39   THE PARTICULARLY SWIFT HEIGHT PLUMMET . . . Richard Steckel, historical
economist at Ohio State University, personal communication, July 2007.

39   NINETEENTH-CENTURY BRITISH BABIES . . . This is the work of James Tanner. See Hall, *Size Matters*, 296.

40   KING FREDERICK WILLIAM I OF PRUSSIA . . . The tale is delightfully told
ibid., 170–172.

40   HE DEVELOPED WHAT ONE BIOGRAPHER . . . Robert Ergang, *The Potsdam
Führer* (New York: Columbia University Press, 1941), quoted ibid., 171.

42   MILITARIES HAVE ALWAYS RECORDED . . . Melvin Grumbach, personal
communication, February 2007. The extensive Dutch records are often
used in medical and historical research.

43   CALLED A YASSIS CURVE . . . *Yassis* stands for Yearly Average Sex and Age
      Specific Increase in Stature. *Yassis* also means "yuck" in Dutch, the re-
      search assistants' opinion of compiling tens of thousands of soldiers'
      heights by hand.

44   THE FATHER OF ANTHROPOMETRIC HISTORY . . . Anthropometry is quite
      old. Its presumed first use arose in *Anthropometria*, 1654, the graduate
      thesis of naturalist Johann Elsholtz, who connected bodily proportions
      to disease risk.

44   FOUR ACADEMICS PLEDGED TO PUT TOGETHER . . . Lydialyle Gibson, "The
      Human Equation," *University of Chicago Magazine*, May–June 2007.

44   AT PARTICULAR CONTENTION WAS HIS CLAIM . . . Fogel had developed his
      age 21 theory by simply subtracting childrens' ages from their mothers'
      on slave population records As critics pointed out, this method would
      inherently miss any lost pregnancies or baby deaths.

44   FOGEL FLED TO LONDON . . . In 1975 Fogel worked with Dr. James Tanner,
      the doyen of growth research, who confirmed Fogel's findings by com-
      paring them to modern pediatric data. Robert Fogel, personal commu-
      nication, June 2007.

45   BIRTH CERTIFICATES INDICATED THAT MOST . . . Theories abound about
      why female slaves were purposely not mated at the earliest fertility: Per-
      haps slaves didn't want their teenagers having babies, and owners went
      along to prevent rebellion. Or perhaps owners were concerned that
      early pregnancy stunted teen girls' growth (slaves' growth was delayed
      due to their childhood malnutrition), thereby limiting a woman's long-
      term productivity.

45   KOMLOS IS NOT TALL . . . Height researchers—a group manically de-
      tailed about height—are uniformly vague about their own heights.
      Fogel described himself as "5'11" in his twenties."

45   KOMLOS FOUND THAT EAST GERMAN GIRLS . . . J. Komlos, P. Kriwy, "Social
      Status and Adult Heights in the Two Germanies," *Annals of Human Bi-
      ology* 29, no. 6 (2002): 641–648.

46   THE STUDENTS AT THE ELITE ROYAL MILITARY ACADEMY . . . Paul Krugman,
      "America Comes Up Short," *New York Times*, June 15, 2007.

46   TO QUANTIFY AN EQUATION . . . This is a layperson's version of an equa-
      tion from a slide presentation prepared by John Komlos and Marco Sun-
      der. Marco Sunder, personal communication, May 2007.

46   STECKEL'S FINDINGS . . . Richard Steckel, personal communication, July
      2007.

47   EVOLUTIONARY PSYCHOLOGIST MARJAANA . . . Marjaana Lindeman, "Height
      and Our Perception of Others," in *Growth, Stature and Psychosocial Well-
      Being*, ed. Urs Eiholzer, et al. (Seattle: Hogrefe & Huber, 1999), 121–30.

Chapter 4. The Secret Life of the World's Tallest

53   CANADIAN ANNA SWAN . . . G. Brown et al., *Dictionary of Canadian Biography* (Toronto: University of Toronto Press, 1966), 865–66.

54   A GUY NAMED EDDIE CARMEL . . . Stacy Abramson, "The Jewish Giant," *All Things Considered*, National Public Radio, October 6, 1999.

57   TO GIVE YOU A SENSE OF HER MASS . . . "What Is Life Like for Sandy Allen, Who Is 7 Feet, 7 Inches Tall?" *20/20*, July 27, 2007.

57   IN HER FIRST LETTER TO GUINNESS . . . "Tallest Woman—Living," Guinness World Records, www.guinnessworldrecords.com/records/human_body/extreme_bodies/tallest_woman_-_living.aspx.

60   HE'S A MEDIA DARLING . . . "World's Tallest Man Saves Dolphin," BBC News, December 14, 2006. The aquarium manager got the idea from a similar feat by NBA player Clifford Ray, 6'9", who saved a dolphin at Marine World in California in 1978.

60   XISHUN GAINED FURTHER ATTENTION . . . "World's Tallest Man Gets Married," BBC News, March 28, 2007.

60   THOUGH HE UNDERWENT PITUITARY SURGERY . . . "Gentle Giant Needs Urgent Surgery," *Age*, May 3, 2004; "Ukrainian Vet Declared World's Tallest Man," Agence France-Presse, August 9, 2007.

60   STADNYK IS ALSO A CONTENDER . . . Sabina Zawadzki, "Hard Life and Isolation for World's Tallest Man," Reuters, August 12, 2007.

Chapter 5. A Brief Interruption for a Tall People Convention

69   THE CALIFORNIA KING MATTRESS . . . Tall Clubs International, "About TCI," http://tall.org/about_tcifoundr.cfm?CFID=591265&XΦTOKEN=92298974.

69   EINFELDT MET HER HUSBAND, GEORGE, . . . Ibid.

Chapter 6. Growing Up Tall

76   EVEN TODAY HARRY POTTER'S HALF WIZARD . . . J. K. Rowling, *Harry Potter and the Sorcerer's Stone* (London: Bloomsbury, 1997), 46–9.

77   GULLIVER IS BAFFLED . . . Jonathan Swift, *Gulliver's Travels* (New York: Penguin Classics, 2003), 31.

79   PUBERTY IS DELAYED . . . D. Nettle, "Women's Height, Reproductive Success and the Evolution of Sexual Dimorphism in Modern Humans," *Proceedings of the Royal Society of London* 269 (2002): 1919–23.

80   TEEN TEASING IS BASED . . . S. Leff, "Bullied Children Are Picked On for Their Vulnerability," *British Medical Journal* 318 (April 1999): 1076.

80   EVEN TEASED BABOONS . . . Stephen S. Hall, *Size Matters* (Boston: Houghton Mifflin, 2006), 163.

Chapter 7. Sports

85   A HANDFUL OF CENTERS ARE SUPER TALL . . . Brook Larmer, "The Creation
      of Yao Ming," *Time Asia*, November 7, 2005.

86   GABRIELLE REECE, THE 6'3" BEACH . . . Karen Karbo, "The Übergirl
      Cometh," *Outside*, October 1995.

86   MID-ATLANTIC TROOPS AVERAGED . . . Brian A'Hearn, "The Antebellum
      Puzzle Revisited," in ed. John Komlos, Joerg Baten, *The Biological Stan-
      dard of Living in Comparative Perspective*, (Shottgart: Franz Steiner Ver-
      lag, 1998), 263.

86   NUMEROUS HEALTH PROBLEMS—VISION LOSS . . . Gina Kolata, "So Big and
      Healthy Grandpa Wouldn't Even Know You," *New York Times*, July 30,
      2007.

87   AS LORI SMITH, THEN NIKE'S . . . Karbo, "Übergirl Cometh."

88   AS REECE PUT IT . . . Ibid.

89   TALLER PEOPLE ARE MUCH LESS STRONG . . . T. Tuvemo et al., "Intellectual
      and Physical Performance and Morbidity in Relation to Height in a Co-
      hort of 18-year-old Swedish Conscripts," *Hormone Research* 52, no. 4
      (1999): 186–91.

Chapter 8. On the Job, Counting Greenbacks

94   WHEN TWO SALESMEN CANDIDATES . . . D. L. Kurtz, "Physical Appearance
      and Stature," *Personnel Journal* 48 (1969): 981–83.

94   THE SAME IS TRUE FOR SCHOOL PRINCIPALS . . . C. A. Bonuso, "Body Type
      A Factor in Hiring School Leaders," *Phi Delta Kappan* no. 64 (1983), 374.

95   TALL WORKERS ARE INSTINCTIVELY PERCEIVED . . . L. A. Jackson, K. S.
      Ervin, "Height Stereotypes of Women and Men," *Journal of Social Psy-
      chology* 132 (1992): 433–45.

95   TALL WOMEN IN PARTICULAR . . . Simon Chu, Kathryn Geary, "Physical
      Stature Influences Character Perception in Women," *Personality and In-
      dividual Differences* 38, no. 8 (June 2005): 1927–34.

95   TALL POLICE OFFICERS' NEW SUPERVISORS . . . D. Lester, D. Sheehan, "Atti-
      tudes of Supervisor Toward Short Police Officers," *Psychological Reports*
      47 (1980): 462.

95   LOOKED AT SEVENTY-ONE WORKPLACE STUDIES . . . Timothy Judge and
      Daniel Cable, "The Effect of Physical Height on Workplace Success and
      Income," *Journal of Applied Psychology* 89, no. 3 (2004): 428–41.

95   TALLS ARE PERCEIVED AS BETTER WORKERS . . . W. E. Hensley, "Height as a
      Measure of Success in Academe," *Psychology: A Journal of Human Be-
      havior* 30 (1993): 40–46.

95   THE BOSSES HEAVILY FAVORED THE TALLER . . . M. Lindeman, L. Sundvik,
      "Impact of Height on Assessments of Finnish Female Job Applicants'
      Managerial Abilities," *Journal of Social Psychology* 134, no. 2 (April 1994):
      169–74.

95   MARJAANA LINDEMAN . . . Marjaana Lindeman, "Height and Our Perception of Others," in *Growth, Stature and Psychosocial Well-being,* ed. Urs Eiholzer, et al. (Seattle: Hogrefe & Huber, 1999), 124.

96   A STUDY OF ACCOUNTING FIRMS . . . J. Ross, K. R. Ferris, "Interpersonal Attraction and Organizational Outcomes," *Administrative Science Quarterly* 26, no. 4 (December 1981): 617–32.

96   TALL INCOME PER INCH TICKS . . . Judge and Cable, "Effect of Physical Height on Workplace Success."

96   A DISTINCTION SHARED BY . . . U.S. Census Bureau, *Statistical Abstract of the United States 2003: Cumulative Percent Distribution of Population by Height and Sex: 1988–94,* 140. Of men ages 30–39, 98.1% are 6'3" or lower.

96   AND ROUGHLY 58 PERCENT OF FUTURE 500 . . . Based on a poll of half of all Fortune 500 CEOs. Malcolm Gladwell, *Blink: The Power of Thinking Without Thinking* (New York: Little, Brown, 2005), 86–87.

96   A THIRTY-YEAR STUDY OF A WEST POINT CLASS . . . Allan Mazur et al., "Military Rank Attainment of a West Point Class," *American Journal of Sociology* 90, no. 1 (July 1984): 125–50.

97   COLIN'S CO-WORKERS GIVE HIM ONE OR TWO FEET . . . Gender researchers are quite interested in personal space because it potentially explains why CEOs are mostly male. People give more space to men than women. The gender difference likely has more to do with height than with women being perceived as weak, says Judy Hall.

99   AS THE WASHINGTON POST PUTS IT . . . Jay Mathews, "The Shrinking Field," *Washington Post,* August 3, 1999.

99   IN 1866 SENATORS AVERAGED . . . Ralph Keyes, *The Height of Your Life* (New York: Warner Books, 1982), 218.

99   TODAY AMERICAN MALE SENATORS AVERAGE . . . Ibid.

103   THERE, TALLS TEND TO MAKE MORE . . . Judge and Cable, "Effect of Physical Height on Workplace Success."

104   THE ODDS OF A MAN WORKING IN SECURITY . . . Anne Case, Christina Paxson, "Stature and Status," *NBER Working Paper Series,* August 2006, 29.

104   BURT REYNOLDS (A DEBATABLE 5'9") . . . Roger Ebert, "What Kind of Playmate is Burt?" *New York Times* March 26, 1972.

106   THE SMITHSONIAN HAS A PHOTO OF HER . . . Photo from 1949. On display online at http://americanhistory.si.edu/juliachild.

107   HER SHOWS ARE AN ADVERTISEMENT . . . Child was among the first of a slew of tall women in media, such as Martha Stewart (5'10"), with a sense of presence and large features. Television plays to larger heads that have expressive eyes and mouths, features naturally attached to taller bodies.

$: A Word on the Costs of Height

109   A TONGUE-IN-CHEEK 2007 PAPER . . . N. Gregory Mankiw, Matthew Weinzierl, "The Optimal Taxation of Height," Working Paper, April 13, 2007.

Chapter 9. Genes, Hormones, and Luck

114 THE VERY FIRST HEIGHT GENE WAS . . . "Scientists Discover Height Gene," BBC News, September 3, 2007.

114 IT CONTROLS THE RELEASE OF A GROWTH HORMONE . . . Nathan B. Sutter et al., "A Single IGF-1 Allele Is a Major Determinant of Small Size in Dogs," *Science* 6 (April 2007): 112–15.

114 THE EXCEPTION IS CHILDREN . . . M. Tauber et. al., "Growth Hormone Secretion in Children and Adolescents with Familial Tall Stature," *European Journal of Pediatrics* 153, no. 5 (May 1994): 311–16.

115 AND SOMETIMES HIGHER LEVELS OF HGH . . . R. G. Rosenfeld, E. O. Reiter, "Normal and Aberrant Growth," in *Williams Textbook of Endocrinology*, 10th ed, (Philadelphia: Sanders, 2003), 1078.

115 WE DO KNOW THAT TALL KIDS PUMP THEM . . . P. Rochiccioli et al., "Correlation of the Parameters of 24-hour Growth Hormone Secretion with Growth Velocity in 93 Children of Varying Height," *Hormone Research* 31, no. 1 (1989): 115–18.

115 GROWTH IS A SPRINGTIME THING . . . Stephen S. Hall, *Size Matters* (Boston: Houghton Mifflin, 2006), 82 and 133.

115 ABOUT 20 PERCENT OF HEIGHT DIFFERENCES . . . Anne Case, Christina Paxson, "Stature and Status," *NBER Working Paper Series*, August 2006.

115 THE OTHER 80 PERCENT . . . K. Silventoinen, "Determinants of Variation in Adult Body Height," *Journal of Biosocial Sciences* 35, no. 2 (2003): 263–85. This paper reviewed a number of height studies, predominantly twin studies.

115 DURING THE DUTCH HUNGER WINTER . . . Sara Stinson, "Growth Variation," in Sara Stinson et al., eds, *Human Biology* (New York: Wiley-Liss, 2000), 438.

116 AS EPIDEMIOLOGIST DAVID BARKER . . . Hall, *Size Matters*, 40.

116 BRITISH DIETING GIRL IS NOT HAVING A SUPER TALL . . . M. Hack et al., "Growth in Very Low Birth Weight Infants to Age 20 Years," *Pediatrics* 112 (July 2003): e30–38; Stinson, "Growth Variation," 439.

116 BABIES ARE THE HEAVIEST . . . Hall, *Size Matters*, 43.

116 ACTUALLY, NEWBORN SIZE HAS ALMOST . . . Barry Bogin, *The Growth of Humanity* (New York: Wiley-Liss, 2001), 71.

116 ECOLOGIST REBECCA SEAR . . . Rebecca Sear et al., "Height, Marriage and Reproductive Success in Gambian Women," *Research in Economic Anthropology* 23 (2004): 203–24.

116 IMMUNIZATIONS ARE KEY TO HEIGHT . . . Melvin Grumbach. Personal communication, February 2007.

116 KIDS WHO ARE SICK OR MALNOURISHED . . . Stinson, "Growth Variation," 439. One example of catch up growth is the mildly malnourished Turkana people of Kenya. Most lag below the American 50th percentile as children, but then at age sixteen, when U.S. girls stop growing, Turkana speed ahead for 2.5 years, ending up nearly the same size.

117 ONCE IN THE THREE-YEAR PUBERTY . . . Naomi Neufeld, personal communication, February 2007; Hall, *Size Matters*, 144.

117 THE TROUBLE IS THAT THIS IS A BALL PARK . . . Z. C. Luo, et al, "Target
Height As Predicted by Parental Heights in a Population-Based Study,"
Pediatric Research 44, no. 4 (October 1998): 563–71.

117 GROWTH EXPERT JAMES TANNER ALSO HYPOTHESIZES . . . Phyllis B.
Eveleth, James M. Tanner, *Worldwide Variation in Human Growth* (Cambridge, U.K.: Cambridge University Press, 1991), 202.

117 A 2007 STUDY FOUND THAT ON AVERAGE . . . Ian Sample, "Study Reveals
How Having An Older Brother Can Make You Shorter," *Guardian*, September 13, 2007.

117 THE DEVELOPING WORLD, WHERE BIG AGRICULTURAL . . . Stinson, "Growth
Variation," 434.

118 BY AGE FIVE THE CHILDREN . . . R. H. Rona et al., "Social Factors and
Height of Primary Schoolchildren in England and Scotland," *Journal of
Epidemiological Community Health* 32, no. 3 (1978): 147–54. This has
been shown in many studies. See Eveleth and Tanner, *Worldwide Variation in Human Growth*, 199.

118 AND YES, BOARDING SCHOOL KIDS GROW MORE . . . Eveleth and Tanner,
Worldwide Variation in Human Growth, 204–05.

118 BUT CHILDREN GROWING UP IN SEVERELY POLLUTED . . . Stinson, "Growth
Variation," 434.

118 LAWRENCE SCHELL HAS FOUND . . . Ibid.

118 AS ONE DOCTOR'S MANUAL EXPLAINED . . . Rosenfeld and Reiter, "Normal
and Aberrant Growth," 1078.

119 EXERCISE STIMULATES GROWTH PLATES . . . Hall, *Size Matters*, 72.

Chapter 10. Tall Health

122 WOMEN ABOVE 5'7" HAVE A 110 PERCENT . . . Demetrius Albanes et al.,
"Adult Stature and Risk of Cancer," *Cancer Research* 48, no. 6 (1988):
1658–62; Phyllis B. Eveleth, James M. Tanner. *Worldwide Variation in Human Growth* (Cambridge: Cambridge University Press, 1991), 210.

122 VERY TALL MEN HOST AT LEAST 30 PERCENT . . . George Davey Smith,
"Height and Mortality from Cancer Among Men," *British Medical Journal* 317, no. 7169 (November 1998): 1351–52.

122 AN 84TH PERCENTILE CHILD HAS A 126 PERCENT . . . D. J. Gunnell, "Leg
Length and Risk of Cancer in the Boyd Orr Cohort," *British Medical
Journal* 317, no. 7169 (1998): 1350–51.

123 TALL MALE CANCER RATES (CHART) . . . The chart combines data from
several large-scale studies: Ibid; G.D. Batty, et al, "Adult Height in relation to Mortality from 14 Cancer Sites in Men in London." *Annals of Oncology* 17, no. 1 (2006): 157–66; G. D. Smith et al, "Height and Risk of
Death Among Men and Women"; Patricia R. Herbert et al, "Adult
Height and Incidence of Cancer in Male Physicians," *Cancer Causes and*

Control 8, no. 6 (1996):591–597; Albanes, "Adult Stature and Risk of Cancer."

123 STOMACH–8 PERCENT . . . The low stomach cancer rate is a function of the fact that short people have higher stomach cancer rates.

123 PROSTATE 7–27 PERCENT (CHART) . . . A range is given because several studies have come up with varying figures. The most well regarded is a study of 22,071 male physicians which found that 6'0" men are 59 percent more likely to get prostate cancer than 5'8" men. Patricia R. Herbert et al, "Adult Height and Incidence of Cancer in Male Physicians"; Luisa Zuccolo et al, "Height and Risk of Prostate Cancer," *Cancer Epidemiology Biomarkers and Prevention* 17 (September 1, 2008):2325–36; "Prostrate Cancer Risk for Tall Men," BBC News, February 22, 2003.

123 COLON 3–25 PERCENT (CHART) . . . Here, also, several large scale studies have produced widely varying figures. Patricia Herbert's study of 22,071 doctors found 6'0" men to be 59% more likely to get colon cancer than 5'8" men.

123 I CALL THE FIRST THE TALL EATING THEORY . . . D. Albanes, "Height, Early Energy Intake and Cancer," *British Medical Journal* 317, no. 7169 (1998): 1331–32.

124 TALL CALORIC INTAKE (CHART) . . . The caloric estimates came from exercise nutritionist, Nancy Clark, personal communication, January 2007.

124 AS A REVIEW IN THE *BRITISH* . . . D. Albanes, "Height, Early Energy Intake and Cancer."

124 HUMAN STUDIES HAVE SHOWN CANCER RATES . . . S. Tretli, M. Gaard, "Lifestyle Changes During Adolescence and Risk of Breast Cancer," *Cancer Causes Control* 7 (1996): 507–12.

124 AND RODENT STUDIES . . . Valter Longo, Caleb Finch, "Evolutionary Medicine: From Dwarf Model Systems to Healthy Centenarians?" *Science* 299, no. 5611 (February 2003): 1342–46.

124 MANY SCIENTISTS POINT TO IGF-I . . . Gunnell, "Leg Length and Risk of Cancer."

124 HIGH IGF-I LEVELS IN HUMANS . . . Michael N. Pollak, et al., "Insulin-like Growth Factors and Neoplasia," *Nature Reviews* 4, no. 7 (July 2004): 505–18.

125 PEOPLE WHO EAT A LOT ARE EXPOSED . . . D. Albanes, "Height, Early Energy Intake and Cancer."

125 ANIMAL-DERIVED FOODS . . . L. Aksgladede, "The Sensitivity of the Child to Sex Steroids," *Human Reproduction Update* 12, no. 4 (July 2006): 341–49.

125 THE SECOND TALL CANCER THEORY . . . Ibid.; Gunnell, "Leg Length and Risk of Cancer."

125 RESEARCHERS HAVE FOUND THAT TWO GROUPS . . . A. Stoll, "Western Diet, Early Puberty and Breast Cancer Risk," *Breast Cancer Research and Treatment* 49, no. 3 (June 1998): 187–93.

125 TALL MEN HAVE MORE ESTROGEN EXPOSURE . . . "Prostate Cancer Risk For Tall Men," BBC News, February 22, 2003. Prostate cancer is frequently

a cancer of old age—which requires living a long time, which tall people do.

125 SIMILARLY, A 2001 BRITISH JOURNAL . . . L. Hilakivi-Clark et al., "Tallness and Overweight During Childhood Have Opposing Effects on Breast Cancer Risk," *British Journal of Cancer* 85 (2001): 1680–84.

125 A THIRD HYPOTHESIS, THE MORE CELLS THEORY D. Albanes, M. Winick, "Are Cell Number and Cell Proliferation Risk Factors for Cancer?" *Journal of the National Cancer Institute* 80 (1988): 772–75.

126 IN ACTUALITY, IT'S SHORT PEOPLE . . . Nieca Goldberg, cardiologist and medical director of the New York University Women's Heart Program, personal communication, May 2007.

127 IMAGINE THE BLOOD GOING FROM HEART . . . H. S. Badeer, "Does Gravitational Pressure of Blood Hinder Flow to the Brain of the Giraffe?" *Biochemical Physiology* 83, no. 2 (1986): 207–11.

127 BOTH BLACKOUTS AND FAINTING ARE . . . Ben Levine, personal communication.

127 OSTEOARTHRITIS IS A DISEASE OF TALLS . . . V. B. Vad, A. L. Bhat, "The Athlete with Early Knee Arthritis," *Physical Medicine and Rehabilitation Clinics of North America* 11, no. 4 (November 2000): 881–94.

Chapter 11. Tall Treatments

129 I MADE MY FIRST APPEARANCE . . . I've since learned that boys visiting the endocrinologist have a much more invasive encounter with an orchidometer, a ring of calibrated balls (literally) meant to gauge testicular volume. I had no idea my visits were so comparatively easy.

129 HORSE-SIZE DOSES OF ESTROGEN . . . Estrogen is a group of sex hormones, primarily estradiol, estriol and estrone. Throughout the book I often say just *estrogen.*

129 ESTROGEN HEIGHT-REDUCTION TREATMENT IS COMMON . . . Rosenfeld and Reiter, "Normal and Aberrant Growth," 1077. The best estimate of how many girls and boys have been treated is tens-to-hundreds of thousands. A lot.

130 A SIMILAR TESTOSTERONE TREATMENT . . . Melvin Grumbach, personal communication, February 2007. The male body breaks down testosterone with an enzyme called aromatase into estradiol, a form of estrogen, which closes the growth plates identically to the girls' treatment.

130 QUETELET DISCOVERED THAT HUMAN HEIGHT . . . Hall, *Size Matters,* 54–58. Hall writes a nice summary of Quetelet and Galton.

130 THE FIRST NATIONAL HEIGHT AND WEIGHT STANDARDS . . . These are the late-nineteenth-century work of Franz Boas.

133 THEY SURMISED THAT ESTROGEN MUST BE THE CAUSE . . . Stenvert L. S. Drop et al., "Sex Steroid Treatment of Constitutionally Tall Stature," *Endocrine Reviews* 19, no. 5 (1998): 546.

133   A DECADE LATER A TEXAS DOCTOR . . . Rosenfeld and Reiter, "Normal and Aberrant Growth," 1077.

133   A HANDFUL OF DOCTORS AND CLINICS . . . A few variations on estrogen were used with widely varying dosages, some including progesterone to cue monthly menstruation. Some early treatments used stilbestrol. They were soon halted because stilbestrol induced carcinoma of the vagina in unrelated treatments. Most doctors settled on oral ethinal estradiol.

134   ONE STUDY CLASSIFIED THE TREATMENTS . . . G. Binder et al., "Outcome in Tall Stature," *European Journal of Pediatrics* 156, no. 12 (1997): 905–10.

135   IN EUROPE STARTING IN THE 1960S . . . Drop et al., "Sex Steroid Treatment of Constitutionally Tall Stature," 546.

135   IN 1977 HEIGHT-REDUCTION TREATMENTS HIT . . . Joyce M. Lee, "Tall Girls," *Archives of Pediatric Adolescent Medicine* 160 (2006): 1035–39.

135   EXACTLY HALF OF THE U.S. DOCTORS . . . Felix Conte, Melvin Grumbach, "Estrogen Use in Children and Adolescents," *Pediatrics* 62, no. 6 (1978): 1091–97.

136   FIRST CAME WORD THAT ESTROGEN . . . Neal D. Barnard, "The Current Use of Estrogens for Growth-Suppressant Therapy in Adolescent Girls," *Journal of Pediatric Adolescent Gynecology* 15, no. 1 (2002): 23–26.

136   A 2003 STUDY OF 1,423 AUSTRALIANS . . . A. Venn et al., "Oestrogen Treatment to Reduce the Adult Height of Tall Girls," *Lancet* 364 (2004): 1513–18.

136   OVARIAN, UTERINE, AND BREAST CANCERS . . . Lise Aksglaede et al., "The Sensitivity of the Child to Sex Steroids," *Human Reproduction Update* 12, no. 4 (2006): 341–49.

136   THE WHOLE RATIONALE BEHIND THE TREATMENT . . . Drop et al., "Sex Steroid Treatment of Constitutionally Tall Stature." As Drop puts it, "Treatment of tall stature is generally based on psychological grounds. From a strict medical point of view, there is no reason for treatment. Therefore, the validity and necessity for treatment are questionable."

136   EXTENSIVE PSYCHOLOGICAL INVESTIGATION . . . Ibid.

136   IN 2003 ELI LILLY RAN STUDIES TO PROVE . . . Hall, *Size Matters*, 243.

137   AS A 2007 STUDY PUT IT . . . Drop et al., "Sex Steroid Treatment of Constitutionally Tall Stature," 552. Other researchers wrote, "of particular concern is the potential contribution to hormone-related malignancy." Neal D. Barnard et al., "The Current Use of Estrogens for Growth-Suppressant Therapy, 23–26.

137   IN A 2002 SURVEY OF 411 U.S. ENDOCRINOLOGISTS . . . Ibid Barnard.

137   IN SWITZERLAND IT'S NOT UNUSUAL . . . Primus Mullis, pediatric endocrinologist at the University Children's Hospital in Bern, Switzerland personal communication. Mullis personally prefers to treat boys estimated over 6'9" and girls predicted 6'5" and above.

138   A 2002 STUDY OUT OF GERMANY . . . R. Decker, et al., "Combined Treatment with Testosterone and Ethinylestradiol in Constitutionally Tall Boys," *Journal of Clinical Endocrinology and Metabolism* 87, no. 4 (2002): 1634–39.

138　In a 1991 study of 539 norwegian girls . . . E.K. Normann et al, "Height Reduction in 539 Tall Girls Treated with Different Dosages of Ethinylestradiol," *Archives of Disease in Childhood*, 66 (1991): 1275–8.

138　In a similar finnish study . . . A. Ignatius et al, "Oestrogen Treatment of Tall Girls," *Acta Paediatrica Scandinavica*, 80 (1991): 712–7.

139　The leg-sawing operation . . . Richard Jones, "The Height of Vanity," *Marie Claire*, May 2003, 92–98.

139　The cornerstone study is from 2006 . . . Roelof J. Odink et al., "Reduction of Excessive Height in Boys by Bilateral Percutaneous Epiphysiodesis Around the Knee," *European Journal of Pediatrics* 165, no. 1 (2006): 50–54.

139　Another, with six boys . . . V. F. Plaschaert et al., "Bilateral Epiphysiodesis Around the Knee as Treatment for Excessive Height in Boys," *Journal of Pediatric Orthopedics* 6, no. 3 (July 1997): 212–14.

140　Other have suggested that instead . . . Drop et al., "Sex Steroid Treatment of Constitutionally Tall Stature."

140　How do you deliver the message . . . Louhiala, "How Tall Is Too Tall?"

140　A 2005 australian study found . . . Priscilla Pryett et al., "Using Hormone Treatment to Reduce the Adult Height of Tall Girls" *Social Science and Medicine* 61, no. 8 (October 2005): 1629–39.

140　One german study . . . P. Louhiala, "How Tall Is Too Tall? On the Ethics of Oestrogen," *Journal of Medical Ethics*, 33 (2007): 48–50. A thought-provoking paper that refers to the German-language study.

140　The pills were never really about . . . Lee, "Tall Girls" 1035–39.

141　Just under half of treated women . . . Pyett et al., "Using Hormone Treatment to Reduce the Adult Height of Tall Girls." The 2005 survey of 844 Australian women found that 42.1 percent of the treated women were unhappy with their decision, due to negative experiences or suspicions of ongoing health effects. And 99.1 percent of those who chose to not be treated were happy with their choice.

Chapter 12. In a Box of One

145　To be big and tall . . . Helen Simpson, "Costume Drama," *New Yorker*, November 15, 1999, 88.

147　People who grow up . . . John Updike, "At War with my Skin," *Self-Consciousness* (Robbinsdale, Minn.: Fawcett, 1990), 45.

150　Sure enough, in the analogous . . . Jan J.V. Busschbach et al., "Some Patients with Idiopathic Short Stature See Their Short Stature as a Problem, but Others Do Not," in *Growth, Stature, and Psychosocial Well-Being*, ed. Urs Eiholzer et al. (Seattle: Hogrefe & Huber: 1999), 27–36.

152　A dutch study of short adults . . . Ibid., 34.

152　Teenage girls who don't like . . . F. J. Bruinsma et al., "Concern About Tall Stature During Adolescence and Depression in Later Life," *Journal of Affective Disorders* 91, (nos. 2–3) (April 2006): 145–52.

153 RATE THE LIKEABILITY OF EVERYONE . . . David E. Sandberg et al., "Height and Social Adjustment," *Pediatrics* 114 (2004): 744–50.

Chapter 13. Into the Bedroom

157 PAWLOWSKI LOOKED AT COUPLING HABITS . . . Boguslaw Pawlowski, "Variable Preferences for Sexual Dimorphism in Height as a Strategy for Increasing the Pool of Potential Partners in Humans," *Biological Sciences* 270, no. 1516 (April 2003): 709–12.

157 MOST PEOPLE COUPLE WITHIN THEIR OWN HEIGHT RANGE . . . B. Pawlowski, "The Biological Meaning of Preferences on the Human Mate Market," *Anthropological Review* 63 (2000): 52.

158 WHEN SHORT WOMEN ARE OVULATING . . . Boguslaw Pawlowski, Grazyna Jasienska, "Women's Preferences for Sexual Dimorphism in Height Depend on Menstrual Cycle Phase and Expected Duration of Relationship," *Biological Psychology* 70, no. 1 (September 2005): 38–43.

158 A STUDY OF 22,000 DATING ADS . . . Guenter Hitsch et al., "What Makes You Click? Mate Preferences and Matching Outcomes in Online Dating," *MIT Sloan Research Paper*, No. 4603–06, February 2006.

158 WITH ALL THESE HOT DATES . . . Pawlowski found tall men's reproductive success by looking at medical records of 4,401 Polish men. B. Pawlowski, et al., "Tall Men Have More Reproductive Success," *Nature* 403, no. 6766 (January 2000): 156.

158 ONCE MARRIED . . . MEN AT EVERY SIZE . . . Pawlowski, "Biological Meaning of Preferences on Human Mate Market," 51.

158 A BRITISH STUDY FOUND THAT RARE IS . . . Daniel Nettle, "Women's Height, Reproductive Success and the Evolution of Sexual Dimorphism in Modern Humans," *Proceedings of the Royal Society of Biological Sciences* 269, no. 1503 (September 22, 2002): 1919–23.

159 EXTREMELY TALL MEN ABOVE AROUND 6'5" . . . Pawlowski, "Biological Meaning of Preferences on Human Mate Market," 52.

159 THE MAJOR SPERM BANKS . . . Jennifer Egan, "Wanted: Few Good Sperm," *New York Times Sunday Magazine*, March 19, 2006.

159 THE RESEARCHERS OF THE DATING AD STUDY . . . Hitsch et al., "What Makes You Click?"

160 IN ONLINE DATING ADS A 6'3" WOMAN . . . Pawlowski, "Biological Meaning of Preferences on Human Mate Market."

160 A STUDY OF 720 AMERICAN COUPLES . . . J.S. Gillis and W. Avis, "The Male-Taller Norm in Mate Selection," *Personality and Social Psychology Bulletin* 3 (1980): 396–401.

160 SIMILAR RESULTS CAME FROM THE . . . Nettle, "Women's Height, Reproductive Success and the Evolution of Sexual Dimorphism in Modern Humans."

160 THE BRITISH BIOLOGIST DAVID NETTLE . . . Ibid.

161 TALL WOMEN ARE A BETTER BET . . . Rebecca Sear et al., "Height, Marriage and Reproductive Success in Gambian Women," *Research in Economic Anthropology* 23 (2004): 203–24.

161 TALL AFRICAN WOMEN DO INDEED HAVE . . . R. Sear, "Height and Reproductive Success: How a Gambian Population Compares to the West," *Human Nature* 17, no. 4 (2006): 405–18.

162 SEAR THINKS MEN'S SPURNING OF TALL WOMEN . . . Sear, Allal, and Mace, "Height, Marriage and Reproductive Success in Gambian Women"; Sear, "Height and Reproductive Success."

162 NOT SURPRISINGLY, WHEN POLLED, MEN SAY THEY . . . Simon Chu, Kathryn Geary, "Physical Stature Influences Character Perception in Women," *Personality and Individual Differences* 38, no. 8 (2005): 1927–34.

164 IN GAMBIA IT'S NOT SO MUCH THAT MEN . . . Sear "Height, Marriage and Reproductive Success in Gambian Women"; Sear, "Height and Reproductive Success."

165 NOT SURPRISINGLY, WHEN PEOPLE CHOOSE MATES . . . Hitsch, et al., "What Makes You Click?"

165 IN A ROOM FULL OF CLASSMATES . . . C. G. Mascie-Taylor, "Assortative Mating in a Contemporary British Population," *Annals of Human Biology* 14, no. 1 (1987): 59–68.

165 A FINNISH STUDY OF 2,100 TWINS . . . Karri Silventoinen et al., "Assortative Mating by Body Height and BMI," *American Journal of Human Biology* 15, no. 5 (September–October 2003): 620–27.

Chapter 14. The Tall Fetish

171 FETISH N. SOMETHING . . . A fetish can also be an inanimate object, but that's another book.

Chapter 15. Retail Therapy

180 THE U.S. MARKET FOR TALL CLOTHING . . . "Men's Apparel by Size Dollars, June 2006–June 2007," NPD Research Group Report.

182 CASUAL MALE XL WAS ONCE . . . David Kiley, "Casual Male Goes XL," *Business Week*, April 3, 2006.

182 TALL MEN'S STORES ARE ALSO MUCH . . . Marie Leone, "A Casual Turnaround," *CFO*, June 20, 2006; Casual Male, *Annual Report 2006*, p. 5.

183 THIS IS WHY MALE TALL STORES ACCOUNT FOR . . . "Men's Apparel by Size Dollars, July 2006-June 2007" NPD Research Group Report.

183 WOMEN TYPICALLY SPEND TWICE WHAT MEN DO . . . "Men's Clothing Sales Up," Associated Press, August 12, 2008, citing NPD Research Group figure that two-thirds of the $155 billion clothing market is women's.

183   AND UNLIKE THE PLUS-SIZE MARKET, WHERE CUSTOMERS . . . Cotton, Inc. "Tall Tales," *Lifestyle Monitor*, August 16, 2001.

186   CASUAL MALE XL'S ANNUAL REPORT IS QUITE BLUNT . . . Casual Male, *Annual Report 2006*, p. 11.

Chapter 16. The Fitting Manifesto

191   THE HEALTH RISKS OF NOT FITTING ARE . . . "Ergonomics and Computer Use," Princeton University Health Services. http://Princeton.edu/uhs/ih_q_a_ergonomics.html.

192   THEN THERE ARE THE ACCIDENTS . . . J.F.M. Molenbroek, *Made to Measure*, Ph.D. thesis, Delft University of Technology, 1994, 287. Also published as a book in Dutch.

192   ECONOMY-CLASS SYNDROME . . . "Economy Class Syndrome and Deep Vein Thrombosis," American Heart Association, http://americanheart.org/presenter.jhtml?identifier=3010041.

193   NO SAFETY REGULATIONS FORCE THEM . . . The International Air Transport Association also doesn't have any regulations on seat spacing. Steve Lott, IATA head of North American Communications, personal communication, July 11, 2007.

194   AIRLINES ARE ACTIVELY CHOOSING . . . U.S. Department of Transportation, Office of the Secretary, "Order of Dismissal to the Petition for Rulemaking of the Tall Club of Silicon Valley," Docket OST 2001–8991, July 29, 2002, 4. Airlines "compete on the basis of lower fares made possible in part by omitting service features offered by other airlines, such as more legroom or meals."

195   EXTRA BODY WEIGHT REDUCES THEIR PROFITS . . . Elizabeth Cohen, "Obesity in the Skies," CNN, September 14, 2006. For safety purposes, the FAA estimates passengers and their shoes, clothing, and wallets at 190 pounds each, assuming that they actually weight less. Many talls weigh more.

195   [DELTA] TOOK THREE WEEKS . . . Emily Crawford, spokesperson for Delta Airlines, personal communication, July 10, 2007.

195   AMERICAN AIRLINES . . . MADE THE SAME . . . Tim Wagner, spokesperson for American Airlines, personal communication, July 5, 2007.

195   UNITED AIRLINES CLAIMED . . . Jeffery Kovick, spokesperson, United Airlines, personal communication, June 29, 2007.

196   A 10 PERCENT INCREASE IN FEMUR LENGTH . . . Richard Steckel, "New Light on the Dark Ages," *Social Science History* 28, no. 2 (Summer 2004): 211–29.

196   THE CLUB FILED LAWSUITS . . . Court of Appeal of the State of California First Appellate District Division Four, *Tall Club of Silicon Valley v. Alaska Airlines et al.*, February 27, 2004.

196   THE DEPARTMENT OF TRANSPORTATION SAID . . . U.S. Department of Transportation, Office of the Secretary, "Order of Dismissal to the Petition for Rulemaking of the Tall Club of Silicon Valley," Docket OST 2001–8991, July 29, 2002, 4.

199 THE ADA IS A VERY NECESSARY . . . The ADA Accessibility Guidelines for Buildings and Facilities. See www.access-board.gov/gs.htm. They inadvertently are quite explanatory of many tall fitting issues.

200 THE SAE GUIDELINES . . . Society of Automotive Engineers International, *Surface Vehicle Recommended Practice* (2003): 1–5.

201 MOLENBROEK RAN AN EXPERIMENT . . . Molenbroek, *Made to Measure*.

202 THE NEEDS OF TALLS . . . Ibid., 286.

202 SINCE THEN THE DEFAULT SIZE . . . Ibid., 288.

205 I MADE A CHART . . . Chart inspired by ibid., 293.

207 I SPENT MY LAST NINE YEARS . . . I should say that for all of Europe's forward-thinking on universal design, much of the continent has lagged in disability accessibility. The Dutch are only recently installing wheelchair ramps onto buses. It's a tricky puzzle for all countries.

Appendix

215 ABRAHAM LINCOLN AND OSAMA BIN LADEN After endless speculation about Lincoln-based on his Marfanoid looks (thin, lanky, elongated head) and clumsy gait, researchers recently found that eleven generations of people descended from Lincoln have a gene mutation for ataxia, a disease unrelated to Marfan. The only way to find out for sure is to test Lincoln's DNA, which opens up a legal, ahem, can of worms. Associated Press. "Disease May Have Caused Lincoln's Gait," *USA Today*, January 27, 2006. Osama Bin Laden's Marfan syndrome is also purely speculative, based on the fact that he's much taller (6'4" or 6'6") than his family and peers, looks quite Marfanoid, uses a cane for possible back problems, and is said to have a heart problem. Mark F. Cohen, "Does Bin Laden Have Marfan Syndrome?" *Salon.com*, November 9, 2001.

About the Tall Author

Arianne Cohen's work has appeared in the *New York Times*, *O*, *Vogue*, *New York*, *Marie Claire*, *Popular Science*, *Fast Company*, the *New York Times Magazine*, and Nerve.com, among other publications. She is the coeditor of the hilarious teen essay collection, *Confessions of a High School Word Nerd*. She previously used her 6'3" frame as a national-level swimmer, and she graduated magna cum laude from Harvard University in 2003. She now lives the tall life in New York City and was, at one point, one half of the country's tallest couple with her 7'2" partner. Visit her tall party at www.tallbook.com.